ARABIC
Phrase book

Nagi El-Bay and Victoria Floyer-Acland

Series Editor: Carol Stanley

D0488730

BBC Books

BBC Books publishes courses in the following languages:

ARABIC	ITALIAN
CHINESE	JAPANESE
FRENCH	PORTUGUESE
GERMAN	RUSSIAN
GREEK	SPANISH
HINDI URDU	TURKISH

For further information write to:
BBC Books
Language Enquiry Service
Room A3116
Woodlands, 80 Wood Lane, London W12 0TT

Published by BBC Books

A division of BBC Enterprises Ltd
Woodlands, 80 Wood Lane, London W12 0TT

ISBN 0 563 36734 2
First published 1993 © Nagi El-Bay & Victoria Floyer-Acland

Set in Times Roman and Lotus (Arabic)
by Typesetters Ltd, Hertford
Text and Cover printed in Great Britain by Clays Ltd,
St Ives Plc

Contents

HOW TO USE THIS BOOK

Communicating in a foreign language doesn't have to be difficult – you can convey a lot with just a few words (plus a few gestures and a bit of mime). Just remember: keep it simple. Don't try to come out with long, grammatically perfect sentences when one or two words will get your meaning across.

Arabic can seem rather more difficult than some other languages because it uses a different alphabet. Don't worry about it: you can still learn to communicate effectively by following the pronunciation guide given in this book, and then you can work on the written language later if you want to. Where you need to understand written words, you will find them in the 'You may see' sections of each chapter, the Menu reader, or in General signs and notices.

Inside the back cover of this book is a list of All-purpose phrases. Some will help you to make contact – greetings, 'please' and 'thank you', 'yes' and 'no'. Some are to get people to help you understand what they're saying to you. And some are questions like 'Do you have . . .?' and 'Where is . . .?', to which you can add words from the Dictionary at the back of the book.

The book is divided into sections for different situations, such as Road travel, Shopping, Health and so on. In each section you'll find
- Useful tips and information
- Words and phrases that you'll see on signs or in print
- Phrases you are likely to want to say
- Things that people may say to you

Many of the phrases can be adapted by simply using another word from the Dictionary. For instance, take the question *il maTaar be^eed* – Is the airport far away? If you want to know if the museum is far away, just substitute the word for museum, *il matHaf* for *il maTaar* to give *il matHaf be*^{a}*eed*.

The pronunciation guide used for the phrases is based on English sounds and is explained in Pronunciation (page 14).

If you want some guidance on how the Arabic language works, see Basic grammar (page 158).

There's a handy reference section (starts on page 168) which contains a list of days and months, countries and nationalities, place names, general signs and notices, conversion tables, national holidays, useful addresses and numbers.

There is a 3,500-word English–Arabic Dictionary, where words are given with both the Arabic script (so you can show it to someone you're talking to) and a simple pronunciation guide.

A concise list of numbers is printed inside the front cover for easy reference (there's also a chapter on Numbers, page 188). At the end of the book is an Emergencies section (which we hope you won't have to use).

Wherever possible, work out in advance what you want to say – if you're going shopping, for instance, write out a shopping list using the Arabic pronunciation guides. If you're buying travel tickets, work out how to say where you want to go, how many tickets you want, single or return etc.

Practise saying things out loud – the cassette that goes with this book will help you to get used to the sounds of Arabic.

Above all – don't be shy! It'll be appreciated if you try to say a few words, even if it's only 'good morning' and 'goodbye' (or the appropriate responses if someone else greets you). In fact, these are the sorts of phrases that are worth memorising as you'll hear them and need to use them all the time.

There are two kinds of Arabic: literary (classical) and spoken.

Classical Arabic is used in writing throughout the Arab world and also on more formal occasions – for speeches, sermons, news broadcasts and so on. Colloquial Arabic is used in everyday speech and varies from country to country within the Arab world.

We have chosen colloquial northern Egyptian Arabic as the basis for this book, because it is the most widely used and understood in the Arab world. Practically everyone in the region is exposed to colloquial Egyptian Arabic, especially through films, cassettes of popular songs and television soap operas. This form of the language is generally held to be the most prestigious spoken variety and whichever country you visit you will find that people can understand and adapt to Egyptian Arabic.

Generally speaking, we have given the classical Arabic forms of words in the 'You may see' sections, since this is the standard written form.

The background information in this book applies generally throughout the Arab world, although obviously there are variations depending on the country you are visiting. Some countries in the region are more relaxed than others on cultural and religious forms of behaviour, the position of women in society, alcohol and so on; it is always wise to speak to the relevant tourist office or embassy before travelling to find out the exact situation in each country.

If you'd like to learn more about Arabic, BBC Books also publishes *Get by in Arabic*. BBC phrase books are also available for the following languages: French, German, Greek, Italian, Portuguese, Spanish and Turkish.

The authors would welcome any suggestions or comments about this book, but in the meantime, have a good trip – رحله سعيده (*reHla saᵃeeda*).

RELIGION AND CULTURE

More than 20 different states make up the Arab world, and they cover a vast geographical area stretching from Morocco on the Atlantic Ocean in the west to Kuwait on the Persian Gulf in the east, and from Syria on the Mediterranean in the north to Oman on the Indian Ocean in the south.

Islam, Christianity and Judaism all started in the area and close links exist between them. Today Islam is the predominant faith, practised by some 100 million Arabs. Muslims, however, acknowledge and respect the teachings of the Torah and the Bible as well as the Islamic holy book the Koran.

The essential element linking all three religions is that there is one God, who is believed to be behind every action, word or thought. Agnosticism or atheism are extremely rare phenomena and derogatory remarks about any aspect of the three religions are not viewed kindly. God is constantly referred to in daily conversations as you'll see in the Arabic phrases referred to in this book. Often Muslims will preface things like eating, drinking, driving, or making a speech with *bismilla*, 'In the name of God', and end by saying *il Hamdoo lilla*, 'Thanks be to God'.

Public behaviour

Arabs greet their friends, relatives and guests with handshakes, embraces and kisses on both cheeks – as long as they're of the same sex, or are immediate family. It's not acceptable to do so otherwise, even for husbands and wives. (Expansive displays of affection between Westerners of opposite sexes will certainly be disapproved of, and stared at.)

Openness and frankness are characteristic of the Arab world. There's little distinction between what's considered personal and what isn't and you'll find that people share much of their lives with each other. This means, for example, that it's quite acceptable to join in anyone's conversation in public to air your personal views.

The Arabic language encourages already frank people to say exactly what they mean. For example, there's no polite way to say 'There appears to be a mistake on this bill'; instead you'd say: 'This bill is wrong' or 'You've made a mistake'.

In some parts of the Arab world – particularly rural or bedouin communities – you'll find that some older cultural traditions and behaviour still prevail. It may cause offence if you use the left hand to eat, give or receive things; others consider it rude to sit with the soles of your shoes pointing at another person.

Tipping

Tipping is a feature of life in the Arab world, and you may find yourself giving tips several times a day – so be sure to carry plenty of loose change. Large numbers of people engaged (officially and unofficially) in providing public services rely on tips (*bae'sheesh*) for their wages. For example, when you arrive at the airport you'll find several people ready to find you a taxi.

Punctuality and appointments

Time is quite flexible in many parts of the Arab world. *bokra* ('tomorrow') often means 'in the near future', while *insha alla* ('if God wills') is more likely to mean 'in the fullness of time'.

It's not a personal insult if people turn up late for appointments

– and don't be surprised if a business meeting intended for two individuals becomes an extended gathering to which other unexpected people have been invited.

Clothing

It's advisable to wear formal clothing to meetings, conferences and dinners. On these occasions it's considered lacking in respect for your hosts to dress too casually, and people are less likely to take you seriously.

During the daytime people will wear a variety of clothes depending on their social class, status, job, religious belief, or whether they're in mourning. Both men and women are expected to cover their bodies, arms and legs with comfortable, loose clothing. In some countries women also cover their heads, and the severity with which standards of dress are imposed on women in particular vary considerably.

Generally speaking, other than on beaches and at swimming pools and sports centres it's offensive not to be reasonably well covered. In most Arab countries it's acceptable for women to wear short sleeves as long as garments are not too tight or revealing, and the knees are covered. However, in Saudi Arabia and most Gulf States it is offensive for a woman to appear in public without being entirely covered with loose dark clothing covering her head, face, body and ankles. Western women should take advice on their wardrobe before travelling.

Women

There are two sets of standards controlling social life in most Arab countries: one for men and one for women. Women are brought up to believe that their whole life must be primarily dedicated to bringing up a family. A strict code of practice concerning their dress and public behaviour protects and ensures the continuation of that role. Women who wear short, tight and revealing clothes cause offence by challenging the social norm, and effectively present themselves as 'sex objects'. They're stared at by men and laughed at by women.

As a visitor, it's worth showing respect for local sensibilities regarding dress, otherwise you'll find yourself receiving a lot of unwelcome attention and even harassment – varying from repeated invitations out for a meal or a drink to more demanding, physical attentions, or even offers of marriage! This is usually as far as it gets since actual physical violence against foreign women is very rare.

If you are harassed, you can start by loudly telling your admirer to leave you alone. If this doesn't work, it's acceptable to seek the assistance of another female – usually you'll receive sympathy and help (even if *she* doesn't approve of your dress).

If you do experience physical violence then ask a woman to take you to a female doctor or nurse. If you wish to contact the police then do so with the assistance of your female friend.

If you're travelling on your own, wear unrevealing clothes, avoid eye contact with men you don't know and ignore personal comments. It also helps to wear a wedding ring and tell everyone that you're married with children even if you aren't, but be prepared to explain why you aren't with your family.

Hygiene hint

If you're visiting remote areas, be sure to take with you any toiletries you might need, including a basic first aid kit, tampons or sanitary towels and antiseptic toilet seat wipes.

Mosques

Mosques, like churches, are places of worship. Most of the ones that you'll want to visit will be of some historical as well as religious value. Lists of interesting mosques should be available at the relevant tourist information office. They will also supply information about access to, and conduct in, mosques by tourists, and especially women. Alternatively, you may find it at the entrance to the mosque. If not, simply copy what other people do. (See Sightseeing, page 127.)

Ramadan

Muslims become Muslims by declaring their faith in one God. Their faith is demonstrated in a variety of ways, including fasting for 30 consecutive days during the holy month of Ramadan. During this period they abstain from food, drink, cigarettes and all bodily pleasures from sunrise to sunset. This, it is believed, releases the soul and stimulates meditation, contemplation and unity with other Muslims.

Ramadan is a time for people to visit each other, to eat and pray together. Shops close early during this month, and in terms of business, Ramadan is a slack period in the Arab world. People are often tired during the day and busy praying and feasting with family and friends in the evening.

During Ramadan most public eating houses will be closed during daylight hours. Some nightclubs which might normally serve alcohol will stop doing so. Christians living in Muslim countries, though not celebrating Ramadan, tend not to eat and drink in public during the daytime out of respect for their Muslim neighbours.

If you arrive in the Arab world during Ramadan make sure you book your breakfast and lunch at one of the 5-star hotels, or find out the names of restaurants which are open during the day. Dinner should not be a problem, since all public eating houses will start re-opening around 6.00–7.00 p.m. in winter, and 8.00–9.00 p.m. in summer.

Ramadan is an exciting time to be out and about during the evening: streets are brightly decorated, shops are open late, and restaurants are crowded with big family parties celebrating into the early hours.

PRONUNCIATION

You don't need perfect pronunciation to be able to communicate – it's enough to get the sounds approximately right. If you want to hear real (Egyptian) Arab voices and practise trying to sound like them, then listen to the cassette.

Arabic pronunciation is quite regular – you can usually tell how a word is pronounced from the way it's written, once you know what each letter (or group of letters) represents. Most of the phrases in this book have been given in a transliterated form, following a system based on English sounds as described below. Hardly any of the Arabic sounds presents any difficulties.

Stress

In speech, some Arabic words are stressed, while others are not. As a general rule, the last but one syllable in a word is stressed, but this is not always the case. For example, the word *sawra* carries equal stress on both syllables.

In this book, a stressed syllable is shown in the pronunciation guide by bold type: *gowzi, molokhaya*. Where no bold type is used, the stress is equal on all syllables.

NB: Stress may change according to the word's ending, and its position in the sentence. It also varies from one country to another.

The following is a guide to the written symbols used and the sounds they represent.

Vowels

		Approx. English equivalent	Shown in book as	Example	
أ		a as in 'hat' (short)	*a*	*gamal*	جمل
	or	a as in 'car' (long)	*aa*	*Taar*	طار
	or	ae as in 'aeroplane'	*ae*	*kitaeb*	كتاب
و		o as in 'doll'	*o*	*foll*	فل
	or	o as in 'know'	*ow*	*yowm*	يوم
	or	oo as in 'boot'	*oo*	*noor*	نور
ى		i as in 'hit'	*i*	*min*	من
	or	ee as in 'keen'	*ee*	*meen*	مين

Other compound vowel sounds used are:

أى		ai as in 'aisle'	*ai*	*raiyiH*	رايح
	or	ay as in 'day'	*ay*	*fayn*	فين
أو		ow as in 'now'	*aw*	*gaw*	جو
		e as in 'egg'	*e*	*hena*	هنا
		e-oo	*ew*	*bitewga*[a]	بتوجع

15

In short words such as *fi* (at, in), *wi* (and) or *li* (to, for), the *i* often disappears when another vowel precedes or follows:

il walad wil bint (the boy and the girl)
fil qahira (in Cairo)

Consonants

Some letters are pronounced differently in colloquial Egyptian from classical Arabic. For example, 'th' is not used for the letter ث in colloquial Egyptian Arabic; instead, it is usually pronounced as a 't' or 's'. The same is true of the letter ذ which is pronounced 'z' as in 'zoo' in classical Arabic, but in colloquial Egyptian Arabic comes out as 'd'.

'Thick' consonants

The capital letters *S*, *T*, *D* and *Z* are used in this book to represent 'heavy' or 'thick' versions of *s*, *t*, *d* and *z*. They're pronounced with the tip of the tongue touching the roof of the mouth against the front teeth, and the rest of the tongue fairly relaxed.

The sound represented by the capital *H* is another 'thick' letter, pronounced with the back of the tongue almost touching the back of the mouth, producing a 'strangled' h sound.

There is no easy equivalent to any of these in English – but don't worry, it's not that difficult to give a fair approximation of the sounds with a bit of practice, and you'll have no problem being understood.

Arabic	Approx. English equivalent	Shown in book as	Example	
ء	glottal stop, as in cockney 'bu'er' or 'Sco'land'	'	ma'aaes	مقاس
ب	b in 'bay'	b	baeb	باب
ت	t in 'tea'	t	taeb	تاب
ث	th in 'think'	th	thawra	ثوره
or	s in 'see'	s	sawra	
ا or	t in 'tea'	t	ta^{a}lab	تعلب
ج	g in 'gap'	g	gamal	جمل
or				
چ	j in 'Jim'	j	jadeed	جديد

ح	'thick' h, as if you're breathing on glass or silver before polishing	*H*	*Haarb*	حرب	
خ	ch in Scottish 'loch'	*kh*	*khabaT*	خبط	
د	d in 'dog'	*d*	*dorg*	درج	
ذ	z in 'zoo' or d in 'dog'	*z* *d*	*zahab* *dahab*	ذهب	
ر	r in 'rabbit', rolled like the Scottish r	*r*	*ragil*	راجل	
ز	z in 'zoo'	*z*	*zatoon*	زيتون	
س	s in 'sign'	*s*	*sabbat*	سبت	
ش	sh in 'shore'	*sh*	*shams*	شمس	
ص	'thick' s	*S*	*maSaSa*	مصاصه	
ض	'thick' d	*D*	*min faDlak*	من فضلك	
ط	'thick' t	*T*	*baTeekha*	بطيخه	
ظ	'thick' z	*Z*	*manZar*	منظر	
ع	almost silent, a sound between a glottal stop and French 'r' (like a very brief gargle)	*a*	*aarabi*	عربى	
غ	a cross between Scottish 'ch' and French 'r'	*gh*	*ghaeli*	غالى	
ف	f in 'food'	*f*	*fannaen*	فنان	

17

ق	not found in English, similar to k but produced further back in the throat	q	qahira	قاهره
ك	k in 'kettle'	k	kalb	كلب
ل	l in 'like'	l	lazeez	لذيذ
م	m in 'meat'	m	midaen	ميدان
ن	n in 'nice'	n	naedi	نادى
ه	h in 'here'	h	haram	هرم
و	w in 'window'	w	waedi	وادى
ى	y in 'yes'	y	yaman	يمن

Note

The sound **v** appears in some words borrowed from other languages, e.g. *video*, pronounced *vidyo*. It is written as ڤ.

The letter ج (geem) is pronounced as a hard **g** (as in 'get') in Egypt, while in most other countries it is soft, more like an English **j**, in which case it is written as ج.

The article ال is normally pronounced *il*, but when it's followed by a word beginning with one of the sounds *t, d, r, z, s, sh, S, D, T, Z, l* or *n*, the *l* sound is often lost, e.g. 'medicine' may be pronounced *adawa* (not *al dawa*), and 'trip' *(il reHla)* becomes *ireHla*.

Where the pronunciation shows double consonants, these must both be pronounced, to give a long sound, e.g. *fannaen* is pronounced *fan-naen*; *Salla* is pronounced *Sal-la*.

If a word ends in a thick consonant and the following word also begins with a consonant, a 'helping' vowel is placed between the two to avoid the difficulty of pronouncing them together, e.g. *noS i keeloo*.

THE ARABIC ALPHABET

The Arabic alphabet has 28 characters. A character has different forms depending on whether it's used by itself or comes at the beginning, middle or end of a word.

Isolated	Initial	Middle	Final	Name pronounced	Shown as
أ	أ	ـا	ـا	*alif*	a, ae, aa
ب	بـ	ـبـ	ـب	*ba'*	b
ت	تـ	ـتـ	ـت	*ta'*	t
ث	ثـ	ـثـ	ـث	*thae'*	th, t
ج	جـ	ـجـ	ـج	*geem* or	g
ج	جـ	ـجـ	ـج	*jeem*	j
ح	حـ	ـحـ	ـح	*Haa'*	H
خ	خـ	ـخـ	ـخ	*khaa'*	kh
د	د	ـد	ـد	*dael*	d
ذ	ذ	ـذ	ـذ	*zael*	z, d
ر	ر	ـر	ـر	*re*	r
ز	ز	ـز	ـز	*zayn*	z
س	سـ	ـسـ	ـس	*seen*	s
ش	شـ	ـشـ	ـش	*sheen*	sh
ص	صـ	ـصـ	ـص	*SaaD*	S
ض	ضـ	ـضـ	ـض	*DaaD*	D
ط	طـ	ـطـ	ـط	*Ta*	T
ظ	ظـ	ـظـ	ـظ	*Zaa*	Z
ع	عـ	ـعـ	ـع	*ᵃayn*	a

غ	غ	ـغـ	غ	*ghayn*	gh
ف	ف	ـفـ	ف	*fa'*	f
ق	ق	ـقـ	ق	*qaaf*	q
ك	ك	ـكـ	ك	*kaf*	k
ل	ل	ـلـ	ل	*laem*	l
م	م	ـمـ	م	*meem*	m
ن	ن	ـنـ	ن	*noon*	n
ه	ه	ـهـ	ه	*ha'*	h
و	و	و	و	*waaw*	w
ى	ي	ـيـ	ى	*ya'*	y

In the Arabic script there are three vowel signs:
 ‑ (a), و (w), ‑ (i). These are written either above or below
the letter to which they belong, e.g.

ªarab عَرب   *ªarabi* عَربى
Saboon صابُون   *bint* بنت

Arabic text is written horizontally, from right to left. There
are no capital letters. Punctuation is the same as in English,
but written back to front, e.g. ، ؟

Arabic composite numerals, on the other hand, are written
from left to right, as in English, e.g. 1993 = ١٩٩٣ ; 25 piastres
= ٢٥ قرش .

GENERAL CONVERSATION

● Formulaic greetings are an essential part of conversation, and there's a special phrase for every time of day and different occasion. References to God are made frequently in daily life, reflecting the strongly held belief that everyone and everything belongs to God (see Religion and culture, page 8). Gratitude and thanks to God are particularly often expressed in the context of greetings and introductions.

● In Arabic, the form of words used can vary, according to whether you're speaking to a man or a woman, or to a group of people (see Basic grammar, page 158). Generally, in this book we've given the forms for speaking to a man and a woman for most phrases (although people will seldom take offence if you use the wrong one). With greetings, however, it's a good idea to learn the different forms.

Different forms are labelled as follows:
(m) if you're male
(f) if you're female
(to m) if you're talking to a man
(to f) if you're talking to a woman
(to group) if you're talking to a group.

● People address each other by their first names, preceded by *sayed* (Mr), *sayeda* (Madam) or *aenisa* (Miss). Respect for learning or rank is shown by replacing one of these three with the appropriate title, such as 'Doctor' *(doktowr* or *doktowra).*

● If you're greeting someone, *assalaamoo ªalaykom* is used when you're visiting, while *ahlan wa sahlan* is used when you're receiving visitors. A big smile always helps to support what you're saying.

● In the morning you say *SabaH il kheer*; the correct reply to this is *SabaH innoor*.

In the evening, the greeting is *misa' il kheer*, to which you reply by repeating the phrase, or by saying *misa' innoor*.

● People will frequently shake hands with you, for example when you arrive at someone's house, when you leave and each time you meet – even if it's later on the same day.

● Arab people use a lot of body language. Physical contact is often an intrinsic part of the greeting amongst intimate friends. Women kiss other women on both cheeks; men do the same amongst themselves. You'll find that Arab people generally come closer when talking to you than is customary in Western societies, and are more ready to embrace members of the same sex. Physical contact with a member of the opposite sex, however – unless they're a blood relative – is not customary (see Religion and culture, page 8).

Greetings

Hello
ahlan wa sahlan

Good morning
SabaH il kheer

Good evening
misa' il kheer

Good night
tiSbaH ᵃala kheer (to m)
tiSbaHi ᵃala kheer (to f)
tiSbaHoo ᵃala kheer
  (to group)

Goodbye
maᵃassalaema

Hello, how are things?
ahlan kayf ilHal

How are you?
izzayak (to m)
izzayik (to f)
izzayokom (to group)

Fine, thanks
kwayyis il Hamdoo lilla (m)
kwayissa il Hamdoo lilla (f)

And how are you? *(said in reply)*
winta izzayak (to m)
winti izzayik (to f)
wintom izzayokom (to group)

You may hear

assalaam ᵃalaykom
Peace be on you
REPLY: *ᵃalaykom assalaam*

ahlan wa sahlan
Welcome
REPLY: *ahlan ahlan*

SabaH il kheer
Good morning
REPLY: *SabaH innoor*

misa' il kheer
Good evening
REPLY: *misa' innoor*

tiSbaH/tiSbaHi ᵃala kheer
Good night
REPLY: *tiSbaH ᵃala kheer* (to m)
tiSbaHi ᵃala kheer (to f)

ma ᵃassalaema
Goodbye
REPLY: *alla yessalemak* (to m)
alla yessalemik (to f)

ahlan kayf ilHal
Hello, how are things?

izzayak/izzayik
How are you?

Introductions

My name is . . .
ismi . . .

This is Mr Brown
isayid brawn

This is Mrs Clark
isayida klark

This is Miss Smith
il aenisa smith

This is my husband
gowzi

This is my wife
miraati

This is my son
ibni

This is my daughter
binti

Pleased to meet you
forSa saᵃeeda

Talking about yourself and your family

(*see* Countries and nationalities, *page 174*)

I am English
ana ingleezi (m)/
ingleezaya (f)

I am Scottish
ana iskotlandi (m)/
iskotlandaya (f)

I am Irish
ana ayrlandi (m)/
ayrlandaya (f)

I am from Wales
ana min waylz

We live in Newcastle
iHna ªaysheen fi nyookasel

I am a student
ana Taalib (m)/*Taaliba* (f)

I am a nurse
ana momarriD (m)/
momarriDa (f)

I work in/for . . .
ana bashtaghal fi . . .

I work in a bank
ana bashtaghal fi bank

I work for a computer firm
*ana bashtaghal fi shirkit
kombyootar*

I work in an office
ana bashtaghal fi maktaeb

I work in a factory
ana bashtaghal fi maSnaª

I am unemployed
ana ªaaTil

I am single
ana ªaezib (m)/*ana mish
metgawiza* (f)

I am married
ana metgawiz (m)/
metgawiza (f)

I am separated
ana monfaSil (m)/
monfaSila (f)

I am divorced
ana meTaala' (m)/
meTaala'a (f)

I am a widower
ana armal

I am a widow
ana armala

I have a son
ªandi walad

I have a daughter
ªandi bint

I have three children
ʿandi talat aTfaal

I don't have any children
maʿandeesh aTfaal

I have one brother
ʿandi akh

I have three sisters
ʿandi talat tekhwaet banaet

I'm on holiday here
ana hena fi 'agaeza

I'm here on business
ana hena fi ma'mooraya

I'm here with my husband
ana hena maʿa gowzi

I'm here with my wife
ana hena maʿa miraati

I'm here with my family
ana hena maʿa ahli

I speak a little Arabic
batkalim ʿarabi baseeT

My husband is . . .
gowzi . . .

My wife is . . .
miraati . . .

My husband is a policeman
gowzi fil bolees

My wife is an accountant
miraati moHassba

My husband works in . . .
gowzi biyishtaghal fi . . .

My wife works in . . .
miraati bitishtaghal fi . . .

My son is five years old
ibni ʿomro khamas sineen

My daughter is eight years old
binti ʿomraha taman sineen

25

You may hear

inta/inti min ay balaed
Where are you from?

ismak ay/ismik ay
What's your name?

bitishtaghal/bitishtaghali ay
What work do you do?

bitedris/bitedresi ay
What are you studying?

metgawiz/metgawiza
Are you married?

ʿandak/ʿandik aTfaal
Do you have children?

ªandak/ªandik ikhwaet
Do you have brothers and sisters?

ªomrohom kaem sana
How old are they?

ªando/ªandaha kaem sana
How old is he/she?

ªomrak/ªomrik kaem sana
How old are you?

da gowzik/SaHbik
Is this your husband/boyfriend?

di miratak/SaHbitak
Is this your wife/girlfriend?

howa laTeef 'awi
He is very nice

haya laTeefa 'awi
She is very nice

raiyiH/raiyHa fayn
Where are you going?

ªayesh/ªaysha fayn
Where are you staying?

ªayesh/ªaysha fayn fi briTanya
Where do you live in Britain?

Talking about their country and yours

(*see* Countries and nationalities, *page 174*)

I like Egypt very much
baHib maSr 'awi

Syria is very beautiful
sorya Helwa 'awi

It's the first time I've been to Saudi Arabia
di awil marra azoor isoªodaya

I come to Oman often
basaefer ªoman kiteer

Do you live here?
inta ªayesh hena (to m)
inti ªaysha hena (to f)

Have you ever been to . . .?
ªomrak roHt (to m)/
ªomrik roHti (to f) . . .

. . . England/Scotland/Ireland/Wales?
. . . *ingilterra/skotlanda/ayrlanda/waylz*

Did you like it?
ªagabetak/ªagabetik

You may hear

ªagabetak/ªagabetik maSr
Do you like Egypt?

di awil marra tezoor/
tezoori lebnaen
Is this your first time in
Lebanon?

'aªid/'aªda hena 'ad ay
How long are you here for?

ay ra'ayak/ra'ayik fi . . .
What do you think of . . .?

ay ra'ayak/ra'ayik fi maSr
What do you think of
Egypt?

bititkalim/bititkalimi
ªarabi kwayyis
Your Arabic is very good

Likes and dislikes

I like . . .
baHib . . .

I like football
baHib korit il qaddam

I like swimming
baHib il ªowm

I like strawberries
baHib il firawla

I don't like . . .
mabaHibish il . . .

I don't like beer
mabaHibish il beera

I don't like theatre
mabaHibish il masraH

Do you like . . .?
teHib (to m)/
teHibi (to f) . . .

Do you like olives?
teHib/teHibi zatoon

Invitations and replies

Would you like . . .?
teHib (to m)/*teHibi* (to f) . . .

Would you like a drink?
teHib tishrab/teHibi tishrabi ay

Would you like something to eat?
teHib taekool/teHibi taekli ay

Would you like to come with us?
teHib/teHibi teegi ma^aana

Would you like to go dancing?
teHib tor'os/teHibi tor'osi

Would you like to go and eat?
teHib/teHibi naekool barra

Yes please
aywa min faDlak (to m)/ *min faDlik* (to f)

No, thank you
la'a shokran

Please leave me alone
law samaHt sebni fi Haeli

Are you going out tonight?
Hatokhrog (m)/ *Hatokhrogi* (f) *ilayla*

What time shall we meet?
net'aebil imta

Where shall we meet?
net'aebil fayn

Good wishes and exclamations

Congratulations!
mabrook
REPLY: *alla yibaerik feek* (to m)
alla yibaerik feeki (to f)
alla yibaerik feekom (to group)

Happy Birthday!
^aeed milaed sa^aeed

Happy Christmas!
^aeed milaed sa^aeed

Happy New Year!
kolisana winta Tayeb (to m)
kolisana winti Tayeba (to f)
kolisana wentom Tayebeen (to group)
REPLY: *winta Tayeb* (to m)
winta Tayeba (to f)
wentom Tayebeen (to group)

Happy Biram! (*see page 183*)
ᵃeed saᵃeed

Blessed Ramadan!
ramadaan kareem
REPLY: *alla akram*

Good luck!
Haz saᵃeed

Have a good journey!
reHla saᵃeeda

Enjoy yourself/yourselves!
atamanna 'an t'aDi/t'aDoo
  wa'at saᵃeed

Bless you! (*including after*
  sneeze)
baarak fikom

Enjoy your meal!
bilhana wishefa

Cheers!
fi SeHetak (to m)
fi SeHetik (to f)
fi SeHetkom (to group)

What a pity!
khoSara

If only!
law

It's no problem
baseeTa

Talking about the weather

The weather's fine
il gaw laTeef

The weather's bad
il gaw weHish

It's very hot
il gaw Haar

It's very cold
il gaw baerid

It's a wonderful day
yowm saᵃeed

I don't like the heat
mabaHibish il Har

I don't like the cold
mabaHibish il bard

Phew, it's hot!
il donya Har

It's very windy!
il reeH shadeed

What's the weather like
  today?
il gaw ay inaharda

Do you think it will rain?
teftekir (to m)/*teftekri* (to f)
  HatnaTar

ARRIVING IN AN ARAB COUNTRY

● You will probably not need to say anything in Arabic unless you are asked the purpose of your visit, or have something to declare at Customs. If you need to say what you have to declare (rather than just showing it), look up the words in the Dictionary.

● You'll need a valid passport and visa to visit any Arab country. You should also have up-to-date vaccination certificates. Check with each country's authorities a few weeks before travelling for the latest information on vaccinations needed; in some cases you won't be allowed to enter the country without the necessary immunisation papers.

● On arrival in some Arab countries you'll be asked how much money you are bringing into the country. For currency and other restrictions (e.g. alcohol), enquire at the relevant tourist office or embassy before departure; as a general rule, you cannot take alcohol into any of the Gulf States.

● When visiting some countries in the area, a valid visa to visit Israel before or after your stay in that country could cause a delay in the immigration or customs procedure. This doesn't apply to Egypt, which has diplomatic relations with Israel.

You may see

الجمرك	Customs
الجوازات	Passport control
الصالة الحمراء	Red hall (goods to declare)

الصالة الخضراء	Green hall (nothing to declare)
جوازات أخرى	Other passports
مرحباً	Welcome

You may want to say

I am here on holiday
ana hena fi 'agaeza

I am here on business
ana hena fi ma'mooraya

It's a joint passport
gawaez saffar moshtarak

I have something to declare
ma^aaya Hagaet tetgamrak

I have this
ma^aaya da

I have two bottles of perfume
ma^aaya izaztayn barfaen

I have two cartons of cigarettes
ma^aaya khartoshtayn sagayyer

I have a receipt (for this)
ma^aaya waS1

Do I have to pay duty on this?
^aalayha Dareeba

You may hear

basborak/basborik min faDlak/faDlik
Your passport, please

'awra'ak/'awra'ik
Your documents

sabab izayaara
What is the purpose of your visit?

inta/inti hena fi shoghl walla 'agaeza
Are you here on business or holiday?

Hato'^aod/Hato'^aodi 'ad ay
How long are you going to stay here?

iftaH/iftaHi ishanTa di min faDlak/faDlik
Please open this bag/suitcase

iftaH/iftaHi ishanTa min faDlak/faDlik
Please open the car boot

ªayzeen nefatesh il ªarabaya
We have to search the car

maªak/maªaki Haga tanya
Do you have any other luggage?

maªak/maªaki mashroobaet koHoolaya
Do you have any alcohol with you?

di ªalayha Dareeba
There is duty to pay on this

taªala/taªali maªaya
Come with me

istanna/istanni hena min faDlak/faDlik
Wait here, please

maªak/maªaki . . .
Have you got . . .?

maªak/maªaki sharayiT vidyo
Have you got any video tapes?

vidyo
A video recorder

kamerit vidyo
A video camera

sagageed Seenee
Chinese rugs

ta'm Seenee
A set of china

dahab
Any gold

maªak/maªaki fatoora/fawateer
Have you got the receipt(s)?

DIRECTIONS

● When you need to ask the way somewhere, the easiest thing is just to name the place you're looking for and add 'please', e.g. *il maTaar min faDlak/faDlik* ('The airport, please?'). Or you can start with 'where is . . .?': *fayn maHatit il otobees min faDlak/faDlik* ('Where is the bus stop, please?'); *fayn il matHaf il islaemi min faDlak/faDlik* ('Where is the Islamic museum, please?').

● If you're looking for a particular address, have it written down in Arabic as well as in its transliteration. In Arabic-speaking countries, addresses are written down with the house number first, followed by the street name and then the apartment numbers, district and town or city name.

7 Pyramid Street	*Sab*ª*a share*ª *il haram*	٧ شارع الهرم
Apartment 24	*sha'a arba*ª*a wi* ª*ishreen*	شقه ٢٤
Giza	*il geeza*	الجيزه
Cairo	*il qahira*	القاهره

● When you're being given directions, listen out for the important bits (such as whether to turn left or right), and try to repeat each bit to make sure you've understood it correctly. If you can't understand something, ask the person to say it again more slowly, *taeni min faDlak/faDlik* ('Again, please'), and *bishwaysh min faDlak/faDlik* ('Slowly, please').

You may see

المحطة الرئيسية	Main station
جامع	Mosque
حارة	Alley
خاص	Private
سوق	Market-place, bazaar

شارع	Street
عبورالمشاه	Pedestrian crossing
قصر	Palace
قلعه	Castle, fortress
كاتدرائيه	Cathedral
كنيسه	Church
متحف	Museum
مترووالأنفاق	Underground railway
محطةاتوبيس	Bus stop
محطه	Station, stop
محطة ترومای	Tram stop
محكمه	(Law) court
معرض	Art gallery, exhibition
ممنوع الدخول	Entrance prohibited
ميدان	Square

You may want to say

Excuse me
law samaHt (to m)
law samaHti (to f)

Pardon?
*ba*ᵃ*d iznak* (to m)
*ba*ᵃ*d iznik* (to f)

Can you repeat that, please?
taeni min faDlak/faDlik

More slowly, please
*bishwaysh min faDlak/
faDlik*

Where are we?
iHna fayn

Where does this road/street
lead to?
*ishare*ᵃ *da birooH lifayn*

Can you show me on the
map?
momkin tewareenee ᵃ*alal
khareeTa*

The station, please?
*il maHaTa min faDlak/
faDlik*

The town centre, please?
wesT il balaed min faDlak/ faDlik

The road to Rabat?
iTaree' lil rabaaT

I want to get to . . .
ªawez (m)/ªawza (f) 'aroH . . .

We want to get to . . .
ªawzeen neroH . . .

I want to get to the airport
ªawez (m)/ªawza (f) aroH il maTaar

We want to get to Aleppo
ªawzeen neroH li Halab

We want to visit the Pyramids
ªawzeen nezoor il ahraam

I want to get to this address
(if you've got it written down)
ªawez/ªawza aroH lil ªenwaen da

Where is/are . . .?
fayn . . .

Where is the tourist office?
fayn maktaeb il siyaHa

Where is the Post Office?
fayn maktaeb il bosTa

Where is the bank?
fayn il bank

Where is the nearest restaurant?
fayn a'rab maTªam

Where is this office?
fayn il maktaeb da

Where are the toilets?
fayn itowalit

Is it far?
beªeed

Is the airport far away?
il maTaar beªeed

How far is it?
masaefit 'ad ay

How long does it take (on foot/by bus)?
Hawaeli 'ad ay (mashi/bil otobees)

Can I go by bus?
momkin aroH bil otobees

Can I get there on foot?
momkin aroH mashi

Can I get there by car?
momkin aroH bil ªarabaya

Is there . . .?
fi . . .

Is there a chemist here?
fi agzakhaena hena

You may hear

mish hena
It's not here

iHna hena
We are here

hena
Here

hinaek
There

roH . . .
Go . . .

roH hinaek
Go over there

soo' . . .
Drive . . .

min hena
This way, Along here

min hinaek
That way, Along there

teHawid yemeen
Turn right

teHawid shimael
Turn left

ªala Tool
Straight on

awil shareª ªalal yemeen
The first street/turning on
   the right

taeni shareª ªalashimael
The second street/turning
   on the left

fi aekhir ishareª
At the end/bottom of the
   street

ªadi il midaen
Cross the square

ªala inaSya
On the corner

taHt
Down, Downstairs

fo'
Up, Upstairs

wara
Behind there

taHt inakhla
Under the palm tree

ªala ikobri
Over the bridge

'abl ishaarit il moroor
Before the traffic lights

baªd igameª
After/Past the mosque

oddaem il madrasa
Opposite the school

lighayit inahr
As far as the river

oddaem il bank
In front of the bank

wara il matHaf
Behind the museum

orayyib min il maTaar
Near/Close to the airport

fil midaen
It's in the square

fi . . .
At/Into/In . . .

fitiga wesT il balaed
Towards the town centre

ᵃadi ikobri
Cross the bridge

khod yemeenak/shimaelak
Take a right/left turn

talit shareᵃ ᵃala (il yemeen)
Take the third exit (on the right)

Hawid ᵃand ishaarit il moroor
Turn off at the traffic lights

fi door itaelit
It's on the third floor

il baeb il awil/il taeni
The first/second door

(mish) beᵃeed
It's (not) far away

orayyib
Very/quite close

khamas da'aye' min hena
It's five minutes away

ᵃishreen keeloo min hena
It's twenty kilometres away

Hatakhod/Hatakhdi il otobees/il 'aTr
You will (have to) catch the bus/train

ROAD TRAVEL

- It is unlikely that you will want to take your car to the Arab world, but if you do, consult motoring organisations for advice. You will need a valid international driving licence, insurance and registration documents.

- If you hire a vehicle, make sure you do so through one of the big international hire firms. They have offices at airports and large 5-star hotels, which are usually staffed by people who speak English. Ensure that you have fully comprehensive insurance which is valid in the country you're visiting. Motor insurance is not compulsory for drivers in many Arab countries, and 'local insurance' is unlikely to do you any good if you actually have an accident.

- Women are not permitted to drive in Saudi Arabia, Libya or the Gulf States.

- Seatbelts and crash helmets are not compulsory, but are advisable.

- You drive on the right in all Middle Eastern countries. Vehicles already on roundabouts have priority over those about to join them.

- Speed limits in Arab countries usually vary up to 100 km per hour for small vehicles and 70 km per hour for trucks and lorries on intercity routes. Main roads, dual carriageways and flyovers will probably have a 60 km per hour limit. In towns the limit is 30 km per hour, but city traffic is usually so congested (for example, in Cairo or Damascus) that no speed limits are necessary! Radars are in place throughout Egypt to check speeding vehicles.

For speed limits and additional information on driving in the country you plan to visit, consult relevant motoring organisations or tourist information centres.

● Some of the best and fastest three-lane motorway networks are found in Saudi Arabia and the Gulf States. There are good motorways in several Arab countries but even some of the main roads can be very rough. On some routes, you may have to pay a small toll (*Dareeba*).

● When there's a road accident, the parties concerned usually sort it out between themselves before continuing with their journies. However, as a foreigner it would be advisable to wait until a traffic policeman arrives. If someone is seriously injured, or the police are called for another reason, they will probably assess the situation and issue an on-the-spot fine, perhaps taking a driver's licence away for a few days as well.

● Petrol (*banzeen*) comes in two grades – 2-star and 4-star or 'super'. Unleaded petrol is not yet available. Diesel (*deezil*) can be found all over the Arab world.

● Parking is not easy in the big capitals. Car parks may be found in main squares, and in Cairo, at least, there are cheap multi-storey car-parks. You may have to tip the car park attendant, whichever country you are in.

● Garages for breakdowns are available, but it may not always be possible to telephone for help. You may have to go and fetch a mechanic yourself. If you break down in the desert, stay with your vehicle until help arrives, and always make sure that you have a plentiful supply of water if you plan a desert journey.

● Beware of inadvertently crossing national borders while driving in the desert; it is often impossible to tell where they actually lie.

You may see

اتجاه واحد	One-way street
استعمل النورالأمامي	Use headlights
اسعاف أولى	First-aid post
اشغال طرق	Road works
إفسح الطريق	Give way
إفسح للسيار	Give way to vehicles from the left
إفسح لليمين	Give way to vehicles from the right
الزم اليمين	Keep right
انتبه	Caution
اوتوستراد	Motorway
بنزين	Petrol
تحويله	Diversion
جمرك	Customs
حدودالسرعه	Speed limit
خطر	Danger
خروج	Exit
دخول	Entry
ديزل	Diesel
سوبر	Super (4-star)
سيارات للأيجار	Cars for hire
ضريبه	Toll
طريق دائرى	Ring road
الطريق الزراعى	Agricultural highway
الطريق الصحراوى	Desert highway
طريق غير ممهد	Uneven road surface
طريق للدراجات	Bicycle path

طريق مسدود	Cul-de-sac, no through road
طريق مغلق	Road closed
عاده	Standard (2-star)
عبور خطر	Dangerous crossroad
عبور سكة حديد	Level crossing
عبور مشاه	Pedestrian crossing
قف	Stop
قنطرة	Viaduct
محطة خدمه	Service/petrol station
مدرسة	School
مشاه	Pedestrians
مغلق	Closed
مفتوح	Open
ممنوع الأنتظار	Parking prohibited
ممنوع التجاوز	No overtaking
ممنوع الدخول	No entry
ممنوع للسيارات اللورى	Closed to heavy goods vehicles
منحنى خطر	Dangerous bend
منطقه اثرية	Archaeological site
موقف انتظار السيارات	Car park
ميكانيكى	Repair shop
نهاية الأوتوستراد	End of highway
هدئ السرعه	Dead slow
وسط البلد	Town/City centre

You may want to say

Where is there a petrol station?	4-star
fayn maHaTit il banzeen	*soobar*

2-star
ada

Diesel
deezil

20 litres of 4-star, please
aishreen litr soobar min faDlak/faDlik

5 pounds' worth of diesel
bi khamsa ginay deezil

Fill it up with 4-star/2-star
fool tank soobar/ada

A can of oil/petrol
aelbit zayt/banzeen

Water, please
maiya min faDlak/faDlik

Air, please
hawa min faDlak/faDlik

Can you change the tyre?
momkin teghaiyyar il kawetch

Can you clean the windscreen?
momkin tinaDaf il izaez

Where is the air?
fayn Trombit il hawa

Where is the car wash?
fayn maw'af ghaseel il saiyaraat

How much is it?
bikaem

Parking

Where can I park?
arkin fayn

Can I park here?
momkin arkin hena

How long can I park here?
momkin arkin hena 'ad ay

How much is it per hour?
bikaem issa'a

Hiring a car

(*see* Days, months, dates, *page 168*)

I want to hire a car
aayiz (m)/*aayza* (f) *a'agar aarabaya*

A small car, please
aarabaya Soghayara min faDlak/faDlik

A medium-sized car
ªarabaya meTawaseTa

A large car
ªarabaya kibeera

An automatic car
ªarabaya otomatik

A car with a driver
ªarabaya bisawae'

For three days
limodit talat tiyaem

For a week
limodit izbooª

For two weeks
limodit izbooªayn

From . . . to . . .
min . . . li . . .

From Monday to Friday
min yowm il itnayn li yowm il gomªa

From 5th December to 12th December
min khamsa disambir li itnashar disambir

How much is it?
bikaem

Per day
fil yowm

Per week
fil izbooª

Per kilometre
fil keeloo

Is mileage (kilometrage) included?
hal il iygaar yeshmal il masaefa

Is petrol included?
hal il iygaar yeshmal il banzeen

Is insurance included?
hal il iygaar yeshmal il ta'meen

Comprehensive insurance cover
ta'meen shaemil

My husband is driving too
gowzi kamaen Haysoo'

My wife is driving too
miraati kamaen Hatsoo'

Do you take credit cards?
bitakhod karnay i'timaen

Do you take travellers' cheques?
bitakhod shikaet siyaHaya

Can I leave the car in Tunis?
momkin aseeb il ªarabaya fi toonis

Can I leave the car at the airport?
momkin aseeb il ªarabaya fil maTaar

How do the controls work?
bitishtaghal izay

Breakdowns and repairs

(*see* Car and bicycle parts, *page 46*)

My car has broken down
ªarabiti bayZa

I think . . .
met-haya'lee . . .

Is there a mechanic around here?
fi mikaneekee orayyib

It's the clutch
il dibriyaj

Can you telephone a mechanic?
momkin teTiSil (to m)/ teTiSli (to f) bil mikaneekee

It's the radiator
il radyater

It's the brakes
il faramil

Can you send a mechanic?
momkin tebªat (to m)/ tebªati (to f) mikaneekee

The car won't start
mish ªayza te'oom

Can you tow the car to the nearest mechanic?
momkin tigor il ªarabaya li a'rab mikaneekee

The battery is flat
il baTarayya naemit

The engine is overheating
il maTowr biyeskhan

It's losing water/oil
na'Sa maiya/zayt

Do you do repairs?
bitSalaH ªarabayaet

I have a puncture
fi khorm fil kawetch

I don't know what's wrong
mish ªarif (m)/ªarfa (f) lay mish bitishtaghal

The . . . doesn't work
il . . . mish biyeshtaghal

I need a . . .
ayiz (m)/*ayza* (f) . . .

Can you repair it (today)?
momkin tiSalaHa (inaharda)

When will it be ready?
HatikhlaS imta

How much will it cost?
Hatitkalif kaem

You may hear

Petrol

teHib/teHibi
What would you like?

'ad ay
How much do you want?

*il moftaeH min faDlak/
   faDlik*
The key, please

Parking

mamnoo^a il inti'Zaar hena
You can't park here

bi . . . fil sa^aa
It's . . . an hour

matedfa^ash
You don't pay

bibalaesh
It's free

fi maw'af saiyaraat hinaek
There's a car park over there

Hiring a car

*teHib/teHibi ^aarabaya
   now^a ay*
What kind of car do you
   want?

limodit 'ad ay
For how long?

limodit kaem yowm
For how many days?

meen ellee Haysoo'
Who is driving?

meen kamaen Haysoo'
Is anyone else driving?

itaman . . .
The price is . . .

fil yowm
Per day

fil izboo ͨ
Per week

rokhSetak/rokhSetik
min faDlak/faDlik
Your driving licence, please

ͨenwaenak/ͨenwaenik ay
What is your address?

il mafateeH ahay
Here are the keys

ragga ͨ il ͨarabaya fool
tank min faDlak/faDlik
Please return the car with a
full tank

ragga ͨ il ͨarabaya issa ͨa
setta
Return the car before six
o'clock

Breakdowns and repairs

mish bitishtaghal lay
What's wrong with it?

ma ͨandeesh qeta ͨ gheyar
I don't have the parts

laezim aTlob qeta ͨ gheyar
I will have to order the parts

Ha tekhalas yowm italaet
It will be ready next Tuesday

Ha titkalif tamaneen ginay
It will cost eighty pounds

Car and bicycle parts

Accelerator	*dawaesit* (f) *il banzeen*	دواسة البنزين
Air filter	*filtar* (m) *il hawa*	فلتر الهواء
Alternator	*monaZim* (m) *il kahraba*	منظم الكهرباء
Battery	*baTarayya* (f)	بطاريه

English	Transliteration	Arabic
Bonnet	*kabboot* (m)	كابوت
Boot	*shanTa* (f)	شنطه
Brakes (front/ rear)	*faramil (amamaya/ khalfaya)* (pl)	فرامل (اماميه/ خلفيه)
Brake cable	*selk* (m) il *faramil*	سلك الفرامل
Brake fluid	*zayt* (m) il *faramil*	زيت الفرامل
Brake hose	*kharToom* (m) il *faramil*	خرطوم الفرامل
Disc brakes	*teel* (m) il *faramil*	تيل الفرامل
Carburettor	*karborayTar* (m)	كاربوريتر
Chain	*ganzeer* (m)	جنزير
Choke	*shafaaT* (m) il *banzeen*	شفاط البنزين
Clutch	*dibriyaj* (m)	دبرياج
Cooling system	*gihaez* (m) il *tabreed*	جهاز التبريد
Distributor	*il mowazi*[a] (m)	الموزع
Electrical system	*gihaez* (m) il *kahraba*	جهاز الكهرباء
Engine	*il maTowr* (m)	الموتور
Exhaust pipe	*shakmaen* (m)	الشاكمان
Fanbelt	*sayr* (m) il *marwaHa*	سير المروحه
Frame (*bicycle*)	*il bodi* (m)	البودي
Front fork	*il dera*[a] (m)	الدراع

Fuel gauge	*mo'ashir* (m) *il banzeen*	مؤشرالبنزين
Fuel pump	*Tromba* (f)	الطرمبه
Fuses	*fyowzaet* (pl)	الفيوزات
Gear lever	*fetays* (m)	فتيس
Gears	*teroos* (pl)	تروس
Gearbox	*ᵃelbit* (f) *il teroos*	علبةالتروس
Handbrake	*farmalit* (f) *il yad*	فرملةاليد
Handlebars	*gadown* (m)	جدون
Headlights	*il noor il ᵃalee* (m)	النورالعالى
Heater	*il dafaya* (f)	الدفايه
Horn	*il kalaks* (m)	الكلكس
Ignition	*il kontakt* (m)	الكونتاكت
Ignition key	*moftaeH* (m) *il kontakt*	مفتاح الكونتاكت
Indicators	*isharaet* (pl)	اشارات
Inner tube	*il 'alb* (m) *il gowani*	القلب الجوانى
Lights (front/ rear)	*il noor (amami/ khalfi)* (m)	النور (امامى/ خلفى)
Lock	*il terbaes* (m)	الترباس
Oil filter	*filtar izayt* (m)	فلترالزيت
Oil gauge	*mo'ashir izayt* (m)	مؤشرالزيت
Pedal	*badael* (m)	بدال
Points	*bowjeehaet* (pl)	بوجيهات
Pump	*Tromba* (f)	طرمبه
Radiator	*radyater* (m)	رادياتر

Radiator hose (top/bottom)	*kharToom* (m) *il radyater* (^a*elwee/asfal*)	خرطوم الرادياتر (علوى/ اسفل)
Reversing light	*noor il marsh aryer* (m)	نورالمارش ارير
Rotor arm	*dawaar* (m) *il moHarik*	دوارالمحرك
Saddle	*korsi* (m)	كرسى
Silencer	*shakmaen* (m)	شاكمان
Spare wheel	^a*agala* (f) *istebn*	عجله استبن
Spark plugs	*bowjeehaet* (pl)	بوجيهات
Speedometer	^a*adaed isor^aa* (m)	عدادالسرعه
Spokes	*silk* (m) *il* ^a*agala*	سلك العجله
Starter motor	*il marsh* (m)	المارش
Steering, steering wheel	*idireksyon* (m)	الدريكسيون
Transmission	*na'l* (m) *isor^aaet*	نقل السرعات
Automatic transmission	*na'l* (m) *tomateekee*	نقل اوتوماتيك
Tyre (front/rear)	*kawetch (amami/ khalfi)* (m)	كاوتش (امامى/ خلفى)
Wheel rim	*iTaSa* (f)	الطاسه
Window	*ishibaek* (m)	الشباك
Windscreen	*il barbareez* (m)	البربريز
Windscreen washer	*maiyit* (f) *il masaHaet*	ماية المساحات
Windscreen wiper	*masaHaet* (pl) *il barbareez*	مساحات البربريز

TAXIS

● Travelling by taxi is usually an easy and convenient way to get about, particularly if you're in a hurry or reluctant to be squashed into a crowded city bus. However it's important to haggle and agree fares in advance or you may find it expensive!

● You can hail taxis in the street, or find them at a taxi rank. It's always best to use registered taxis. In Bahrain, they're easily spotted by their orange side wings; in Cairo, they're black with white side wings.

● Some taxis have meters, but – even if you find a driver who is willing to use his – it's still a good idea to ask what the fare will be. More usual practice is to haggle over the fare, much as you would in a market stall; start at rock bottom and don't be afraid to stand your ground! It's better to agree a price before getting into a taxi and write it down to save disagreements later.

● For urban taxis with meters, there should be a fixed starting charge. There may be extra charges at night, on weekends and public holidays. Extras for luggage, airport pick-ups etc. may not be shown on the meter.

● A tip of 10% or so is usual.

● Sharing a taxi is a routine practice, so don't be afraid to hail one that's already got a passenger – and don't be surprised if the taxi you're in stops for someone else. If you get into a taxi that's already got a passenger, first make sure you agree how much your fare should be. In Jordan and Egypt, sharing a taxi is a popular way of travelling and many taxis make regular daily runs along set routes both in towns and throughout the country.

● Write clearly, in capital Roman letters, the address of your destination. If it's at all complicated or off the tourist track, try to have it written in Arabic as well.

You may want to say

(see also Directions, page 33)

Is there a taxi rank around here?
fi maw'af taksi orayyib min hena

I need a taxi
ªayiz (m)/*ªayza* (f) *taksi*

Can you call me a taxi, please?
momkin tenadeelee taksi min faDlak/faDlik

Now
delwa'ti

Can you book me a taxi for tomorrow at nine o'clock?
momkin teHgiz (to m)/*teHgizi* (to f) *li taksi lebokra issaªa tesªa*

To go to the airport
lil maTaar

The airport, please
il maTaar min faDlak/faDlik

The train station
maHaTit issekal Hadeed

The bus station
maHaTit il otobees

The Hotel Alexandria, please
hotayl il iskinderayya min faDlak/faDlik

To this address, please
il ªenwaen da min faDlak/faDlik

Is it far?
beªeed

How much will it cost?
tamaen ireHla 'ad ay

I am in a hurry
ana mistaªgil (m)/ *ana mistaªgila* (f)

Stop here, please
wa'af hena min faDlak/ faDlik

Can you wait, please?
momkin testanaeni min faDlak/faDlik

How much is it?
Hissaebak/Hissaebik kaem

That is too much
kiteer 'awi

I will give you . . .
Hadilak/Hadilik . . .

I will give you ten dinars
Hadilak/Hadilik ^aashra dananeer

There is a mistake
il Hissaeb mish mazboot

On the meter it's 50 riyals
il ^aaddad biy'ool khamseen riyal

You said the journey would cost only five pounds
inta 'olt/inti 'olti ireHla Hatitkalif khamsa ginay bas

You said that the fee included the luggage
inta 'olt/inti 'olti il'ogra teshmal il shonaaT

Keep the change
khalli il ba'ee

Can you give me a receipt?
momkin teddeenee waSl

For five pounds
bi khamsa ginay

52

You may hear

Hawaeli ^aashra keeloo min hena
It's about ten kilometres away

taman ireHla Hawaeli . . .
It will cost about . . .

talaeta ginay
It's three pounds

AIR TRAVEL

● There are regular flights between the major cities throughout the Arab world.

● At airports and airline offices, you'll generally find someone who speaks English, but be prepared to say a few things in Arabic.

● Signs at major airports will be in French and/or English and Arabic.

● Generally, children under 16 pay 50% of the adult fare in the Arab world.

● International car hire firms have offices at major airports where you can arrange to hire or pick up cars.

You may see

ادفع	Push
إجزب	Pull
استعلامات	Information
الجمرك	Customs
الرجاء ربط الأحزمة	Fasten seatbelts please
الرحلات الداخليه	Domestic departures
الرحلات الدوليه	International departures
الصالة الحمراء	Goods to declare (Red hall)
الصالة الخضراء	Nothing to declare (Green hall)
اوتوبيس (وسط البلد)	Buses (to the town/city centre)
بوابة	Gate

تأخير	Delay
تاكسى	Taxis
تواليت	Toilets
جوازات أخرى	Other passports
خروج	Exit
دخول	Entrance
رقابة الجوازات	Passport control
سيارات للأيجار	Car hire
صالة الأمتعة	Luggage reclaim hall
صالة السفر	Departure (lounge)
مكتب تحويل العملة	Bureau de change
ممنوع التدخين	No smoking
وصول	Arrivals

You may want to say

(*see also* Numbers, *inside front cover*; Days, months, dates, *page 168*; *and* Time, *page 172*)

Is there a flight (from Cairo) to Khartoum?
fi Taiyaara (min ilqahira) lil kharToom

Today
inaharda

This morning
inaharda iSobH

This afternoon
inaharda ba^ad iDohr

Tomorrow (morning/ afternoon)
bokra (iSobH/ba^ad iDohr)

Do you have a timetable of flights to Tunis?
^aandak (to m)/^aandik (to f) gadwal mawa^aeed il reHlaet ila Toonis

What time is . . .?
. . . issa^aa kaem

What time is the first flight to Marrakesh?
awil reHla li marakesh issa^aa kaem

The next flight
il reHla illi ba^ad keda

The last flight
il reHla il 'akheera

What time does it arrive (in Tripoli)?
yewSal (Tarablos) issa^aa kaem

A ticket to Bahrain, please
tazkara lil baHrayn min faDlak/faDlik

Two tickets to Cairo
tazkartayn lil qahira

Single
tazkara raiyiH

Return
raiyiH gay

First class/Economy class
daraga 'oola/daraga tanya

For the eleven o'clock flight
reHlit issa^aa Hidashar

I want to cancel my reservation
^aawez (m)/^aawza (f) alghee il Hagz

I want to change my reservation
^aawez/^aawza aghaiyyar il Hagz

What is the number of my flight?
raqam il reHla 'ay

What time must I be at the airport?
awSal il maTaar issa^aa kaem

Which gate/hall is it?
anhi madkhal/Saala

Is there a delay?
fi ta'kheer

Where is the luggage from the flight from London?
fayn il shonaaT illi weSlit min landan

My luggage is not here
mish la'ee shonaaTi

Is there a bus to the centre of town?
fi otobees biyewaSal li wesT il balaed

You may hear

teHib to'ᵃod/teHibi to'ᵃodi ganb il shibaek
Would you like a seat by the window?

teHib to'ᵃod/teHibi to'ᵃodi ganb il mamar
Would you like a seat on the aisle?

bitdakhan/bitdakhani
Do you smoke?

il Taiyaara Hat'oom issaᵃa . . .
The flight will be called/board at . . . (time)

bawaeba raqam sabᵃa
Gate number seven

tazkartak min faDlak/tazkartik min faDlik
Your ticket, please

gawaez isaffar/basbor min faDlak/faDlik
Your travel documents/passport, please

kart il rekoob min faDlak/faDlik
Your boarding card, please

iwSifli ishonaaT bitaᵃtak/bitaᵃtik
What does your luggage look like?

tazkarit ishonaaT min faDlak/faDlik
The reclaim tag, please

reHla
Flight

il neda' il akheer
Final call

ta'kheer
Delay

bawaeba
Gate

TRAVELLING BY TRAIN

• Railways in the Arab world are generally state-owned. The extent of the rail network and standards of comfort on trains vary from country to country. It is worth checking the rail service with the appropriate tourist office before you travel.

In some countries trains run 24 hours a day, and there are inter-city express trains.

• Passenger seating is usually in three categories: *daraga 'oola* (first class), *daraga tanya* (second class) and *daraga talta* (third class). The third class, with its cramped, uncomfortable wooden seats and friendly atmosphere, still exists but is being phased out in many countries. First class compartments and carriages are usually air-conditioned, have dining facilities and washrooms, and can be attractively furnished as well as being well-equipped.

• Long-distance trains have two classes of sleeper: 'tourist' (*siyaHee*) and 'ordinary' (*ªada*), which costs half as much. They must be booked in advance, from railway stations or travel agents.

• Discounted tickets may be available for children, students and senior citizens. Students should carry an International Student Card with them. For information on any other offers that may be available to overseas visitors, contact the relevant tourist office well in advance of travel.

• You can take bicycles or animals on trains in most Arab countries, but you should book well in advance.

• Main central stations are often well equipped with washing facilities, toilets, eating places, lost property offices and Tourist Information Centres. As a rule there are no left luggage facilities on stations.

● Beware of theft on trains, particularly on well-travelled tourist routes. When travelling, take all the usual precautions with your valuables.

You may see

استعلامات	Information
بوفيه	Buffet
تاكسى	Taxis
تذاكر	Tickets
تواليت	Toilets
جداول السفر	Train timetables
جرس انذار	Alarm
حجرةالأنتظار	Waiting room
حجز	Reservations
درجة اولى	First class
درجة ثانية	Second class
درجة ثالثه	Third class
درجة سياحية	Tourist class
خروج	Exit
رجال	Gentlemen
رحلة	Trip
رصيف	Platform
سفر	Departures
عربةالأكل	Dining car
عربةالبضاعة	Luggage van
عربةالنوم	Sleeping car
محطةالسكه الحديد	Railway station
مدخل	Entrance

مدير المحطة	Station master
ممنوع الدخول	No access
مكتب الحجز	Booking office
مكتب المفقودات	Lost property office
نساء	Ladies
وصول	Arrivals

You may want to say

Information

Is there a train to Fez?
fi 'aTr li faes

Do you have a timetable of
  trains to Luxor?
fi gadwal saffar li lo'Sor

What time . . .?
. . . issaᵃa kaem

What time is the train to
  Idfoo?
'aTr idfoo issaᵃa kaem

What time is the first train
  to Aleppo?
awil 'aTr Halab issaᵃa kaem

The next train
il 'aTr illi baᵃd keda

The last train
akheer 'aTr

What time does it arrive (at
  Amman)?
yewSal (ᵃamaen) issaᵃa kaem

What time does the train
  from Port Said arrive?
*'aTr borsaᵃeed biyewSal
  issaᵃa kaem*

The train to Khartoum,
  please
*'aTr il kharToom
  min faDlak/faDlik*

Which platform?
raSeef nemra kaem

Does this train go to
  Riyadh?
il 'aTr da biyroH irriyaaD

Is this a direct route?
il khaT da mobaeshir

Where do I change trains?
aghaiyyar il 'aTr fayn

Tickets

(*see* Time, *page 172*; Numbers, *inside front cover*)

One/Two tickets to Luxor, please
tazkara/tazkartayn li lo'Sor min faDlak/faDlik

Single
tazkara raiyiH

Return
raiyiH gay

For one adult/two adults
tazkara ªada/tazkartayn ªada

And one child/two children
wi Tefl/wi Teflayn

First class/Second class
daraga 'oola/daraga tanya

For the ten o'clock train to Cairo
'aTr issaªa ªashra lil qahira

For the express to Alexandria
sareeª lil iskinderayya

I want to reserve a seat
ªayiz (m)/ªayza (f) aHgiz korsi

I want to reserve two seats to Amman
ªayiz/ªayza aHgiz korsiyayn li ªamaen

I want to reserve a sleeper
ªayiz/ªayza aHgiz fi ªarabayit inowm

How much is it?
bikaem

On the train

I have reserved a seat
ana Hagazt korsi

I have reserved a sleeper
ana Hagazt fi ªarabayit inowm

Is this seat taken?
il korsi da faaDi

Excuse me
ªan iznak (to m)/ªan iznik (to f)

Where is the dining-car?
fayn ªarabayit il 'akl

Where is the sleeping-car?
fayn ªarabayit inowm

Where is the buffet?
fayn il boffay

Have we arrived at Amman?
woSelna ªamaen

May I open the window?
momkin aftaH ishibaek

How long does the train
stop here?
il 'aTr Ha yow'af hena 'ad ay

May I smoke?
momkin adakhan

Where are we?
iHna fayn

Can you tell me when we
get to Aswan?
*momkin te'olli lama
newSal aswan*

You may hear

Information

biy'oom issaªa ªashra wi noS
It leaves at 10.30

*biyewSal issaªa arbaªa ila
ªashra*
It arrives at ten to four

*laezim teghaiyyar/
teghaiyyari fi TanTa*
You have to change trains
at Tanta

raSeef raqam arbaªa
It's platform number four

Tickets

(*see* Time, *page 172*; Numbers, *inside front cover*)

*ªayiz tisafir/ªayza tisafri
imta*
When do you want to
travel?

raiyiH walla raiyiH gay
Single or return?

bitdakhan/bitdakhani
Do you smoke?

ªayiz tergaª/ªayza tergaªi imta
When do you want to return?

bi ªishreen ginay
(It's) 20 pounds

il 'aTr da daraga 'oola bas
That train is first class only

BUSES AND COACHES

● As well as town and city bus services, there are many buses between towns and villages throughout the Arab world. Inter-city buses and coaches are also available. Bus travel is cheap and popular and wherever you travel, you can be sure that they will be crowded with passengers.

● There are seldom any timetables, especially in rural districts: you just have to sit and wait, or ask someone when the bus is due.

● Bus fares are usually paid to a conductor. Coach fares are paid for either at the main coach station or to a conductor on the coach. You can buy bus passes in Egypt and Morocco, which allow unlimited travel at discounted prices, normally for one week or one month periods.

You may see

أخرج من الباب الأوسط	Alight by the centre door
ادخل من الباب الأمامى	Enter by the front door
اشترى تذكرة السفر قبل	Buy your ticket before
ركوب الأتوبيس	boarding the coach
خروج	Exit
دخول	Entrance
لاتتحدث مع السائق	Do not talk to the driver
محطة اوتوبيس	Bus stop

You may want to say

(for sightseeing bus tours, see Sightseeing, *page 127)*

Where is the bus stop/
    station?
fayn maHatit il otobees

Is there a bus to the
    Pyramids?
fi otobees lil haram

What number is the bus to
    the station?
*il otobees illi biyroH il
    maHaTa nemra kaem*

How often do they run?
biyeegee kol 'ad ay

What time is . . .?
. . . issa^aa kaem

What time is the coach to
    Alexandria?
*otobees iskinderayya
    issa^aa kaem*

What time is the first bus to
    Maadi?
*awil otobees lil ma^aadi
    issa^aa kaem*

The next bus
il otobees illi ba^ado

The last bus
akheer otobees

What time does it arrive?
biyewSal issa^aa kaem

Where can I buy a ticket?
ashteri tazkara min ayn

Where does the bus to the
    town centre leave from?
*otobees noSil balaed
    biy'oom minayn*

Does the bus to the airport
    leave from here?
*otobees il maTaar biy'oom
    min hena*

Does this bus go to
    Ar Raml Square?
*il otobees da biyroH
    midaen iraml*

Can you tell me where to
    get off?
momkin te'olli anzil fayn

Is this the stop for the
    Mohamed Ali Mosque?
*di maHaTit game^a
    mahamad ^aali*

The next stop, please
*il maHaTa il gaya
    min faDlak/faDlik*

Open the door, please!
*iftaH/iftaHi il baeb
min faDlak/faDlik*

Excuse me, may I get by?
*ᵃan iznak/iznik momkin
'ᵃadi*

One ticket to Cairo, please
*tazkara lil qahira
min faDlak/faDlik*

Two single tickets to Rabat
tazkartayn raiyiH lil rabaaT

A return to Amman
ᵃamaen raiyiH gay

How much is it?
bikaem

You may hear

*otobees wesT il balaed min
il maHaTa di*
The bus to the centre leaves
from that stop there

*otobees sabaᵃa wi khamseen
biyroH il maHaTa*
The 57 goes to the station

maᵃak/maᵃaki tazakir
Have you got tickets?

biy'oom kol ᵃashar da'ayi'
It goes every ten minutes

*biy'oom issaᵃa itnashar wi
noS*
It leaves at 12.30

biyewSal issaᵃa itnayn
It arrives at 2.00

raiyiH walla raiyiH gay
Single or return?

Hatenzil/Hatenzili hena
Are you getting off here?

il maHaTa illi gaya
It's the next stop

fatitak/fatitik il maHaTa
You've missed the stop

UNDERGROUND TRAVEL

● Cairo has an underground system, of which the first stretch of line opened in 1987. Called *metro il anfa'*, it is both very clean and very safe, and relatively easy to use. It has a single line, and most of the stops are actually above ground – which can make it a good and relaxing way of seeing something of the city. The trains run at five-minute intervals. Station names are written in both Arabic and Roman script.

● Tickets – which cost very little – are bought at manned ticket offices, rather than from machines, so you will need to have a few words of Arabic ready. You can buy cheap season tickets, and children pay half price.

You may see

تذاكر	Tickets
خروج	Exit
دخول	Entrance
متروالأنفاق	Underground (metro)
ممنوع التدخين	No smoking

You may want to say

Do you have a map of the
  underground?
fi khareeTa li metro il anfa'

One/Two, please
*waHid/itnayn
  min faDlak/faDlik*

Which platform is it for
  Helwan?
anhi raSeef li Hilwaen

Which stop is it for the
  Pyramids?
anhi maHaTa lil ahraam

Where are we?
iHna fayn

Is this the stop for the
railway station?
*da maw'af maHaTit il
sekkal Hadeed*

Does this train go to
Tahreer Square?
*il metro da biyroH midaen
itaHreer*

You may hear

il maHaTa illi gaya
It's the next stop

il maHaTa illi fatit
It was the last stop

fatitak/fatitik il maHaTa
You've missed the stop

BOATS AND FERRIES

● Egypt is renowned for its river cruises. There are long- and short-distance cruises by boat and steamer on the river Nile, which stretches for over 1,000 kilometres from the Nile Delta in the north to Aswan and Abu Simbel Temple in the south. The trip up the Nile from Cairo to Aswan is not to be missed if you have the time. It lasts approximately three days.

● You can also find boat trips from Latakia, Alexandria, Algiers, Port Said and all along the north African coast on the Mediterranean, and from Suez and Ismalia on the Red Sea. Mediterranean cruisers also go all the way to Cyprus, Greece, Venice, Naples, Genoa and Marseilles from all the major north African ports.

● There are ferries around Port Said and Port Tewfik and between various towns on the Nile.

You may see

اطواق نجاه	Lifebelts
رحلات حول الخليج	Trips around the bay
رحلات فى النيل	Trips on the Nile
فيلوكه	Felucca
مراكب	Boats
مرسى	Pier
معديه	Ferry
ميناء	Port, harbour
كباين	Cabins

You may want to say

(*see* Time, *page 172*)

Is there a boat to Tripoli today?
fi markib li Tarablos inaharda

Is there a ferry to Aswan?
fi maᵃadaya li aswan

Are there any boat trips?
fi reHlaet nahraya (on river)/*baHaraya* (by sea)

What time . . .?
. . . issaᵃa kaem

What time is the boat to Casablanca?
markib idaar ilbayDa issaᵃa kaem

What time is the first boat?
il markib il awalanaya issaᵃa kaem

The next boat
il markib illi gaya

The last boat
il markib il akhranaya

What time does it arrive?
HatewSal issaᵃa kaem

What time does it return?
Hatergaᵃ issaᵃa kaem

How long is the crossing?
bitᵃadi fi 'ad ay

Where is the ferry for Port Tewfik?
fayn maᵃadayit bortawfee'

Where does the boat for Algiers leave from?
il markib illi raiyHa algazae'ir Hat'oom minayn

Where can I buy tickets?
ashteri itazakir minayn

Is the sea rough today?
il baHr hayig inaharda

Tickets

Four tickets to Suez, please
arbaᵃ tazakir lisoways min faDlak/faDlik

Two adults and two children
itnayn ᵃada wi itnayn aTfaal

Single
tazkara raiyiH

Return
raiyiH gay

I want to book tickets for
a cruise to Luxor
ayiz (m)/*ayza* (f)
*aHgiz tazakir li reHla
inahraya li lo'Sor*

I want to book a cabin
*ayiz/ *ayza aHgiz kabeena*

For one person
nafar waHid

For two people
nafarayn

For a family
*lil *ayla*

How much is it?
bikaem

On board

I have reserved a cabin
ana Hagazt kabeena

I have reserved two berths
ana Hagazt sereerayn

Where are the cabins?
fayn il kabayin

Where is cabin number 20?
*fayn kabeena nemra
ishreen

Can we go out on deck?
*momkin no'af *ala saT-H
il markib*

You may hear

---

*fi markib yowm il itnayn
wil khamees*
There are boats on
Mondays and Thursdays

*il ma*adaya illi raiyHa
komombo Hat'oom
issa*a tes*a*
The ferry to Komombo
leaves at nine o'clock

Haterga issa*a arba*a wi
noS*
It returns at half past four

*markib asyoot Hat'oom
min marsa raqam itnayn*
The boat to Asiut leaves
from pier number two

il baHr haedee
The sea is calm

il baHr hayig
The sea is rough

AT THE TOURIST OFFICE

● There are tourist information offices all over Cairo, Alexandria, Luxor and Aswan. Look for the name 'Misr Travel': the organisation has branches in most 5-star and 4-star hotels. They will be able to supply leaflets about sights worth seeing, and will also book hotel rooms and transport.

In Arabic, Misr Travel is مصرللسياحه *(miSr lilsiyaHa)*.

● In Jordan, Syria and the Gulf States tourist information is available from Ministry of Tourism desks in 5-star and 4-star hotels, the airport and some tourist sites.

● Tourist offices in Morocco are located in the centre of towns and offer free city maps indicating the main tourist sites.

You may see

إدارة الأستعلامات	Department of Information
استعلامات	Information
خرائط	Maps
دليل	Guides
رحلات بمرشد	Guided Tours
قسم الحجز	Reservations
مصرللسياحه	Misr Travel
وزاره السياحه	Ministry of Tourism

You may want to say

(*see* Directions, *page 33*; Sightseeing, *page 127*; Time, *page 172*)

Where is the tourist office?
fayn maktaeb isiyaHa

Do you have . . .?
ªandak (to m)/
   ªandik (to f) . . .

Do you have a plan of the town?
ªandak/ªandik khareeTa lil balaed

Do you have a map of the area?
ªandak/ªandik khareeTa lil mante'a

Do you have a list of hotels and restaurants?
ªandak/ªandik lista lil hotilaet wil maTaªim

Do you have a list of campsites?
ªandak/ªandik lista li moªaskaraat ishabaeb

Can you recommend a cheap hotel?
momkin tikhtar (to m)/
   tikhtari (to f) li hotayl rekheeS

Can you recommend a restaurant?
momkin tikhtar/tikhtari li maTªam

Can you book a hotel for me?
momkin teHgiz (to m)/
   teHgizi (to f) li hotayl

Can you find a room for me?
momkin teHgiz/teHgizi li 'owda

I want a room overlooking the Nile
ªayiz/ªayza 'owda ªalal neel

With a bathroom
bi Hammaem

A single room
'owda bisereer mofrad

A twin-bedded room
'owda bisereerayn

A double room
'owda mozdawaga

Where can I change sterling/travellers' cheques/dollars?
aghaiyyar isterleenee/
   shikaet siyaHaya/
   dolaraat fayn

71

Where can I hire a bicycle?
*'a'agar *agala fayn*

Have you got information
about . . .?
*andak/*andik
ma*loomaet *an . . .*

Have you got information
about the Roman ruins?
*andak/*andik ma*loomaet
an il athaar il romanaya

Have you got information
in English?
*andak/*andik ma*loomaet
bilingleezi*

What is there to see here?
fi ay hena

Do you have any leaflets?
*andak/*andik manshooraat*

Where is the archaeological
museum?
fayn matHaf il athaar

Can you show me on the
map?
*momkin tewareenee *alal
khareeTa*

When is the National
Theatre open?
*il masraH il qawmi
biyeftaH issa*a kaem*

Are there any excursions?
fi reHlaet

You may hear

*momkin asa*dak/asa*dik*
Can I help you?

inta ingleezi/inti ingleezaya
Are you English?

almaeni/almanaya
German?

inta/inti min ay balaed
Where are you from?

*a*id/a*da hena 'ad ay*
How long are you going to
be here?

naezil/naezla fayn
Where are you staying?

*ayiz/*ayza hotayl daraga
kaem*
What grade of hotel do you
want?

khamas negoom/arba
negoom*
5-star/4-star

ªayiz/ªayza 'owda fi bansyown
Would you like a room in a private house?

teHib/teHibi 'owda bi Hammaem
Would you like a room with a bathroom?

teHib/teHibi 'owda ªalal neel
Would you like a room overlooking the Nile?

fi maSr il 'adeema
It's in the old part of Cairo

ACCOMMODATION

● There is a wide range of accommodation throughout the Arab world. In Egypt, hotels are not officially graded, unless they belong to international chains such as Hilton, Sheraton, Meridian etc., in which case they will be 4- or 5-star; standards of other hotels vary enormously.

Jordan and Syria boast a wide range of accommodation, from deluxe hotels to small inn-type *pensions*. There are also tourist 'rest houses' near major tourist attractions and on main highways; these are mainly owned by the Ministry of Tourism.

Saudi Arabia and all the Gulf States have mainly large, deluxe hotels, with prices to match.

Morocco and Tunisia, on the other hand, have hotels across the range, the majority graded according to the European star system. The prices of all but 5-star hotels are fixed by the government. Lists of hotels and campsites are provided free of charge at national tourist offices.

● You may find 'bed only' hotels (*fondoq*), and for those who wish to experience life with a local family, there are many *pension* (*bansyown*) rooms available. Tourist offices may help.

● You may also rent a flat or an apartment. Rents vary enormously, depending particularly on location. Where possible rent apartments that are known to you through recommendation, rather than at random. You will probably find an opportunity here to practise your haggling skills!

● There are very few youth hostels in Arab countries; those that do exist are mainly in Cairo, Alexandria, Marrakesh, Rabat and Damascus. They are very cheap.

● When you book in anywhere you will be asked for your

passport which the proprietor has to show to the police before it can be returned to you. As a general rule, however, always keep your passport, money and valuables on you.

● Campsites aren't widespread in the Arab world, but you do find them in the more popular tourist areas, especially in Morocco. They are almost invariably near beaches or rivers, and facilities are usually very basic.

Information requested on a registration card

First name	الأسم الأول
Family name	اسم العائلة
Address	العنوان
Nationality	الجنسية
Occupation	الوظيفة
Date of birth	تاريخ الميلاد
Place of birth	محل الميلاد
Passport number	رقم جوازالسفر
Issued at	صدر من
Arrived from	وصل من
Further destination	مسافر إلى
Date	التاريخ
Signature	التوقيع

You may see

أستراحة	Rest house
استقبال	Reception
أطلب خدمة	Call for service
إقامة كاملة	Full board

الدور الأرضى	Ground floor
الدور الأول	First floor
الدور الثانى	Second floor
بنسيون	Pension
بيت شباب	Youth hostel
بيت ضيافه	Guest house
تواليت	Toilets
جراج	Garage
حجرة الأكل	Dining-room
حجرات للأيجار	Rooms for rent
حمام	Bathroom
خروج (طوارئ)	(Emergency) exit
دش	Showers
روم سرفيس	Room service
زبالة	Rubbish
سراير	Beds
صالون	Lounge
غسيل	Laundry
فندق	Bed only hotel
كهرباء	Electricity
كومبليه	Full up
للأيجار	To let
لوكاندة	Hotel
مصعد	Lift
معسكر	Campsite
مياه صالحه للشرب	Drinking water
نصف إقامه	Half board
هوتيل	Hotel
هوتيل لوكس (خمس نجوم)	Luxury hotel (five stars)

You may want to say

Booking in and out

I've reserved a room
Hagazt 'owda

I've reserved two rooms
Hagazt 'owdtayn

My name is . . .
ismi . . .

Do you have a room?
*^aandak (to m)/
^aandik (to f) 'owda*

A single room
'owda bisereer mofrad

A twin-bedded room
'owda bisereerayn

A double room
'owda mozdawaga

For one night
layla waHda

For two nights
layltayn

With bath/shower
bi Hammaem/dosh

How much is it?
bikaem

Per night
filayla

Per week
fil izboo^a

Is there a reduction for
children?
fi takhfeeD lil aTfaal

Is breakfast included?
il fiTaar maDmoon

A room at the back, please
*'owda fil khalf
min faDlak/faDlik*

A room overlooking the
sea, please
*'owda ^aalal baHr
min faDlak/faDlik*

Can I see the room?
momkin ashoof il 'owda

It's too expensive
ghaeli 'awi

Do you have anything
cheaper?
*^aandak/^aandik Haga
arkhaS*

Do you have anything
bigger?
*^aandak/^aandik Haga
akbar*

Do you have anything smaller?
*aandak / *aandik Haga aSghar*

I'd like to stay another night
kamaen layla min faDlak / faDlik

I am leaving tomorrow morning
ana mashi bokra iSobH

The bill, please
il fatoora min faDlak / faDlik

Do you take credit cards?
*momkin adfa*a bi karnay i'timaen*

Do you take travellers' cheques?
*momkin adfa*a bi shikaet siyaHaya*

Can you recommend a hotel in Jeddah?
momkin tikhtar (to m) / tikhtari (to f) li hotayl fi gadda

Can you phone them to make a booking, please?
momkin teHgiz (to m) / teHgizi (to f) li bil tilifown

In hotels

(*see* Problems and complaints, *page 151*; Time, *page 172*)

Where can I park?
arkin fayn

Do you have a cot for the baby?
aandokom sereer Tefl

Do you have facilities for the disabled?
*aandokom khadamaet lil mo*aawiqeen*

Is there room service?
fi qesm li room servis

Can I have breakfast in the room?
momkin afTar fil 'owda

What time is breakfast?
*il fiTaar issa*a kaem*

What time is dinner?
*il *aasha issa*a kaem*

What time does the hotel close?
*il hotayl bi ye'fil issa*a kaem*

I'll be back very late
*ana Harga*a mit'akhar*

(Key) number 42, please
(moftaeH) nemra itneen wi arbᵃeen min faDlak/ faDlik

Are there any messages for me?
fi rasayel ᵃashani

Where is the bathroom?
fayn il Hammaem

Where is the dining-room?
fayn otil akl

Can I leave this in the safe?
momkin aseeb da fil khazna

Can you give me my things from the safe?
momkin akhod Hagti min il khazna

Can you wake me at eight o'clock?
momkin tiSaHeenee issaᵃa tamanya

Can you order me a taxi?
momkin toTlob (to m)/ toTlobi (to f) li taksi

For tomorrow at nine o'clock
issaᵃa tesᵃa iSobH

Can you clean this jacket for me?
momkin tinaDafli (to m)/ tinaDafeelee (to f) il jaketta di

Can you book me a babysitter?
momkin teHgiz/teHgizi li galeesit aTfaal

Can you put it on the bill?
momkin tiHoT (to m)/ tiHoTi (to f) da ᵃala il fatoora

Room number 21
'owda nemra waHid wi ᵃishreen

I need another pillow
ana ᵃayiz (m)/ᵃayza (f) kamaen makhadda

I need a towel
ana ᵃayiz/ᵃayza fooTa

Camping

Is there a campsite around here?
fi moᵃaskar hena

Where can I put the tent?
aHoT il khayma fayn

Where are the showers?
fayn il dosh

Is there an extra charge for the showers?
fi ogra ziyaeda lil dosh

Where are the toilets?	Is there a laundry-room?
fayn il towalit	*fi 'owda lil ghaseel*
Where are the dustbins?	Is the water drinkable?
fayn SafayiH izibaela	*il maiya di SalHa lil shorb*

Self-catering accommodation

(*see* Directions, *page 33*; Problems and complaints, *page 151*)

I have rented a villa	Where is the stopcock?
ana 'agart vila	*fayn il maHbas*
It's called Sun Villa	Where is the fusebox?
ismaha vilit ishams	*fayn Sandoo' il fayash*
I have rented an apartment	How does the cooker work?
ana 'agart sha'a	*il botagaez biyeshtaghal izay*
We're in number 11	How does the water-heater
iHna fi raqam Hidashar	work?
	il sakhaen biyeshtaghal izay
My name is . . .	
ismi . . .	Is there air conditioning?
	fi takyeef
What is the address?	
ay il ᵃenwaen	Is there a spare gas bottle?
	fi amboobit botagaez
How do I get there?	*iDafaya*
aroH izay	
	Are there any more
Can you give me the key,	blankets?
please?	*fi baTateen ziyaeda*
momkin teddeenee il	
moftaeH min faDlak/	What day do they come to
faDlik	clean?
	biyenaDafoo imta
Where is . . .?	
fayn . . .	

Where do I put the rubbish?
aHoT izibaela fayn

When do they collect the rubbish?
biyakhdoo izibaela imta

Where can I contact you?
aTeSil beek fayn

Are there any shops round here?
fi maHalaet hena

You may hear

momkin asa^adak/asa^adik
Can I help you?

ismak/ismik ay
What's your name, please?

kaem layla
For how many nights?

kaem nafar
For how many people?

bi Hammaem walla min ghayr Hammaem
With bath or without bath?

aesif/asfa iHna komblay
I'm sorry, we're full

basborak/basborik min faDlak/faDlik
Your passport, please

momkin temDi hena min faDlak/faDlik
Can you sign here, please

il shaghaela biteegee kol yowm
The maid comes every day

momkin aegi yowm il gom^a
I can come on Friday

biyeegoo yowm ba^d yowm
They come every other day

biyelemmo izibaela kol yowm
They collect the rubbish every day

TELEPHONES

- Local calls can be made from public telephones, which are usually found in district post offices, larger shops and in main squares. Some kiosks also allow you to make local calls. You may be able to make long-distance and international calls from your hotel if you are staying in one of the large international chains; otherwise, go to the central telephone office.

- To call abroad you usually dial 00, followed by the country code; for the UK it's 44. Follow this with the city code minus the 0, and then the number you want. For example, to call central London from Egypt, dial 00 44 71, then the number.

- Phone cards are available in some countries; they can be purchased from Post Offices or central telephone offices.

- You start a telephone conversation by greeting your respondent and sending your best wishes to all his/her family. You'll receive similar greetings, to which your response should always be accompanied by *il Hamdoo lilla*, 'thanks be to God'. (See Greetings, page 22.)

You may see

اسعاف	Ambulance
تليفون	Telephone
بوليس	Police
مصلحة التليفونات	Telephone company
مكالمات دوليه	International calls
مكالمات محلية	Local calls
مطافئ	Fire brigade

You may want to say

Is there a telephone?
fi tilifown

Where is the telephone?
fayn itilifown

Can I make a phone call,
please?
*momkin atkalim fi tilifown
min faDlak/faDlik*

Do you have change for the
telephone?
*ªandak (to m)/ªandik (to f)
fakka li tilifown*

Do you have a phone card,
please?
*ªandak/ªandik biTa'a lil
tilifown min faDlak/
faDlik*

Do you have the Cairo
telephone directory?
*ªandak/ªandik daleel
tilifownaet il qahira*

I want to call England
*ªayiz (m)/ªayza (f) akalim
ingilterra*

Hello
allow

Mr Osman, please
*ilostaz ªosman min faDlak/
faDlik*

Extension number 121,
please
*tawSeela raqam maya
waHid wi ªishreen*

It's Mrs Howard (speaking)
ana madam howard

It's Stephen (speaking)
ana stefaen

My name is . . .
ismi . . .

When will he/she be back?
*Hayergaª/Hatergaª issaªa
kaem*

I'll call later
*Hakalimak baªdayn (to m)/
Hakalimik baªdayn (to f)*

Can I leave a message for
him/her?
*momkin aseeblo/aseeblaha
risaela*

Please tell him/her that
(your name) called
*o'llo/o'llaha . . . itkalim
min faDlak/faDlik*

I am in the Hotel Alexandria
ana fi hotayl iskinderayya

My telephone number is . . .
nemrit tilifowni . . .

83

Can he/she call me?
momkin yekalimni/
  tekalimni

Can you repeat that, please?
taeni min faDlak/faDlik

Slowly
bishwaysh

We were cut off
il khaT it'aTa[a]

How much is the call?
bikaem il mokalma

You may hear

alow
Hello?

aywa
Yes?/Speaking

meen biyetkalim/bitetkalim
Who's calling?

sanya waHda min faDlak/
  faDlik
One moment, please

istanna/istanni min faDlak/
  faDlik
Please wait

HawaSalak/HawaSalik
I'm putting you through

il khaT mashghool
The line's engaged

teHib tintaZir/teHibi
  tintaZiri
Do you want to hold on?

mafeesh rad
There's no answer

mish mawgood/mawgooda
He/She is not in

innemra ghalaT
You've got the wrong
  number

CHANGING MONEY

• The Egyptian unit of currency is the pound, which is made up of 100 piastres. Syria has the lira, also made up of 100 piastres. Jordan, Bahrain, Kuwait have the dinar; Saudi Arabia, Qatar and Oman the riyal; and Morocco and the United Arab Emirates the dirham. (Each country's currency has a different rate of exchange, although the names are the same.)

• Generally speaking, when you arrive anywhere in the Arab world, except the Gulf States, you will have to declare all currency – local or foreign – that you bring in with you, and you should keep all exchange and purchase receipts in case these are checked when you leave to make sure the amounts correspond. Some countries limit or forbid the import or export of the local currency.

• Banking hours vary throughout the region, but banks are usually open between 9.00 a.m. and 1.30 p.m., Saturday to Thursday. However some bank branches remain open until 8.00 p.m., and have an afternoon break between 2.00 p.m. and 4.00 p.m.

It is advisable to check bank opening hours before departure, to avoid being caught out without any money (although big international hotels will often exchange cash or travellers' cheques for you). Banking hours may vary during Ramadan.

• In some countries changing money in banks can be a lengthy, frustrating and even confusing process. You may find it quicker and easier to change money at hotel or travel offices' exchange counters, where possible.

• Dollars are preferred to sterling throughout the Arab world, but you should not experience any problems in using either –

in the form of cash or travellers' cheques. It's often handy to have a small dollar or sterling note in reserve in case you get caught out without any local currency; you may find a shopkeeper who is happy to change it for you at more or less the going rate.

● You can get money with credit cards from some banks and exchange centres, but cash dispensers are not widely used. Large international hotels should accept payment by credit card.

● Apart from banks, there are now official money-changing centres (*maktaeb taHweel ªomla*) in Egypt, so don't make any back-street deals on money – this is illegal, and you would probably lose out on the exchange rate in any case.

You may see

بنك	Bank
بيع عملات أجنبيه	Foreign currency sales
خروج	Exit
دخول	Entrance
فاتح	Open
شراء عملات أجنبيه	Foreign currency purchases
شيكات سياحيه	Travellers' cheques
مغلق	Closed
مكتب تحويل عمله	Exchange, Bureau de change
مواعيد العمل	Opening hours

You may want to say

(see Numbers, inside front cover)

I'd like to change some
   pounds sterling
ayiz (m)/*ayza* (f)
   aghaiyyar isterleenee

I'd like to change some
   travellers' cheques
*ayiz/*ayza aghaiyyar*
   shikaet siyaHaya

I'd like to get some money
   with this credit card
*ayiz/*ayza aTalla* filoos*
   *ala karnay il i*timaen*

What's the exchange rate
   today?
nesbit il taghyeer 'ad ay
   inaharda

Can you give me some
   change, please?
momkin tedeenee fakka
   min faDlak/faDlik

Can you give me five
   twenty-dinar notes?
momkin tedeenee khamas
   *war'aet bi *ishreen dinar*

I'm at the Palace Hotel
ana fi hotayl balas

I'm staying with friends
*ana 'a*id ma*a aS-Haab*

The address is . . .
*il *enwaen . . .*

You may hear

basborak/basborik
   min faDlak/faDlik
Your passport, please

*ayiz tighaiyyar/*ayza*
   tighaiyyari 'ad ay
How much do you want to
   change?

*enwaenak/*enwaenik*
   min faDlak/faDlik
Your address, please?

ism il hotayl min faDlak/
   faDlik
The name of your hotel,
   please?

imDi hena min faDlak/
   faDlik
Sign here, please

roH shibaek iSarf min
   faDlak/faDlik
Please go to the cashier

EATING AND DRINKING

● Eating is a major element of social life in the Arab world. It is a means of welcoming friends and relatives, and even of showing off. People are very hospitable and generous even when they can't afford it (and expect reciprocal generosity at a later date).

● Lunch is eaten around two to three o'clock and is usually the main meal of the day. Meat, vegetables, rice and fruit are served. When entertaining, many different dishes are usually offered – and you'll find that, if you're invited to someone's home, you're expected to eat large quantities of everything. Great pride is taken in home-cooked food.

● Is is usual in Arab countries for a variety of appetizers to be served before the main meal. Called *mezza*, they are small plates of hors d'œuvres of all kinds: meats, vegetables, pickles, fish and so on.

● Whether you're eating in a private house or in anywhere but the smartest of restaurants, all the dishes available will be served at once; you just help yourself periodically to whatever you want from the dishes in the middle of the table.

● There are many different types of public eating places throughout the Arab world. Some of these are restaurants that specialize in particular kinds of food, such as charcoal-grilled lamb, fish and seafood, or pigeon. *kafiterya* are snack bars that sell sweets and desserts, and/or fresh fruit drinks, such as sugar cane and mango drinks.

● Some eating places open all day, and some open for lunch and then from 6.00 p.m. till late in the evening.

● The most popular foods for a sit-down or take-away snack are *fool* and *falafel*.

fool is a kind of broad bean that is soaked overnight and boiled. It's served in small bowls or in Arabic bread, with salad and tahini paste.

falafel is made from the same beans, but they are minced and mixed with herbs and garlic, made into small balls, fried, and served with Arabic bread and salad. Another common name for *falafel* is *Ta^cmaya*.

● *koshari* (brown lentils mixed with rice, fried onions and chili sauce) is another popular cheap dish. *bamya* (okra), *molokhaya* (a green leaf cooked in rabbit, chicken or meat stock) and stuffed peppers or aubergines (*maHshi*) are also very popular.

● In Egypt and elsewhere in the Arab world there are many coffee houses (*'ahwa*), which are open all day and offer their guests only strong black tea, Turkish coffee and the 'hubbly bubbly' (*sheesha*). Here men meet to chat and play backgammon, cards and dominoes.

● Vegetarians will find they're well catered for since meat-free dishes are part of the regular weekly diet for rich and poor alike in the Arab world.

● There's a great deal of similarity and overlap between Mediterranean food (such as Greek, Italian and Turkish dishes) and Arab food, especially in Egypt, Lebanon, Syria, Morocco, Algeria and Tunisia. Pasta dishes, soups, moussaka, baklava, *kataifi* and *konaefa* are some examples.

● Muslims do not eat pork. In those countries such as Egypt and Lebanon which have sizeable Christian populations, pork is available in some shops.

● A staple part of the Arab diet is bread, of which there are three main kinds: 'Arabic bread' (*^caysh baladi*) which is made of wheat dough and is flat (like pitta bread); 'foreign' or French bread (*^caysh fino*); and Lebanese bread (*^caysh shami*) which is also like pitta bread but is thicker.

• Tea and coffee are drunk extensively in the Arab world. Tea (*shay*) is brewed until it is black and is served very sweet, either plain or with mint (*bine ªnaª*), milk (*bilaban*), or with a variety of roots and spices such as ginger, caraway or cinnamon. If you want it without sugar, ask for *shay saeda*. English-style tea may be found in 4- and 5-star hotels and restaurants.

• The thick black Turkish coffee is served in small cups and saucers; be sure not to stir it once it arrives, or you will end up with a mouthful of grains! It comes ready-sugared (if you want it that way) and will automatically be made extremely sweet unless you ask for it the way you like it: *'ahwa saeda* – without sugar; *'ahwa ªalal reeHa* – with very little sugar; *'ahwa mazbooT* – medium sweet; *'ahwa ziyaeda* – very sweet. Instant coffee (*neskafay*) is also available but is not widely drunk in most Arab countries.

• Alcohol is prohibited by Islam and is usually not available in shops in Muslim countries. In practice, attitudes towards alcohol vary considerably: in Saudi Arabia, the sale or public consumption of alcohol is severely punished; in other countries such as Egypt, Morocco and Jordan – where there are sizeable populations of non-Muslims – it's not so frowned upon. In most Arab countries you'll find alcoholic beverages in 4- and 5-star hotels, nightclubs and duty-free shops. In some countries it is also available in some grocery stores and restaurants.

• Juice bars are very popular throughout the Arab world. They have a wide range of fruits to choose from, and the juice is freshly squeezed while you wait.

You may see

أخدم نفسك	Self-service
بار	Bar
تواليت	Toilets, cloakroom
حلويات شاميه	Lebanese and Syrian sweets
سمك	Fish and seafood restaurant
قائمة السياح	Tourist menu
قهوه	Coffee shop
كافيتيريا	Café (or similar)
كبابجي	Charcoal-grilled lamb
محل آيس كريم	Ice-cream parlour
محل عصير	Juice bar
مطعم	Restaurant
مطعم ساندوتشات	Sandwich bar
مطعم فول و فلافل	Fool and falafel restaurant
مطعم كشري	Koshari restaurant
نقبل كروت الأتمان	We accept credit cards

You may want to say

Are there any inexpensive
   restaurants around here?
fi maTa^aim rekheeSa hena

One . . . please
*waHid . . . min faDlak/
   faDlik*

Another/More . . .
. . . *kamaen*

A little more, please
*showaya kamaen
   min faDlak/faDlik*

A little less
a'al showaya

For me
^aashaeni

For him
^aashano

For her
ashanha

For them
ashanhom

For the baby
alashaen il baybi

This, please
da min faDlak/faDlik

Two of these, please
*itnayn . . . min faDlak/
faDlik*

Do you have . . . ?
andak (to m)/*andik*
(to f) . . .

What do you have to eat?
*andak/*andik ay lil akl*

What do you have for
dessert?
*andak/*andik ay lil Helw*

Is/Are there any . . . ?
fi . . .

What do you recommend?
tinsaH bi ay

Do you have any typical
local dishes?
*andak/*andik aTba'
sha*baya*

What is this?
ay da

How do you eat this?
bitaeklo da izay

Cheers!
fi seHetak (to m)/
fi seHetik (to f)/
fi seHetkom (to group)

Enjoy your meal!
bilhana wishefa

Thank you, same to you
shokran winto kamaen

Nothing else, thanks
il Hamdoo lilla shokran

The bill, please
*il fatoora min faDlak/
faDlik*

Where are the toilets?
fayn itowalit

Bars and cafés

A coffee, please
'ahwa min faDlak/faDlik

A white coffee, please
*'ahwa bilaban min faDlak/
faDlik*

Two Turkish coffees, please
*itnayn 'ahwa torki
min faDlak/faDlik*

With sugar
bil sokkar

Without sugar
saeda

A mint tea
shay bine^ana^a

A hot chocolate
kakaw

Mineral water
maiya ma^adanaya

Fizzy water
maiya fawaara

Still water
maiya ^aada

A fizzy orange
^aaSeer borto'an fawar

What fruit juices do you have?
^aandak/^aandik ^aaSeer ay

A mango juice, please
^aaSeer manga min faDlak/faDlik

A milk-shake
milk shayk

A beer/Two beers
beera/itnayn beera

A glass of (local) red wine
kaes nebeet aHmar (maHaeli)

A gin and tonic
jin wi tonik

With ice
bil talg

A cake
kayka

Some mezza, please
mezza min faDlak/faDlik

A toasted sandwich, please
sandawich towst min faDlak/faDlik

What rolls do you have?
^aandak/^aandik sandawichaet ay

A chicken roll, please
sandawich firaekh min faDlak/faDlik

Two (white) cheese rolls, please
itnayn sandawich gebna (bayDa) min faDlak/faDlik

Two falafel sandwiches, please
itnayn sandawich falafel min faDlak/faDlik

Do you have ice-creams?
^aandak/^aandik 'ays kreem

Chocolate, coffee and banana, please
kakaw 'ahwa wi mowz min faDlak/faDlik

A little of . . .
showayit . . .

Booking a table

I want to reserve a table for two people
ªayiz (m)/*ªayza* (f) *aHgiz tarabayza linafarayn*

For nine o'clock
issaªa tesªa

For tomorrow at half past eight
bokra issaªa tamanya wi noS

I have booked a table
Hagazt tarabayza

My name is . . .
ismi . . .

In restaurants

A table for four, please
tarabayza li arbaªa tinfar min faDlak/faDlik

Outside/On the terrace, if possible
fil tiras law samaHt

Excuse me! *(to call the waiter/waitress)*
ªan iznak/iznik

The menu, please
il menyoo min faDlak/faDlik

The wine list, please
listit inebeet min faDlak/faDlik

Do you have a set price menu?
ªandak/ªandik menyoo bilistit il asªar

Do you have vegetarian dishes?
ªandak/ªandik aTbaa' nabataya

The tourist menu (at 12 pounds), please
menyoo isoyaH (bi itnashar ginay) min faDlak/faDlik

For the starter . . .
lil aperateef . . .

Kofta, please
kofta min faDlak/faDlik

Tuna and olives, please
*toona wi zatoon
min faDlak/faDlik*

For the first course . . .
lil kors il awalaeni . . .

The fish soup, please
*shorbit issamak
min faDlak/faDlik*

Kebab, please
kabaeb min faDlak/faDlik

For the second course . . .
lil kors itaeni . . .

The roast chicken, please
*firaekh fil forn min faDlak/
faDlik*

The okra, please
il bamya min faDlak/faDlik

Are vegetables included?
bil khoDar

With rice
bil roz

With chips
bil baTaaTis il miHammar

And a mixed/green salad
wi SalaTit khoDar

For dessert . . .
lil Helw . . .

Semolina cake, please
*basboosa min faDlak/
faDlik*

Baklava, please
baqlaewa min faDlak/faDlik

A peach, please
khowkha min faDlak/faDlik

What cheeses are there?
*ᵃandak/ᵃandik geban
nowᵃay*

Excuse me, where is the
moussaka?
*law samaHt fayn Talab il
misa'aᵃa*

More bread, please
*ᵃaysh kamaen min faDlak/
faDlik*

More chips, please
*baTaaTis miHammar
kamaen min faDlak/
faDlik*

A bottle of red wine
izaezit nebeet aHmar

A litre of white wine
litr nebeet abyaD

Half a litre of red wine
noS litr nebeet aHmar

(for ordering coffee, see
page 90)

It's very good
Helw 'awi

It's really delicious
lazeez 'awi

This is burnt
da maHroo'

Do you accept credit cards?
bite'bal karnay i'timaen

This is not cooked
da mish maTbookh

Can I pay with travellers' cheques?
momkin adfa^a bi shikaet siyaHaya

No, I ordered the chicken
la'a ana Talabt il firaekh

The bill, please
il fatoora min faDlak/faDlik

Excuse me, the bill is wrong
law samaHt fi ghalaT fil fatoora

You may hear

Bars and cafés

ay khedma
Can I help you?

HaDir
Right away

teHib taekol ay/teHibi taekli ay
What would you like to eat?

^aandena . . .
We have . . .

teHib tishrab ay/teHibi tishrabi ay
What would you like to drink?

. . . Helw 'awi inaharda
The . . . is very delicious today

teHib/teHibi talg
Would you like ice?

Tabbakhna biye^amil . . . lazeez/lazeeza 'awi
Our chef makes very tasty . . .

fawar walla ^aaedi
Fizzy or still?

Restaurants

kaem nafar
How many are you?

likaem nafar
For how many people?

laHza waHda min faDlak/ faDlik
Just a moment, please

teHib/teHibi ay
What would you like?

lil aperateef
For the starter

lil kors il awalaeni
For the first course

lil kors itaeni
For the second course

teHib tishrab ay/teHibi tishrabi ay
What would you like to drink?

meen Talab . . .
Who is the . . . for?

teHib/teHibi Helw walla 'ahwa
Would you like dessert, or coffee?

teHib/teHibi likayr
Would you like a liqueur?

khedma tanya
Anything else?

MENU READER

All the words and phrases below are listed in Arabic
alphabetical order.

General phrases

Hors d'œuvres	*aperateef*	أبراتيف
Breakfast	*ifTaar*	إفطار
Egg dishes	*aTbaq bayD*	أطباق بيض
À la carte	*a la kart*	الا كارت
Main courses	*il akla il ra'isaya*	الأكله الرئيسيه
Service included	*il khedma maDmoona fil Hissaeb*	الخدمه مضمونه فى الحساب
Tax included	*il Dareeba maDmoona fil Hissaeb*	الضريبه مضمونه فى الحساب
First courses	*il Talab il awil*	الطلب الأول
Second courses	*il Talab il taeni*	الطلب الثانى
Cheeses	*geban*	جبن
Desserts	*Halawayaet*	حلاويات
Vegetables	*khoDar*	خضار
Poultry	*dawaegin*	دواجن
Fish	*samak*	سمك
Snacks	*snak*	سناك

Salads	*salaTaat*	سلطات
Soups	*shorba*	شوربه
Dinner	*ªasha*	عشاء
Lunch	*ghada'*	غداء
Hors d'œuvres	*faetiH lil shahaya*	فاتح للشهيه
Fruit	*fak-ha*	فاكهه
Price list	*qa'imit il asªaar*	قائمةالأسعار
Tourist menu	*qa'imit il Taªaam lil soyaH*	قائمةالطعام للسياح
Menu of the day	*qa'imit il yowm*	قائمة اليوم
Coffees and teas	*'ahwa wi shay*	قهوه و شاى
Meat	*laHm*	لحم
Drinks	*mashroobaet*	مشروبات
Soft drinks	*mashroobaet khafeefa*	مشروبات خفيفه
Alcoholic drinks	*mashroobaet koHoolaya*	مشروبات كحولية
Alcoholic drinks	*mashroobaet roHaya*	مشروبات روحية
Wines	*nebeet*	نبيت

Soups

Vegetables, garlic and meat broth	*molokhaya*	ملوخيه
Pea soup	*shorbit bisilla*	شورية بسله
Onion soup	*shorbit baSal*	شورية بصل

Vegetable soup	*shorbit khoDar*	شوربة خضار
Fish soup	*shorbit samak*	شوربة سمك
Noodle soup	*shorba bil shi^araya*	شوربة بالشعريه
Tomato soup	*shorbit TamaTim*	شوربة طماطم
Lentil soup	*shorbit ^aads*	شوربة عدس
Chicken soup	*shorbit firaekh*	شوربة فراخ
Meat soup	*shorbit laHm*	شوربة لحم

Main meat and poultry dishes

Cutlet	*iskalob*	إسكالوب
Beefsteak	*boftaek*	بوفتيك
Pigeon	*Hamaem*	حمام
Stuffed pigeon	*Hamaem maHshi*	حمام محشى
Grilled pigeon	*Hamaem mashwi*	حمام مشوى
Turkey	*deek roomi*	ديك رومى
Roast beef	*rozbeef*	روز بيف
Lamb chops	*riyash*	ريش
Spicy sausages	*sogo'*	سجق
Strips of meat cooked on spit	*shawarma*	شاورمه
Chicken	*firaekh*	فراخ
Fillet	*filetto*	فيليتو
Chicken	*faerkha*	فرخه
Barbecued meat	*kebaeb*	كباب
Liver	*kibda*	كبده
Kidney	*kalaewi*	كلاوى

Meatballs with cracked wheat	*kobaeba*	كبيبه
Meatballs	*kofta*	كفته
Chops	*kostalaeta*	كستليته
Chicken broth and yoghurt	*kishk*	كشك
Meat	*laHm*	لحم
Veal	*laHm bitillo*	لحم بتلو
Lamb	*laHm Daani*	لحم ضانى
Camel	*laHm gamali*	لحم جملى
Beef	*laHm kandooz*	لحم كندوز
Minced meat	*laHm mafroom*	لحم مفروم
Stuffed	*maHshi*	محشى
Grilled	*mashwi*	مشوى
Meat and aubergines	*ma'looba*	مقلوبه
Moussaka	*misa'aªa*	مسقعه
Vegetables, garlic and rabbit, chicken or beef broth	*molokhaya*	ملوخية
Shank, knuckle	*mowza*	موزه

Fish

Prawns	*gambari*	جمبرى
Oysters	*gaendofli*	جندوفلى
Fish	*samak*	سمك

Fish braised with onion, served with rice	*samak Sayadiyya*	سمك صياديه
Sole	*samak moosa*	سمك موسى
Nile perch	*qishr bayaD*	قشر بياض
Crab	*kaborya*	كابوريا
Charcoal-grilled chunks of fish	*kebaeb samak*	كباب سمك
Deep-fried fish balls	*koftit samak*	كفته سمك
Lobster	*kaeraekaend*	كركند
Red mullet	*morgaen*	مرجان

Egg dishes

Eggs	*bayD*	بيض
Egg with pastoorma (beef cured with spices and garlic)	*bayD bil basToorma*	بيض بالبسطرمه
Egg mayonnaise	*bayD bil mayonayz*	بيض بالمايونيز
Hard boiled eggs, rice and tomato sauce	*shaekshooka*	شكشوكه
Omelette (thick)	*ᵃaegga*	عجه
Cheese omelette	*ᵃaegga bil gebna*	عجه بالجبنه
Omelette with mince	*ᵃaegga bil laHma*	عجه باللحمه

Vegetables, pulses and cereals

English	Transliteration	Arabic
Asparagus	*asparagas*	أسباراجاس
Okra	*bamya*	بامية
Aubergine	*bitingaen*	بازنجان
Cracked wheat	*borghol*	برغل
Peas	*bisilla*	بسله
Onions	*baSal*	بصل
Potatoes	*baTaTis*	بطاطس
Beetroot	*bangar*	بنجر
Garlic	*towm*	ثوم
Watercress	*gargeer*	جرجير
Carrots	*gazar*	جزر
Chickpeas	*Homoos*	حمص
Artichokes	*kharshoof*	خرشوف
Rice	*roz*	ارز
Leeks	*koraat*	كرات
Lettuce	*khas*	خس
Cucumber	*khiyaar*	خيار
(Sweet)corn	*dora*	ذره
Olives	*zatoon*	زيتون
Spinach	*sabaenikh*	سبانخ
Pickled vegetables	*Torshi*	طرشي
Tomatoes	*TamaTim*	طماطم
Beans (pulses)	*faSolya*	فاصوليا
French (green) beans	*faSolya khaDra*	فاصوليا خضراء
Radishes	*figl*	فجل
Green peppers	*filfil akhDar*	فلفل أخضر

103

Pimento	*filfil Haemi*	فلفل حامى
Beans (brown)	*fool*	فول
Cauliflower	*'arnabeeT*	قرنبيط
Cabbage	*koronb*	كرنب
Celery	*karafs*	كرفس
Marrow/courgettes	*kowsa*	كوسه
Cracked wheat	*koskosi*	كسكسى
Lentils, rice and pasta	*koshari*	كشرى
Turnips	*lift*	لفت
Beans in tomato sauce (chilled)	*lobya bil zayt (mosalagga)*	لوبيا بالزيت (مثلجه)
Stuffed vegetables	*maHshi khoDar*	محشى
Vine leaves	*wara' ᵃinaeb*	ورق عنب

Salads

Salad	*salaTa*	سلطه
Egyptian salad	*salaTa baladi*	سلطه بلدى
Potato salad	*salaTit baTaTis*	سلطة بطاطس
Egg salad	*salaTit bayD*	سلطة بيض
Yoghurt, cucumber, mint and garlic salad	*salaTit zaebaedee*	سلطة زبادى
Mixed salad	*salaTa khaDra*	سلطه خضراء
Cucumber salad	*salaTit khiyaar*	سلطة خيار
Tomato salad	*salaTit TamaTim*	سلطة طماطم
Celery salad	*salaTit karafs*	سلطة كرفس
Cracked wheat salad	*taboola*	تبولة

Desserts

Raisin cake with warm milk	om ªali	أم علي
Ice cream	ays kreem	أيس كريم
Semolina cake	basboosa	بسبوسه
Nuts, raisins, wheat and milk	bileela	بليله
Flaky pastry with nuts (baklava)	baqlaewa	بقلاوه
Pastries dipped in rose water	zalabiya	زلابية
Shredded flaky pastry with nuts and honey	konaefa	كنافه
Pastry filled with nuts	aTayif	قطايف
Turkish delight	malban	ملبن
Rice or cornflour pudding	mahalabaya	مهلبيه

Cheeses

White cheese	**gebna bayDa**	جبنه بيضاء
Cottage cheese	**gebna rikotta**	جبنه روكته
Hard cheese	**gebna roomi**	جبنه رومى
Thick, creamy cheese	**gebna qaerish**	جبنه قريش
Salted curd cheese	**gebna malHa**	جبنه مالحه

Goat's milk cheese	*gebna min laban almi^aeez*	جبنه من لبن المعيز
Curd cheese with olive oil	*labna*	لبنه
Hard, salty, mature cheese	*mish*	مش

Fruit

Pineapple	*ananaes*	أناناس
Oranges	*bortoqan*	برتقال
Plums	*baerqooq*	برقوق
Watermelon	*baTikh*	بطيخ
Dates	*balaH*	بلح
Apples	*toffaeH*	تفاح
Figs	*teen*	تين
Guava	*gawaefa*	جوافه
Peaches	*khowkh*	خوخ
Pomegranates	*rommaan*	رمان
Raisins	*zibeeb*	زبيب
Melon	*shammaem*	شمام
Grapes	*^ainaeb*	عنب
Strawberries	*firawla*	فراوله
Cherries	*kerayz*	كريز
Pears	*kommitra*	كمثرى
Lemons/Limes	*lamoon*	ليمون
Apricots	*mishmish*	مشمش
Mangoes	*manga*	مانجه

| Bananas | *mowz* | موز |
| Tangerines | *yostafaendi* | يوسف افندى |

Miscellaneous

Parsley	*baqdoonis*	بقدونس
Eggs	*bayD*	بيض
Garlic	*towm*	ثوم
Cheese	*gebna*	جبنه
Nutmeg	*gowzit iTeeb*	جوزة الطيب
Cardamon	*Habahaen*	حبهان
Mixed herbs	*khalTit a^ashaeb*	خلطة أعشاب
Basil	*reeHaen*	ريحان
Thyme	*za^atar*	زعتر
Yoghurt	*zabaedi*	زبادى
Butter	*zebda*	زبده
Olive oil	*zayt zatoon*	زيت زيتون
Sesame seed	*semsem*	سمسم
Sugar	*sokkar*	سكر
Hot chilli	*shaTa*	شطة
Honey	*^aasal*	عسل
Bread	*^aaysh*	عيش
'Arabic' bread	*^aaysh baladi*	عيش بلدى
'French' bread	*^aaysh fino*	عيش فينو
'Lebanese' bread	*^aaysh shami*	عيش شامى
Spice	*^aoToor*	عطور
Pepper	*filfil*	فلفل
Sweet pepper	*filfil Helw*	فلفل حلو

Peanuts	*fool soodaeni*	فول سودانى
Cinnamon	*qerfa*	قرفة
Clove	*qoronfil*	قرنفل
Curry	*kary*	كارى
Cream	*kraym*	كريم
Coriander	*kozbara*	كزبره
Cumin	*kamoon*	كمون
Watermelon seeds	*leb*	لب
Jam	*mirabba*	مربى
Salt	*malH*	ملح
Rose water	*maiyit zahr*	ماء الزهر
Flower water	*maiyit ward*	ماء الورد
Mint	*ne^{a}na^a*	نعناع

108 Methods of cooking

Steamed	*bil bokhaar*	بالبخار
In sauce	*bil SalSa*	بالصلصه
Baked	*fil forn*	فى الفرن
Marinated	*mitaebil*	متبل
Stuffed	*maHshi*	محشى
Chopped	*mikharraT*	مخرط
Smoked	*modaekhkhaen*	مدخن
Roasted	*rosto*	روستو
Braised	*misaebbik*	مسبك
Boiled, poached	*maeslooq*	مسلوق
Grilled	*mashwi*	مشوى

Barbecued	*mashwi ªalal faHm*	مشوى على الفحم
Creamed	*maDroob*	مضروب
Minced	*mafroom*	مفروم
Fried	*maqli*	مقلى
Cured	*mimaellaH*	مملح

Drinks

Brandy	*brandi*	براندى
Beer	*beera*	بيره
in a can	*fi ªelba*	فى علبه
bottled	*fi zogaega*	فى زجاجه
Flask	*tormos*	ترمس
Gin and tonic	*jin bi maiyit itonik*	جن بالماء التونيك
Sweet	*Helw*	حلو
Dry	*dray*	دراى
Herb drink	*kharoob*	خروب
In the bottle	*fi zogaega*	فى زجاجه
Tea	*shay*	شاى
Herb tea	*shay aªshaeb*	شاى أعشاب
Camomile tea	*shay bil sheeH*	شاى بالشيح
Tea with milk	*shay bil laban*	شاى باللبن
Tea with lemon	*shay bil lamoon*	شاى بالليمون
Mint tea	*shay bil neªnaª*	شاى بالنعناع
Iced tea	*shay mosalag*	شاى مثلج
Still	*ªada*	عاده

English	Transliteration	Arabic
Arak	^aarak	عرق
(Fresh) fruit juice	^aaSeer fawakih (Taza)	عصير فواكه (طازه)
Pineapple juice	^aaSeer ananaes	عصير اناناس
Orange juice	^aaSeer borto'an	عصير برتقال
Tamarind juice	^aaSeer tamrhindi	عصير تمرهندي
Grapefruit juice	^aaSeer grebfroot	عصير جريب فروت
Sugar cane juice	^aaSeer qaSab	عصير قصب
Lemon juice	^aaSeer lamoon	عصير ليمون
Apricot juice	^aaSeer mishmish	عصير مشمش
Mango juice	^aaSeer manga	عصير منجه
Banana juice	^aaSeer mowz	عصير موز
Sparkling, fizzy	fawaar	فوار
Fizzy soft drinks	mashroobaet fawaara	مشروبات فواره
Fizzy orange	borto'al fawaar	برتقال فوار
Fizzy lemon	lamoon fawaar	ليمون فوار
Vodka	vodka	ڤودكا
Coffee	'ahwa	قهوه
coffee with milk	'ahwa bil laban	قهوه باللبن
long black coffee, less strong than traditional Turkish coffee	'ahwa khafeefa	قهوه خفيفه
without sugar	'ahwa saeda	قهوه ساده
medium-sweet	'ahwa mazboot	قهوه مظبوط

very sweet	'ahwa ziyaeda	قهوه زياده
iced coffee	'ahwa mosalagga	قهوه مثلجه
instant coffee	'ahwa neskafay	قهوه نسكافيه
Hot chocolate	kakaw	كاكاو
Glass	koob	كوب
Coca cola	koka kola	كوكا كولا
Milk	laban	لبن
Liqueurs	likayr	ليكير
almond liqueur	likayr lowz	ليكير اللوز
Lemonade	limonada	ليموناده
Martini	marteenee	مارتيني
Soft drinks	mashroobaet khafeefa	مشروبات خفيفه
Water	maiya	مياه
tonic water	maiya il tonik	مياه التونيك
soda water	maiya il Sowda	مياه الصودا
mineral water	maiya ma^adanaya	مياه معدنيه
Milk shake	milk shayk	ملك شيك
Wines	nebeet	نبيت
white (wine)	(nebeet) abyaD	(نبيت) ابيض
red (wine)	(nebeet) aHmar	(نبيت) أحمر
sparkling (wine)	(nebeet) fawaar	(نبيت) فوار
rosé (wine)	(nebeet) rozay	(نبيت) روزاى
table (wine)	(nebeet) sofra	(نبيت) سفره
Whisky	wiski	ويسكى

SHOPPING

- You'll probably do most of your shopping in small shops, bazaars *(sooq)*, open markets, from street merchants and a few supermarkets.

- In general shops are likely to be open from 9.00 a.m. until 10.00 p.m. Some close during the afternoon between 3.00 and 6.00 p.m., especially during the hotter months. They are closed one day a week, either Friday or Sunday, depending on whether the proprietor is Muslim or Christian. Opening times may be different during Ramadan.

- In most countries in the Arab world, you can buy stamps at post offices, from anywhere that sells postcards, from general stores *(khordawaeti)*, or from street corner kiosks. The style of postboxes varies from country to country: you may need to ask where your local postbox is. Alternatively mail can be posted at post offices and major hotels.

- Fruit and vegetables can be bought from small shops, or from market stalls. You will also find individuals – usually on street corners – who will sell you one or more particular type of vegetable out of a basket. If you buy from them or from markets you will have to haggle over the prices. As a rough guide, start off by offering half the asking price.

- You will also come across markets, called *sooq*, *bazaar* or *kasba*, throughout the region. They sell a variety of goods, from clothes, jewellery, antiques, artefacts and souvenirs to fruit and vegetables.

- In Arab countries it's essential to be prepared to haggle over the price of purchases. Traders aim to get as high a price as possible for their goods – and they also see bargaining as something of a game, which both sides should join in and enjoy.

If you don't participate, you'll end up paying much more than you should.

The main rule of haggling is to keep your sense of humour and smile at all times. All tactics may be employed to disarm your 'opponent', such as: flattery (of the person/their country), emotional blackmail, expressions of horror and disappointment, feigned departure, and so on. You may also be able to improve your side of the deal by asking for a similar item with a better standard of finish, asking for another small item to be included in the price, or even just by walking away shaking your head. You can always come back later, if they don't come after you.

● Kiosks selling local and foreign cigarettes, films, postcards, newspapers, sweets and soft drinks are found all over the towns and cities of the Arab world. They open all hours and often, in the bigger cities, the proprietors speak English.

● Always be prepared to pay for your purchases in cash. Travellers' cheques may be acceptable in bazaar shops selling tourist goods. Cheques and credit cards are not widely used outside hotels, railway stations, travel agents and airports.

● A *makwagi* is someone who irons your clean clothes for you. Their small shops are found all over town. Neither dry cleaners nor launderettes are common in the Arab world.

● When you go shopping, make sure you take a bag for your purchases; few shops or stalls provide them.

You may see

أجزجى	Duty chemist
اجزاخانه	Pharmacy
أخدم نفسك	Self-service

أدوات كهربائيه	Electrical goods
اسطوانات كاسيت	Records, cassettes
الدورالأول	First floor
الدورالثاني	Second floor
الدورالثالث	Third floor
الدورالرابع	Fourth floor
انتيكات	Antiques
اوكازيون	Sales
بدرون	Basement
بقاله	Grocer's
بائع الورد	Florist's
بائع السجاير	Tobacconist's
تخفيضات	Reductions
جزاره	Butcher's
جواهرجي	Jeweller's
حداد	Ironmonger's
خباز	Baker's
خرداواتي	Stationer's
خروج (طوارئ)	(Emergency) exit
خضري	Greengrocer's
ساعاتي	Watchmaker's
سعرالقطعه	Retail price
سماك	Fishmonger's
سمك	Fish
سوبر ماركت	Supermarket
سوق	Shopping centre
صراف	Cashier
صندوق بريد	Postbox
طوابع	Stamps on sale

عرض خاص	Special offer
عطور	Perfumery
فاتح	Open
فكهانى	Fruiterer's
كوافير	Hairdresser's
لبان	Dairy
مأكولات صحيه	Health foods
مشروبات روحيه	Off-licence
مصنوعات جلديه	Leather goods
مغلق	Closed
مكتب بريد	Post Office
مكتبه	Bookshop
ملابس	Clothes
منتجات رياضيه	Sports goods
موبيليا	Furniture
نظاراتى	Optician
هدايا	Gifts
هدايا تذكارية	Souvenirs

You may want to say

General phrases

(*see also* Directions, *page 33*; Problems and complaints, *page 151*; Numbers, *inside front cover*)

Where is the main shopping area?
fayn il soo'

Where is the pharmacy?
fayn il agzakhaena

Is there a grocer's shop around here?
fi ba'ael hena

Where can I buy batteries?
ªayiz (m)/*ªayza* (f) *ashteri baTarayaet*

What time does the baker's open?
il khabaez biyeftaH issaªa kaem

What time does the post office close?
il bosTa bite'fil issaªa kaem

What time do you open in the morning?
bitiftaHoo issaªa kaem iSobH

What time do you close in the afternoon?
biti'filo issaªa kaem baªd iDohr

What time do you re-open?
bitiftaHoo issaªa kaem

What time do you close in the evening?
biti'filo issaªa kaem bilayl

Do you have . . .?
ªandak (to m)/
ªandik (to f) . . .

Do you have stamps?
ªandak/ªandik Tawaabiª

Do you have any halva?
ªandak/ªandik Halaewa

How much is it?
bikaem

How much is this?
bikaem da

How much are these?
bikaem dowl

I don't understand
mish fahim (m)/*mish fahma* (f)

Can you write it down (here) please?
momkin tiktibha (hena) min faDlak/faDlik

It's too expensive
da ghaeli 'awi

Have you got anything cheaper?
ªandak/ªandik Haga arkhaS

I don't have enough money
maªandeesh filoos kifaya

That's still too much
la' da kiteer 'awi

It's cheaper over there
isseªr arkhaS hinaek

I won't give you more than . . .
Hadilak/Hadilik . . . aekhir kalaem

I will give you two pounds only
Hadilak/Hadilik itnayn ginay bas

Is this your best price?
aekhir kalaem

It's a deal
itafa'na

Can you keep it for me?
momkin teHgizhaeli

I'm just looking
ana bas bakhod fekra

That one, please
da min faDlak/faDlik

Two, please
itnayn min faDlak/faDlik

Three, please
talaeta min faDlak/faDlik

Not that one – this one
mish da – da

There's one in the window
fi waHid fil vatreena

That's fine
kwayyis

Nothing else, thank you
bas keda shokran

I'll take it
Hashteree

I'll think about it
Hafakkar showaya

Do you have a plastic bag, please?
aandak/aandik shanTa blastik min faDlak/faDlik

Can you wrap it, please?
momkin tilefhaeli min faDlak/faDlik

With plenty of paper
bi wara' kiteer

I'm taking it to England
Hakhdoo ingilterra

It's a gift
hidaya

Where is the cashier?
fayn iSaraaf

Do you take credit cards?
bitakhod karnay i'timaen

Do you take travellers' cheques?
bitakhod shikaet siyaHaya

I'm sorry, I don't have any change
aesif (m)/*asfa* (f) *maaandeesh fakka*

Can you give me a receipt, please?
iddeenee waSl min faDlak/faDlik

Buying food and drink

A kilo of . . .
keeloo . . .

A kilo of grapes, please
*keeloo ªenab min faDlak/
faDlik*

Two kilos of oranges, please
*itnayn keeloo borto'an
min faDlak/faDlik*

Half a kilo of tomatoes,
please
*noSikeeloo TamaTim
min faDlak/faDlik*

A hundred grams of . . .
meet graam . . .

A hundred grams of white
cheese, please
*meet graam gebna bayDa
min faDlak/faDlik*

Two hundred grams of
olives, please
*meetayn graam zatoon
min faDlak/faDlik*

A piece of cheese, please
*Hetit gebna min faDlak/
faDlik*

Five slices of corned beef,
please
*khamas transhaat bolobeef
min faDlak/faDlik*

A bottle of mineral water,
please
*izaezit maiya maªdanaya
min faDlak/faDlik*

Fizzy water
maiya fawaara

A (small) carton of milk,
please
*kartownit laban (Soghayara)
min faDlak/faDlik*

Two cans of beer, please
*ªelbitayn beera min faDlak/
faDlik*

A bit of that, please
*Hetta min da min faDlak/
faDlik*

A bit more
kamaen Hetta

A bit less
Hetta a'al

What is this?
ay da

What's in this?
da fi ay

Can I try it?
momkin adoo'

At the chemist's

Aspirins, please
asbireen min faDlak/faDlik

Plasters, please
blaster min faDlak/faDlik

Do you have something
   for . . .?
ªandak (to m)/*ªandik*
   (to f) *dawa li . . .*

Do you have something for
   diarrhoea?
*ªandak/ªandik dawa lil
   is-hael*

Do you have something for
   mosquito bites?
*ªandak/ªandik dawa Ded
   ªaDit ibaªooD*

Do you have something for
   period pains?
*ªandak/ªandik dawa lil
   ªaeda ishahraya*

Buying clothes and shoes

I want a skirt
ªayiz (m)/*ªayza* (f) *gonella*

I want a shirt
ªayiz/ªayza 'amees

I want some sandals
ªayiz/ªayza Sandal

Size 40
ma'aaes arbiªeen

Can I try it on?
momkin 'a' eesoo

Do you have a mirror?
fl miraya

I like it
ªagibni

I like them
ªagbinni

I don't like it
mish ªagibni

I don't like them
mish ªagbinni

I don't like the colour
ilown mish ªagibni

Do you have it in other
   colours?
*ªandak/ªandik 'alwaen
   tanya*

It's too big
kibeer 'awi

Have you got a smaller size?
ªandak/ªandik m'aaes aSghar

It's too small
Soghayar 'awi

Have you got a bigger size?
ªandak/ªandik m'aaes akbar

They're too big
kobar 'awi

They're too small
Soghayareen 'awi

Miscellaneous

Five stamps for England, please
khamas Tawaabiª lingilterra min faDlak/faDlik

A box of matches, please
ªelbit kabreet min faDlak/faDlik

For postcards
li koroot bosTa

A film like this, please
film zay da min faDlak/faDlik

For letters
li gawabaet

A film for this camera
film lil kamira di

Three postcards, please
talat koroot bosTa min faDlak/faDlik

Do you have any English newspapers?
ªandak/ªandik garayid ingleezi

You may hear

ay khedma
May I help you?

'ad ay
How much would you like?

teHib/teHibi ay
What would you like?

kaem waHid/waHda
How many would you like?

tamaem
Is that all right?

ay khedma tanya
Anything else?

aesif/asfa khaeliS
I'm sorry, we're sold out

aesif/asfa iHna 'afleen
I'm sorry, we're closed now

HaniftaH (taeni) kamaen rob^a sa^aa
We (re-)open in fifteen minutes

teHib alifo/alifaha lak (to m)
teHibi alifo/alifaha lik (to f)
Do you want me to wrap it for you?

idfa^a ^aand iSaraaf min faDlak/faDlik
Please go to the cashier

^aandak/^aandik fakka
Do you have any change?

inta miHtaeg/inti miHtaega roshetta
You need a prescription

m'aaesak/m'aaesik kaem
What size are you?

kart bosTa walla gawaeb
For postcard or letter?

. . . now^a/no^aha ay
What sort of . . .?

il kamira no^aha ay
What sort of camera do you have?

^aayiz/^aayza anhi now^a film
What sort of film do you want?

da bi khamsa ginay bas
This is for five pounds only

^aashaenak/^aashaenik arba^aa ginay bas
For you, it's only four pounds

la'a mish momkin
No, that's not possible

BUSINESS TRIPS

● Business hours in the Arab world are roughly from 7.30 a.m. until 2.30 p.m.; businesses are closed on Fridays and sometimes Sundays.

● The public sector keeps the same hours, but offices may also be closed on Saturdays.

● You'll probably be doing business with the help of interpreters or in a language everyone speaks, but you may need a few Arabic phrases to cope at a company's reception desk.

● When you arrive for an appointment, all you need do is say who you've come to see and give your name or hand over your business card. However, if you're not expected you may need to make an appointment or leave a message.

● Generally speaking, once you have met a business contact you will address them by their job title, plus first name, e.g. *doktowr ahmad* (Doctor Ahmed), *mohandis awad* (Engineer Awad), *ostaeza fawzaya* (Professor Fawzaya).

You may see

استعلامات	Information
استقبال	Reception
البدرون	Basement
الدورالأرضى	Ground floor
الدورالأول	First floor
الدورالثانى	Second floor
الدورالتالث	Third floor
الدورالرابع	Fourth floor

خروج (طوارئ)	(Emergency) exit
سلم	Stairs
شركه محدوده	Limited liability company
عاطل	Out of order
مدخل	Entrance
مصعد	Lift
ممنوع التدخين	No smoking
ممنوع الدخول	No entry
ممنوع الدخول لغيرالمسموح لهم	No entry to unauthorised persons

You may want to say

(*see also* Days, months, dates, *page 168*; Time, *page 172*)

Mr Ibrahim, please
*isayid ibraheem
min faDlak/faDlik*

Mrs Fathaya, please
*isayida fatHaya
min faDlak/faDlik*

Miss Fatima Mubarak,
please
*il'aenisa fatma moobarak
min faDlak/faDlik*

The manager, please
*il modeer min faDlak/
faDlik*

My name is . . .
ismi . . .

My company is . . .
shirketi . . .

I have an appointment with
Mr Sami Awad
*ªandi maªaed maªa isayid
sami ªawad*

I don't have an appointment
maªandeesh maªaed

I'd like to make an
appointment with Miss
Khadiga Mahmood
ªayiz (m)/*ªayza* (f) *aHadid
maªaed maªa il'aenisa
khadeega maHmood*

I am free this afternoon at one thirty
ana faaDi (m)/*faDya* (f) *inaharda ba*ª*d iDohr issa*ª*a waHda wi noS*

I'd like to talk to the export manager
ª*ayiz*/ª*ayza akalim modeer itaSdeer*

What is his name?
ismo ay

What is her name?
ismaha ay

When will he be back?
*Hayerga*ª *imta*

When will she be back?
*Hatirga*ª *imta*

Can I leave a message?
momkin aseeb risaela

Can you ask him/her to call me?
momkin yeTlobni/teTlobni

My telephone number is . . .
nemreti . . .

I am staying at the Hotel Luxor
ana naezil (m)/*nazla* (f) *fi hotayl lo'Sor*

Where is his/her office?
maktaebo/maktaebha fayn

I am here for the exhibition/trade fair
ana hena ª*alashan aHDar il ma*ª*raD itogaeri*

I am here for the conference
ana hena ª*alashan aHDar il mo'tamar*

I have to make a phone call (to Britain)
laezim akalim (briTanya)

I have to send a telex
*laezim ab*ª*at teleks*

I have to send a fax
*laezim ab*ª*at faks*

I need someone to type this letter for me
ª*ayiz*/ª*ayza Had yeTba*ª*li igawaeb da*

I want to send this by post/ courier
ª*ayiz*/ª*ayza Had yeb*ª*at da bil bosTa/kooryer*

I need to photocopy this
ª*ayiz*/ª*ayza aSawar da*

I need an interpreter
ª*ayiz*/ª*ayza motargim*

You may hear

*ismak/ismik ay
    min faDlak/faDlik*
Your name, please?

*ism ishirka ay min faDlak/
    faDlik*
The name of your company,
    please

ªandak/ªandik maªaed
Do you have an
    appointment?

ªandak/ªandik kart
Do you have a card?

*laHza waHda min faDlak/
    faDlik*
(Wait) one moment, please

*Ha'ollo inak waSalt/
    inik waSalti*
I'll tell him you're here

*Ha'ollaha inak waSalt/
    inik waSalti*
I'll tell her you're here

*Haykoon maªaek/maªaeki
    Haelan*
He will be with you in a
    moment

*Hatkoon maªaek/maªaeki
    Haelan*
She will be with you in a
    moment

*itfaDal o'ªod/itfaDali
    o'ªodi*
Please sit down

*itfaDal idkhol/itfaDali
    idkholi*
Go in, please

min hena
Come this way

isayid ªali mish mawgood
Mr Ali is not here

il'aenisa nadya kharagit
Miss Nadia is out

*isayida zakaraya Hatergaª
    issaªa Hidashar*
Mrs Zacharaya will be back
    at eleven o'clock

kamaen noS issaªa
In half an hour

kamaen saªa
In an hour

*khod il asansayr lil dowr
    italit*
Take the lift to the third
    floor

imshi fil mamar
Go along the corridor

awil/taeni baeb
It's the first/second door

ªalal shimael/yemeen
On the left/right

itfaDal/itfaDali
Come in!

'owda raqam toltomaya wi
  ªishreen
Room number 320

SIGHTSEEING

● You can get information about all the sights worth seeing in most countries from the relevant national tourist office in London (see Useful addresses, page 184) and from local tourist offices. The latter should also be able to tell you about sightseeing tours in cities and tourist areas, some with English-speaking guides.

● Opening hours for historic sites vary throughout the region, but are mostly around 9.00 a.m. to 5.00 p.m. They are usually closed on Fridays.

● Cairo is known as the city of a thousand minarets, but there are beautiful mosques all over the Arab world which you could visit. However, note that in the Gulf States and Libya you must ask permission.

To enter a mosque, your shoulders, arms and legs should be fully covered. Women should wear a headscarf, and avoid wearing tight clothing. Shoes must be taken off at the entrance. Photographs can usually be taken outside prayer times, with permission. During prayers avoid walking in front of standing or kneeling worshippers, and talk quietly. Watch what other people are doing and you'll soon learn what you can and cannot do inside a mosque.

You may see

استعلامات	Information
تذاكر	Tickets
خريطه	Map
خطر	Danger

ركوب الجمال	Camel rides
رحلات بمرشد	Guided tours
مغلق	Closed
فاتح	Open
ممنوع التصوير	No photography
ممنوع الدخول	No entry
ممنوع اللمس	Do not touch
منطقه خاصه	Private area
مواعيدالزياره	Visiting hours
هدايا تذكاريه	Souvenirs

You may want to say

(*see also* At the tourist office, *page 70, for asking for information, brochures etc.*)

Opening times

(*see* Time, *page 172*)

When is the museum open?
il matHaf biyeftaH issaªa kaem

What time do the Pyramids open?
il ahraam biteftaH issaªa kaem

What time does the gallery close?
il maªraD biye'fil issaªa kaem

Is it open every day?
biyeftaH kol yowm

Can we visit the mosque?
momkin nezoor il gameª

Visiting places

One/Two, please
waHid/itnayn
min faDlik/faDlik

For two adults and one
child, please
itnayn ªadee wi Tefl
min faDlik/faDlik

Are there reductions for
children?
fi takhfeeD lil aTfaal

For students
lil Talaba

For pensioners
lili ªalal maªash

For the disabled
lil moªawaqeen

For groups
lil magmooªaet

Are there guided tours (in
English)
fi raHalaet bi morshid
bilogha (il ingleezaya)

Can I take photos?
momkin akhod Sowar

Would you mind taking a
photo of us, please?
momkin takhod Soora lena
min faDlik/faDlik

When was this built?
itbana imta

Who painted that picture?
min rasam iSoora di

In what year?
fi sanat kaem

What is this flower called?
il warda di ismaha ay

What is that bird called?
il ªasfoora di ismaha ay

Where are the toilets?
fayn itowalit

Where can I get a drink?
ashteri mashroob minayn

Sightseeing excursions

What tourist excursions are
there?
ay anwaª ireHlaet
issayaHaya ªandokom

Are there any excursions to
the Aswan dam?
fi reHlaet lisad aswan

What time does it leave?
tebda' issaᵃa kaem

How long does it last?
ireHla 'ad ay

What time does it get back?
Hanergaᵃ issaᵃa kaem

Where does it leave from?
bitebda' minayn

Does the guide speak English?
il morshid biyetkalim ingleezi

How much is it?
bikaem

Are there camel rides?
fi rekoob gimael

You may hear

il matHaf maftooH kol yowm maᵃada yowm il gomᵃa
The museum is open every day except Friday

ma'fool yowm isabt
It is closed on Saturdays

il maᵃbad itbana fil ᵃasr il klasseekee
The temple was built in the Classical period

il ahraam itbanat talat talaef sana abl il milaed
The Pyramids were built in the third millennium BC

di ayqoona li . . .
It's an icon by . . .

fi reHlaet kol yowm talat wi khamees
There are excursions every Tuesday and Thursday

il otobees Hayemshi issaᵃa ᵃashra min . . .
The coach leaves at ten o'clock from . . .

ENTERTAINMENTS

● The most popular spectator sport throughout the Arab world is football. Most professional sports fixtures take place on Fridays and Sundays.

● Evening performances at theatres, cinemas, musical events etc. usually start late – around 9.00 p.m. It is customary to give a small tip to theatre and cinema ushers.

● Many British and American films are shown throughout the Arab world, usually subtitled.

● The most common venues for entertainment are 'casinos' which are not gambling houses, but places where the whole family goes to have a meal and watch a small orchestra, stand-up comedian, belly dancer or folk dancing troupe. Most of these are found in the centre of the larger cities throughout the Arab world, in 5-star international hotels, on Nile cruise boats and at the seaside. They usually stay open till 2.00 a.m. or even later.

● Nightclubs offer music, dancing, dinner, belly dancing and so on for couples and single men. These are found mainly in Rabat, Marrakesh, Damascus, Amman, Cairo and Alexandria.

● Gambling is illegal in the Gulf States. If you fancy a flutter elsewhere in the Arab world, try one of the big international hotels.

You may see

إستاد	Stadium
استراحه	Interval
الحجز مقدماً	Advance booking

اوبرا	Opera house
باب	Door
مترجم بالعربيه	With Arabic subtitles
بحر	Sea
بلكون	Balcony, circle
تذاكر لحفله اليوم	Tickets for today's performance
تواليت	Toilets
ديسكو	Discothèque
درجه اولى	Stalls
ارض السباق	Racecourse
سباق الخيل	Horse racing
سيرك	Circus
سينما	Cinema
صف	Row
عرض مسائى	Evening performance
عرض مستمر	Continuous performance
فيلم	Film
كازينو	'Casino' nightclub
كومبليه	Sold out
لوج	Boxes
ماتينيه	Matinée
مسرح	Theatre
ممنوع الدخول بعد بدايةالعرض	No entry once the performance has begun
منصه	Stand

You may want to say

What's on

(*see* Time, *page 172*)

Where can we go tonight?
nis-har fayn ilayla

Is there a discothèque
    around here?
fi disko hena

Is there any entertainment
    for children?
fi tarfi lil aTfaal

What's on tonight?
fi ay ilayla

What's on tomorrow?
fi ay bokra

At the cinema
fil sinema

At the theatre
fil masraH

Who is performing?
meen biyemasil

Who is singing?
meen biyghani

Does the film have subtitles?
il film motargam

Is there a football match on
    Sunday?
fi matsh kowra yowm il Had

Who are playing?
meen biyel^aab

What time does the show
    start?
Hayebda' il^aarD issa^aa kaem

What time does the concert
    end?
il Hafla tintehi issa^aa kaem

How long does the
    performance last?
il Hafla modet-ha 'ad ay

Tickets

Where can I get tickets?
ageeb tazakir minayn

Can you get me tickets for
the concert?
*momkin tigebli tazakir lil
Hafla*

For the football match
limatsh korit il qaddam

For the theatre
lil masraH

Two, please
itnayn min faDlak/faDlik

Three for tonight, please
*talaeta ilayla di
min faDlak/faDlik*

Two for the eight o'clock
screening, please
*itnayn lil sa*a tamanya
min faDlak/faDlik*

Are there any seats left for
Saturday?
fi tazakir faDla liyowm isabt

I want to book a box for
four people
*ayiz (m)/ayza (f) aHgiz
loj li arba*a tinfaar*

I want to book two seats
ayiz/ayza aHgiz korsiyayn

For Friday
*yowm il gom*a*

In the stalls
fil daraga il 'oola

In the balcony
fil balkon

What price are the tickets?
bikaem il tazakir

Do you have any cheaper
seats?
fi tazakir arkhaS

That's fine
kwayyis

At the show/game

Where is this seat, please?
*fayn il korsi da min faDlak/
faDlik*

Where is the bar?
fayn il bar

Where are the toilets?
fayn il towalit

A programme, please
brogram min faDlak/faDlik

Where can I get a
   programme?
ashteri brogram minayn

A cushion, please
*makhadda min faDlak/
   faDlik*

Is there an interval?
fi istiraHa

You may hear

*momkin tishteri tazakir
   hena fil hotayl*
You can buy tickets here in
   the hotel

fi maktaeb isiyaHa
At the tourist office

fil istaed
At the stadium

biyebda' issaⁿa tamanya
It begins at eight o'clock

limodit saⁿtayn wi robⁿ
It lasts two and a quarter
   hours

yentehi issaⁿa tesⁿa wi noS
It ends at half past nine

*fi istiraHa ⁿishreen
   de'ee'a*
There is a twenty-minute
   interval

ⁿayizhom li imta
When would you like them
   for?

*fil daraga il' oola walla fil
   balkon*
In the stalls or in the
   balcony?

(indicating on seating plan)
fi korsiyayn hena
There are two here

aesif/asfa . . . komplay
I'm sorry, the tickets are
   sold out

*momkin ashoof tazkartak/
   tazkartik*
May I see your ticket?

SPORTS AND ACTIVITIES

● In Egypt water sports are widely practised in the region around the Red Sea, on the river Nile, near Suez and along the Mediterranean. In Morocco and Tunisia water sports are available on the Atlantic and Mediterranean coasts. In Jordan deep-sea diving is available in Aqaba.

● There is plenty of freshwater fishing along the Nile Delta and the Euphrates. There is also fishing in the Red Sea and along the Mediterranean.

● Sports clubs offering facilities for swimming, tennis, squash, volleyball, basketball, table tennis and golf are available for tourists in and around the larger cities and tourist areas. Ask at the local tourist information centre or at your hotel for details.

Sports activities for women are not available in the Gulf States, except on sites owned by multi-national companies. Female tourists can go swimming in the Gulf away from public view.

● Some of the many fine beaches along the Mediterranean and Red Sea are privately owned, but the majority are open to the public. There are no clothing restrictions for men or women in Egypt, Syria, Tunisia or Morocco, as long as costumes worn are not *too* revealing. Elsewhere, take your cue on dress and behaviour from the locals (see Religion and culture, page 8).

You may see

بلاج	Beach
بلاج خاص	Private beach
بلياردو	Billiards

تنس	Tennis
جنازيوم	Gymnasium
حمام سباحه (داخلي)	(Indoor) swimming pool
خاص	Private
خطر	Danger
ركوب الجمال	Camel rides
سكواش	Squash
كرة السله	Basketball
(مدرسة) التزحلق الشراعى	Windsurfing (school)
مراكب للأيجار	Boat hire
مراكب شراعيه للأيجار	Sailboats for hire
ممنوع السباحه	No swimming
ممنوع الصيد	No fishing
ملعب كرة قدم	Football pitch
نادى	Sports centre

You may want to say

General phrases

Can I/we . . .?
momkin . . .

Can we hire bikes?
momkin ni'aggar ªagal

Can I go fishing?
momkin arooH aStaaD

Can I go horse-riding?
momkin arkab HiSena

Can I go on a camel ride?
momkin arkab gamal

Can I go canoeing?
momkin a'adif

Where can I/we . . .?
. . . fayn

Where can we play tennis?
momkin nelªab tenis fayn

I don't know how to . . .
mish ba^araf . . .

I don't know how to ride a camel
mish ba^araf arkab gamal

Do you give lessons?
momkin akhod derooS

I'm a beginner
ana lessa mobtadi'

I'm quite experienced at . . .
ana khabeer fi . . .

How much is it per hour?
bikaem fil sa^aa

How much is it for the whole day?
bikaem fil yowm

How much is it per game?
bikaem il matsh

Are there special rates for children?
fi takhfeeD lil aTfaal

Can I hire a boat?
momkin a'agar markib

Can I hire rackets?
momkin a'agar maDarib

Can I hire fishing lines?
momkin a'agar sinnara

Is a licence needed?
ana miHtaeg rokhSa

Where can I get a licence?
ageeb rokhSa minayn

Is it necessary to be a member?
hal Daroori akoon ^aodw

138

Beach and pool

Can I swim here?
momkin a^aoom hena

Can I swim in the sea?
momkin anzil il baHr

Is the sea dangerous?
il baHr khaTar

Can children swim in the sea safely today?
momkin ilaTfaal yenzelool baHr inaharda

You may hear

inta/inti mobtadi'
Are you a beginner?

te^araf ti'adif/te^arafi ti'adifi
Do you know how to canoe?

issa^aa bi khamsa ginay
It's five pounds per hour

*laezim tedfa^a/tedfa^ai
mo'addam ^aashra ginay*
You have to pay a deposit
of ten pounds

aesif/asfa mafeesh makaen
I'm sorry, we're booked up

*momkin terga^a/terga^ai
kamaen showaya*
You'll have to come back
later

laezim tegeeb/tegeebi Soora
You need a photograph

laezim rokhSa
You need a licence

HEALTH

Medical details – to show to a doctor

(Tick where appropriate, or fill in details)	Self الطالب	Other members of family/party عائلته/ أصدقائه

Blood group فصيلة الدم

Asthmatic ربو

Blind أعمى

Deaf أطرش

Diabetic سكر

Epileptic صرع

Handicapped معوق

Heart condition أمراض القلب

High blood pressure ارتفاع ضغط الرم

Pregnant حامل

Allergic to: ضد حساسيه

Antibiotics مضادات حيويه

Penicillin بنسلين

Cortisone كورتيزون

Medicines أدويه

Self الطالب _____

Others عائلته/ أصدقائه _____

● Before travelling, make sure you have had the necessary immunisations, and don't forget to take vaccination certificates with you (see Arriving in an Arab country, page 30).

● Your local Department of Health office can provide information about medical and dental care abroad. Make sure you have good medical insurance if you're travelling to the Arab world. If you need treatment, you'll have to pay in cash and reclaim the payment from your insurance company when you return to Britain, so be sure to obtain receipts.

● Make sure you take supplies of medicines you need regularly, as well as something for the treatment of common travellers' complaints such as diarrhoea and mosquito bites.

● Chemists are generally highly trained and can often help with minor disorders and injuries. In an emergency, drugs which are available only on prescription in Britain may be obtainable over the counter at chemists in most Arab countries, but you should ensure that you know exactly what you need and the dosage. If in doubt, go to a doctor.

● Most hospitals in the region are state-owned and run, but there are also many private hospitals. There's a significant difference between the two in levels of hygiene, standards of service, degree of attention given, and comfort.

Hospitals in the Gulf are of the highest standards, often boasting state-of-the-art medical equipment and staffed by Egyptian, Palestinian and sometimes European doctors.

● Throughout the Arab world all doctors will have studied medicine in English and should therefore be able to communicate reasonably well with you.

● If you need to indicate where pain is, you can simply point and say 'it hurts here' (*andi waga* *hena*) – if necessary adding the Arabic for the appropriate part of the body (see list, page 148).

● Most complaints experienced by visitors are related to food
and drink. You should avoid drinking anything but boiled or
bottled water – and remember that also applies to ice in drinks.
Refrain also from swimming in rivers or canals.

It is usually best to avoid eating salads or fruit salads in
restaurants. Where possible, peel fruit yourself immediately
before eating it, or else wash it carefully in bottled water.

Be wary of eating food sold in open markets, especially in
summer. If you buy food to prepare yourself, make sure it's
kept in a well-sealed container – cockroaches are a particular
nuisance, especially in humid areas and by the sea.

● The other main cause of problems is the sun – take a hat,
sunglasses and sunblock cream with you and avoid
over-exposure.

You may see

استعمل قبل	Use before (*date*)
اسعاف	Ambulance
اسعافات اوليه	First aid post
العياده الخارجيه	Surgery, Out-patients
خدمات الطوارئ	Emergency services
دكتور	Doctor
دكتور إسنان	Dentist
عياده	Clinic
سموم	Poison
قسم الحوادث	Casualty
لاتبلع	Do not swallow
للأستعمال الخارجي فقط	For external use only

مستشفى	Hospital
مواعيد العياده	Surgery hours
رج قبل الأستعمال	Shake before use

You may want to say

At the doctor

I need a doctor
ayiz (m)/*ayza* (f) *doktowr*

Please call a doctor
iTlobli doktowr
  min faDlak/faDlik

Is there a female doctor?
fi doktowra

It's my husband
gowzi

It's my wife
miraati

It's my friend
SaHbi (m)/*SaHbiti* (f)

It's my son
ibni

It's my daughter
binti

Your symptoms

I feel unwell
ana ayaen (m)/*ayaena* (f)

It hurts here
biyewga hena

I have earache
widaeni bitewgani

Someone else's symptoms

He/She feels unwell
howa ayaen/haya ayaena

He/She is unconscious
oghma alay/alayha

It hurts here
biyewga hena

He/She has earache
widno bitewgao/
  widnaha bitewgaha

I have a sore throat
*zowri biyewga*ª*ni*

He/She has a sore throat
*zoro biyewga*ª*o/*
   *zorha biyewga*ª*ha*

I have a temperature
ª*andi Haraara*

He/She has a temperature
ª*ando/*ª*andaha Haraara*

I have diarrhoea
ª*andi is-hael*

He/She has diarrhoea
ª*ando/*ª*andaha is-hael*

I feel dizzy
Hasis (m)/*Hassa* (f)
   bi dowkha

He/She feels dizzy
ª*ando/*ª*andaha dowkha*

I have been sick
istafraght

He/She has been sick
istafragh/istafraghit

I can't sleep
mish 'aedir (m)/
   'aedra (f) *anaem*

He/She can't sleep
mish 'aedir yinaem/
   'aedra tinaem

I can't breathe
mish 'aedir/'aedra atnafis

He/She can't breathe
mish 'aedir yitnafis/
   'aedra titnafis

My . . . is bleeding
ª*andi nazeef fi . . .*

It's broken
itkasar

It's sprained
itlawa

I have cut myself
ª*awart nafsi*

I have burnt myself
Hara't nafsi

I have been stung by an
  insect
*Hashara lasa*ª*itni*

He/She has been stung by
  an insect
*lasa*ª*ito/lasa*ª*it-ha Hashara*

I have been bitten by a
  dog/snake
*aDeni kalb/ti*aben*

He/She has been bitten
  by a dog/snake
*aDoo/*aDaha kalb/ti*aben*

I have been bitten by a
  scorpion
*aDetni *a'rabba*

He/She has been bitten by
  a scorpion
*aDetoo/*aDetha *a'rabba*

You may hear

*fayn il waga*a*
Where does it hurt?

*biyewga*a/bitewga*a hena*
Does it hurt here?

*biyewga*a/bitewga*a 'awi*
Does it hurt a lot?

*b'aelak *ayaen/
  b'aelik *ayaena 'ad ay*
How long have you been
  feeling ill?

*aandak/*aandik kaem sana*
How old are you?

*aando/*aandaha kaem sana*
How old is he/she?

iftaH bo'ak/iftaHi bo'ik
Open your mouth

*i'la*a hedoomak min faDlak/
  i'la*i hedoomik min faDlik*
Get undressed, please

bitakhod/bitakhdi adwaya
Are you taking any
  medicines?

*aandak/*aandik Hasasaya li
  ay adwaya*
Are you allergic to any
  medicine?

*khadt/khadti taT*aeem Ded
  il tetnas*
Have you been vaccinated
  against tetanus?

akalt/akalti ay inaharda
What have you eaten today?

Hadilak/Hadilik roshetta
I am going to give you a
  prescription

*khod/khodi Habaya talat
  marraat fil yowm*
Take a tablet three times a day

*ba*a d il akl*
After meals

'abl il nowm
At bedtime

molawas/molawassa
It is infected

145

Hadilak/Hadilik Ho'na
I have to give you an injection

meHtaeg/meHtaega ghoraz
I have to give you some stitches

laezim takhod/takhdi isha^aa
It is necessary to do an X-ray

^aayiz/^aayza ^aayenit dam/bowl
I need to take a blood/urine sample

galak/galik Sadma 'albaya
You have had a heart attack

^aandak/^aandik tasamom
You have food poisoning

^aandak/^aandik gafaef
You are dehydrated

laezim tishrab/tishrabi sawa'il kiteera
You must drink plenty of liquids

Soom limodit yowm waHid
Don't eat for a day

laezim testerayaH/testerayaHi
You must rest

laezim tor'od/tor'odi talat tiyaem
You must stay in bed for three days

irga^a/irga^ai kamaen khamas tiyaem
You must come back in five days' time

laezim teroH/teroHi il mostashfa
You will have to go to hospital

Hala khafeefa
It is nothing serious

inta saleem/inti saleema
There is nothing wrong with you

ilbis hedoomak/ilbisi hedoomik
You can get dressed again

You may want to say

At the dentist

I need a dentist
ªayiz (m)/*ªayza* (f)
  doktowr sinaen

I have toothache
sinaeni bitewgaªni

This tooth hurts
sineti di bitewgaªni

I have broken a tooth
sineti itkasarit

I have lost a filling
il Hashw Teleª

I have lost a crown/cap
il taeg Teleª

He/She has toothache
*ªando/ªandaha wagaª fi
  issinaen*

He/She has broken a tooth
kasar/kasarit sinna

He/She has lost a filling
il Hashw Teleª

He/She has lost a crown/cap
il taeg Teleª

Can you fix it temporarily?
*momkin tiSalaH-ha
  mo'aqatan*

Can you give me an
  injection?
momkin teddeenee Ho'na

Can you give him/her an
  injection?
*momkin tedeelo/tedelha
  Ho'na*

This denture is broken
il sinna di maksoora

Can you repair it?
momkin tiSalaH-ha

How much will it cost?
bikaem

You may hear

*iftaH bo'ak min faDlak/
  iftaHi bo'ik min faDlik*
Open your mouth, please

meHtaeg/meHtaega Hashw
You need a filling

Hadilak/Hadilik Ho'na
I'll give you an injection

Hakhlaªha lak/lik
I have to extract it

Parts of the body

ankle	*rosgh ilqaddam* (m)	رسغ القدم
appendix	*moSraan aªwar* (m)	مصران أعور
arm	*deraeª* (m)	ذراع
back	*Dahr* (m)	ظهر
bladder	*il masaena* (f)	مثانه
blood	*dam* (m)	دم
body	*gism* (m)	جسم
bone	*ªaDma* (f)	عظمه
bottom	*deryer* (m)	ديرير
bowels	*ilaHsha'* (pl)	الأحشاء
breast	*Sadr* (m)	صدر
buttocks	*ardaef* (m)	ارداف
cartilage	*kartlij* (m)	كارتلاج
chest	*Sadr* (m)	صدر
chin	*da'n* (m)	ذقن
ear	*wedn* (f)	ودن
elbow	*kooª* (m)	كوع
eye	*ªayn* (f)	عين
face	*wag-h* (m)	وجه
finger	*Sobaª* (m)	صباع
foot	*qaddam* (m)	قدم
genitals	*aªDa' ginsaya* (m pl)	أعضاء جنسيه
gland	*ghodda* (f)	غدة
hair	*shaªr* (m)	شعر
hand	*yad* (f)	يد
head	*ras* (m)	رأس

heart	*'alb* (m)	قلب
heel	*ka°b* (m)	كعب
hip	*redf* (m)	ردف
jaw	*fak* (m)	فك
joint	*mafSal* (m)	مفصل
kidney	*kelwa* (f)	كلوه
knee	*rokba* (f)	ركبه
leg	*regl* (m)	رجل
ligaments	*arbeTa* (m pl)	أربطه
lip	*sheffa* (f)	شفة
liver	*kebd* (m)	كبد
lung	*re'a* (m)	رئه
mouth	*fam* (m)	فم
muscle	*°aDala* (f)	عضله
nail	*Dofr* (m)	ظفر
neck	*ra'aba* (f)	رقبة
nerve	*°aSab* (m)	عصب
nose	*manakheer* (f)	مناخير
penis	*°oDw izzkoora* (m)	عضوالذكوره
private parts	*ala°Da' il ginsaya* (m pl)	الأعضاءالجنسيه
rectum	*fatHit il sharag* (f)	فتحةالشرج
rib	*Del°* (m)	ضلع
shoulder	*ketf* (m)	كتف
skin	*geld* (m)	جلد
spine	*°amood il fa'ri* (m)	العمودالفقرى
stomach	*me°da* (f)	المعده
tendon	*awtar* (m pl)	اوتار

testicles	*khawaSi* (f pl)	خواصى
thigh	*fakhd* (m)	فخد
throat	*zowr* (m)	زور
thumb	*Soba^a il ibhaem* (m)	صباع الأبهام
toe	*Soba^a iregl* (m)	صباع الرجل
tongue	*lisaen* (m)	لسان
tonsils	*lewaz* (f pl)	لوز
tooth	*sinna* (f)	سنه
vagina	*raHim* (m)	رحم
wrist	*rosgh* (m)	رسغ

PROBLEMS AND COMPLAINTS

● Generally, there are two police forces in Arab countries, one dealing with traffic control and the other with law and order. In Egypt, for example, the main police force wear green uniforms, while the traffic police wear black in winter and white in summer.

● Special 'tourist police' may be found at some archaeological sites.

● If you're attacked or have something stolen, you should contact the police immediately. Ask for the nearest police station (*fi ism bolees orayyib*), and if possible find someone who speaks English to help you – unless you're near a tourist site it's unlikely that any policeman will be able to speak English. In Morocco, Tunisia and Algeria, however, you may find one who understands French.

● If you're a woman and are assaulted, you may want to find another woman to talk to. In this case it's probably best to go to the nearest hospital and ask to see a female doctor (who will probably speak at least some English) or nurse. She will advise you what to do and may also be willing to accompany you to the police station. Arab women are very helpful and supportive, and will nearly always respond positively to a fellow woman in distress.

● In case of emergencies, check what the local emergency telephone numbers are when you arrive.

You may see

اسعاف	Ambulance station
البوليس السياحى	Tourist police

عاطل	Out of order
قسم البوليس	Police station
مستشفى	Hospital
مطافئ	Fire station

You may want to say

(for car breakdowns, see page 44; Emergencies, page 300)

General phrases

Can you help me?
momkin tisaªidni

Can you fix it (quickly)?
momkin tiSalaHoo (bisorªa)

When can you fix it?
HatiSalaHoo imta

Can I speak to the manager?
momkin akalim il modeer

There's a problem with . . .
fi moshkila . . .

There isn't/aren't any . . .
mafeesh . . .

I want (need) . . .
ªayiz (m)/*ªayza* (f) . . .

. . . doesn't work
. . . *bayiZ* (m)/*bayZa* (f)

. . . is broken
. . . *maksoor* (m)/*maksoora* (f)

I can't . . .
mish 'aedir (m)/
   'aedra (f) . . .

It wasn't my fault
mish ghalTiti

I have forgotten my . . .
neseet . . .

(My) . . . is lost
. . . *Daª* (m obj)/
   Daªit (f obj)

Someone has stolen (my) . . .
Had sara' . . .

I can't find . . .
mish laeªee (m)/*la'ya* (f) . . .

This isn't mine
mish bitaeªee (m)/*bitaªti* (f)

152

Where you're staying

There isn't any (hot) water
mafeesh maiya (sokhna)

There isn't any toilet paper
mafeesh wara' towalit

There isn't any electricity
mafeesh kahraba

There aren't any towels
mafeesh fowaT

I want another pillow
ªayiz/ªayza kamaen makhadda

I want another blanket
ªayiz/ªayza kamaen baTanaya

I want a light bulb
ªayiz/ªayza lamba

The light doesn't work
inoor bayiZ

The shower doesn't work
idosh bayiZ

The lock is broken
itirbaes maksoor

The switch on the lamp is broken
moftaeH inoor maksoor

I can't open the window
mish ªarif (m)/ªarfa (f) aftaH ishibaek

I can't close the window
mish ªarif/ªarfa a'fil ishibaek

I can't turn the tap off
mish ªarif/ªarfa a'fil il Hanafaya

I can't turn the tap on
mish ªarif/ªarfa aftaH il Hanafaya

The toilet doesn't flush
isafown bayiZ

The wash-basin is blocked
il HowD masdood

The wash-basin is dirty
il HowD wesikh

The room is . . .
il 'owda . . .

The room is too dark
il 'owda Dalma 'awi

The room is too small
il 'owda Soghayara 'awi

There's a lot of noise
fi dawsha kiteer 'awi

It's too hot in the room
il 'owda Har 'awi

The air conditioning doesn't work
itakyeef bayiZ

The air conditioning is too
cold
itakyeef baerid 'awi

The bed is not comfortable
il sereer mish moreeH

In cafés and restaurants

This is raw
da nay

This is burnt
da maHroo'

This is cold
da baerid

I didn't order this, I
ordered . . .
*ana maTalabtish da ana
Talabt . . .*

This glass is cracked
il kobbaya di maksoora

This is dirty
da wesikh

This smells bad
reHto weHsha

This tastes bad
Ta ªmo weHish

This bill is wrong
il fatoora di ghalaT

In shops

I bought this here
(yesterday)
ishtarayt da hena (imbariH)

Can you change this for
me?
momkin tighaiyyarli da

I want to return this
ªayiz (m)/*ªayza* (f)
aragaª da

I want to exchange this
ªayiz/ªayza aghaiyyar da

Can you give me a refund?
momkin astarid filoosee

Here is the receipt
il waSl aho

The material has a flaw
il 'omash fi ªayb

There is a hole
fi khorm

This isn't fresh
da mish Taza

There is a stain/mark
fi ªalaema

The lid is missing
il ghaTa mish mawgood

Forgetting and losing things and theft

I have forgotten my ticket
neseet itazkara

I have forgotten the key
neseet il moftaeH

I have lost my wallet
il maHfaZa Daaªit

I have lost my driving licence
irokhSa Daaªit

We have lost our rucksacks
shonaaT iDahr Daaªoo

Where is the lost property
    office?
fayn maktaeb il mafqoodaet

Where is the police station?
fayn ism ibolees

Someone has stolen my
    handbag
Had sara' shanTit eedee

Someone has stolen my car
Had sara' ªarabeetee

Someone has stolen my
    money
Had sara' filoosee

If someone is bothering you

Leave me alone!
sebni fi Haelee

Go away, or I'll call the
    police
*Hatemshi walla aTlob
    ibolees*

There is someone bothering
    me
fi waHid biyedaye'ni

There is someone following
    me
fi waHid biyemshi waraya

Helpful and unhelpful replies

*laHza min faDlak/
faDlik*
Just a moment, please

Tab^aan
Of course

Hageeb lak waHid
I'll bring you one

Hageeb lak kamaen waHid
I'll bring you another one

Haelan
Right away

HaSalaHoo lak/lik bokra
I'll fix it for you tomorrow

aesif/asfa mish momkin
I'm sorry, it's not possible

mish shoghli ana
I am not the person
responsible

iHna malnaesh da^awa
We are not responsible

ballagh ibolees
You should report it to the
police

aham shay' te^amelo . . .
The best thing you can do
is . .

insha' alla
God willing!

il Hamdoo lilla
Thanks be to God!

(*The last two are both
common, positive replies*)

Questions you may be asked

ishtarayto imta
When did you buy it?

ma^aaek il waSl
Do you have the receipt?

HaSalit imta
When did it happen?

Da^ait minak/minik fayn
Where did you lose it?

itsara'it fayn
Where was it stolen?

momkin towSifli/towSifili . . .
Can you describe . . .?

momkin towSifli shanTitak/towSifili shanTitik
Can you describe your bag?

momkin towSifli/towSifili il ªarabaya
Can you describe the car?

no ªha ay
What make is it?

nemrit-ha ay
What is the registration number?

sakin fayn
Where are you staying?

ªenwaenak/ªenwaenik ay
What is your address?

nemrit 'owdtak/'owdtik ay
What is your room number?

raqam basborak/basborik ay
What is your passport number?

ªandak/ªandik ta' meen
Have you got insurance?

momkin temla iTalab da
Please fill in this form

BASIC GRAMMAR

Classical Arabic, the language in which the Muslim holy book the Koran was written, dates back to the seventh century. All 23 Arab nations use this written form of the language, with only minor variations from country to country. The colloquial – spoken – language, used in this book, is used in Egypt and will be understood in most Arabic-speaking countries, and the basic rules of grammar which follow apply wherever you are.

Arabic is written from right to left. Each word is based on three 'root' letters, from which as many as ten different forms of the word may be derived (although some of them seem very far removed in meaning from the original word).

If you learn to read the Arabic script, you'll find that you'll often be able to guess the meaning of a word from its root letters. For example, the root letters of the word for book, *kitaeb*, are *k*, *t* and *b*. 'Write' is *katab*, 'writer' is *kaetib* and 'office' is *maktaeb* – all based on the same three letters.

Nouns

Arabic nouns are either masculine or feminine. As a rule, feminine nouns end in -*a*, or less commonly -*at*. Often the feminine form of a word is formed by adding one of these endings to the masculine, e.g.:

Masculine	Feminine	
Taalib	*Taaliba*	student
moddaris	*moddarissa*	teacher

However, there are many 'irregular' feminine nouns, such as:

bint	girl	*'om*	mother

Names of towns and countries are nearly always feminine.

Plurals

In Arabic the endings of nouns change in the plural. For 'regular' nouns you add -*een* to masculine nouns, and -*aet* to feminine nouns, e.g.:

Masculine	Feminine	
mohandis	*mohandissa*	engineer
mohandiseen	*mohandissaet*	engineers

'Irregular' nouns have no set rules for forming the plural – it's a matter of learning them as you go along, e.g.:

Singular		Plural	
kart	card	*koroot*	cards
bayt	house	*biyoot*	houses
baSala	onion	*baSal*	onions
shanTa	bag	*shonaaT*	bags

NB: There's a special plural for when you are referring to two of something: you add -*ayn* to the end of masculine words, and -*tayn* to feminine ones, e.g.:

layla	night	*layltayn*	two nights
sereer	bed	*sereerayn*	two beds
tazkara	ticket	*tazkartayn*	two tickets

Articles

The definite article ('the') in Arabic is *il*. This is the same for masculine and feminine, singular and plural. There is no indefinite article ('a' or 'an').

Meanings often depend on the position of *il* – and whether it is used at all. For example:

bayt	a house
il bayt	the house
il bayt il kibeer	the big house
il bayt kibeer	the house is big

Possessives ('my', 'your', 'his', 'her', etc.)

Arabic adds a range of endings to nouns to denote possession:

	Masculine	Feminine
my	-i	-ti
your (s)	-ak	-ik
his/her/its	-o	-ha
our	-na	-tna
your (pl)	-kom	-kom
their	-hom	-t-hom

For example:

shanTiti	my bag
basboro	his passport
reHlatna	our trip
kamirat-hom	their cameras

If the 'possessive' noun is accompanied by an adjective, this must be preceded by the definite article (*il*), e.g.:

kitaeb kibeer a big book   *kitaebi il kibeer* my big book

Adjectives

In Arabic, adjectives come after the noun. They 'agree' with it – that is, they have different endings according to whether the noun is masculine or feminine, singular or plural.

For 'regular' adjectives, you add *-a* to the masculine singular to make the feminine singular, e.g.:

il otobees il kibeer (m)	the big bus
il Taiyaara il kibeera (f)	the big aeroplane

For plurals, when referring to things (as opposed to people), adjectives have the feminine singular ending, e.g.:

Singular	Plural	
maTᵃam (m)	*maTaaᵃim*	cheap
rakheeS	*rakheeSa*	restaurant(s)
shanTa (f) *khaDra*	*shonaaT khaDra*	green bag(s)

When referring to people, adjectives have plural endings as appropriate: *-een* for masculine, *-aat* or *-aet* for feminine, e.g.:

walad (m) *Soghayar*	*aewlad Soghayareen*	little boy(s)
bint (f) *Helwa*	*banaet Helwaet*	pretty girl(s)

There are also 'irregular' adjectives, in which the whole word changes according to gender and number, e.g.:

tarabayza (f) *kibeera*	*tarabizaat kobaar*	big table(s)
walad (m) *shaeb*	*aewlad shabaeb*	young boy(s)

Personal pronouns

Subject pronouns are often omitted in Arabic, the context usually making it clear who or what is being referred to. They're sometimes used to give special emphasis, and it's also useful to learn them so that you can avoid misunderstandings.

I	*ana*
you (*masculine singular*)	*inta*
you (*feminine singular*)	*inti*
he/it	*howa*
she/it	*haya*
we	*iHna*
you (*plural*)	*intoo*
they	*homma*

Object pronouns ('me', 'him', 'her', 'us', etc.) are the same as the subject pronouns.

Indirect object pronouns ('to me', 'to him', etc.) are added to the ends of verbs. They are:

to me	*li*
to you (*masculine singular*)	*lo*
to you (*feminine singular*)	*liha*
to him/it	*lo*
to her/it	*liha*
to us	*lina*
to you (*plural*)	*lokom*
to them	*lohom*

For example:

olli min faDlak	Tell me please
Hab^aatlokom gawabaet	I'll send you (*pl*) letters

Demonstratives ('this', 'that')

Arabic doesn't differentiate between 'this' and 'that' but there are masculine and feminine forms, depending on the gender of the noun. There is also a plural form.

da	this/that (*masculine*)
di	this/that (*feminine*)
dowl	these/those

For example:

il bayt da kibeer	That house is big
di madeena qadeema	This is an old city
il madeena di qadeema	This city is old
bikaem dowl	How much are these?

Verbs

Verbs in Arabic have different forms according to the subject of the verb, the gender of the subject, and the tense. All verbs are derived from a 'root' of three letters (see page 158), and the different forms are made by changing the beginning, middle and/or end of the root. For example, the root of 'travel' is the letters **s**, **f**, **r**. Once you know the root of a verb, you can work out the various forms – most follow the pattern below.

There is no infinitive form of Arabic verbs (the equivalent of 'to . . .'), so in the Dictionary verbs are given in the 'he' and 'she' present tense forms.

Present tense

I travel	*asaefir*
You (*m*) travel	*tisaefir*
You (*f*) travel	*tisafri*
He/it travels	*yisaefir*
She/it travels	*tisaefir*
We travel	*nisaefir*
You (*pl*) travel	*tisafroo*
They travel	*yisafroo*

Past tense

I travelled	*safirt*
You (*m*) travelled	*safirt*
You (*f*) travelled	*safirti*
He/it travelled	*safir*
She/it travelled	*safrit*
We travelled	*safirna*
You (*pl*) travelled	*safirtom*
They travelled	*safrom*

Future tense

The future tense of most verbs is formed by placing *Ha-* in front of the present tense form:

I will travel	*Hasaefir*
You (*m*) will travel	*Hatsaefir*
You (*f*) will travel	*Hatsafri*
He/it will travel	*Haiysaefir*
She/it will travel	*Hatsaefir*
We will travel	*Hansaefir*
You (*pl*) will travel	*Hatsafroo*
They will travel	*Haiysafroo*

To give another example, the root letters of 'book' ('make a reservation') are **H, g, z**. Using the patterns above, 'I book', for instance, is *aHgiz*; 'we booked' is *Hagezna*; 'she will book' is *HateHgiz*.

Irregular verbs

There are a number of 'irregular' verbs in Arabic, which do not follow the pattern above. Two of the most useful are given below, in their present tense.

'To want'

I want	*ªawez*
You (*m*) want	*ªawza*
You (*f*) want	*ªawza*
He/it wants	*ªawez*
She/it wants	*ªawza*
We want	*ªawzeen*
You (*pl*) want	*ªawzeen*
They want	*ªawzeen*

'To come'

I come	*gay*
You (*m*) come	*gay*
You (*f*) come	**gaya**
He/it comes	*gay*
She/it comes	**gaya**
We come	*gayeen*
You (*pl*) come	*gayeen*
They come	*gayeen*

'To be'

Arabic has no verb 'to be'; the subject is simply followed by the rest of the sentence, without a verb. For example:

I am a student	*ana Taalib*
He is a doctor	*howa doktowr*

To say 'there is' or 'there are' you use the word *fi*, e.g.:

fi korsi   There is a chair   *fi tazakir*   There are tickets

The past tense of 'to be' is:

I was	*kont*
You (*m*) were	*kont*
You (*f*) were	**konti**
He/it was	*kaen*
She/it was	**kaenit**
We were	*konna*
You (*pl*) were	*kontom*
They were	*kaeno*

'To have'

Arabic has no verb 'to have' either. Instead, one of two words can be used to indicate possession. These are *^aand* meaning 'have' ('possess') and *ma^a* meaning 'have with . . .' (at the present time). They are used with a suffix:

	'have'	'have with . . .'
I have	*^aandi*	*ma^aaya*
You (*m*) have	*^aandak*	*ma^aaek*
You (*f*) have	*^aandik*	*ma^aaeki*
He/it has	*^aando*	*ma^aa*
She/it has	*^aandaha*	*ma^aaha*
We have	*^aandena*	*ma^aaena*
You (*pl*) have	*^aandokom*	*ma^aakom*
They have	*^aandohom*	*ma^aahom*

^aandi ^aarabaya	I own a car
ma^aaya ^aarabaya	I've got a car with me

momkin

One useful word to remember is **momkin**. Used with the present tense of any verb, it means 'can I?', 'is it permitted?', e.g.:

momkin arkin hena	Can I park here?
momkin tiSawar di	Can she photocopy this?

Negatives

The negative in Arabic is formed in one of two main ways. With verbs *ma-* is put in front of the verb, and *-sh* after it, e.g.:

fi kalb	There is a dog	*mafeesh kalb*	There is no dog

With adjectives and adverbs *mish* is put before the word, e.g.:

da momkin	This is possible
da mish momkin	This is not possible

Questions

Questions in written Arabic end with a back-to-front question mark: ؟ . In speech a question is usually indicated simply by the voice rising at the end of the statement. However you can also make a sentence into a question by putting *hael* at the beginning:

il gaw Helw	The weather is good
hael il gaw Helw	Is the weather good?

Question words can come at the beginning or end of a sentence, e.g:

What is your name?		*ismak ay*
	or	*ay ismak*

Question words include:

fayn	where?		*lay*	why?
imta	when?		*izzay*	how?
ay	what?		*ay*	which?
meen	who?			

Prepositions

Some of the most frequently used prepositions in Arabic are:

ªala	on/over		*'abl*	before
min	from		*baªd*	after
fi	in(to)/in/at		*li*	to
fo'	over		*wara*	behind
taHt	under		*amaem*	before
ªan	about			

DAYS, MONTHS, DATES

Days

Monday	*yowm il itnayn*
Tuesday	*yowm italaet*
Wednesday	*yowm il arba^a*
Thursday	*yowm il khamees*
Friday	*yowm il gom^{a}a*
Saturday	*yowm isabt*
Sunday	*yowm il Had*

Months

January	*yanayer*
February	*fabrayer*
March	*maeris*
April	*ibreel*
May	*mayo*
June	*yonyo*
July	*yolyo*
August	*aghostos*
September	*sebtambir*
October	*oktobar*
November	*novambir*
December	*disambir*

Seasons

Spring	*irabee^a*
Summer	*iSayf*
Autumn	*il khareef*
Winter	*isheta*

General phrases

day	*yowm*
week	*izboo^a*
fortnight (two weeks)	*izboo^ayn*
month	*shahr*
six months	*set osh-hor*
year	*sana*

today	*inaharda*
tomorrow	*bokra*
day after tomorrow	*ba^d bokra*
yesterday	*imbariH*
day before yesterday	*awil imbariH*

(in the) morning	*iSobH*
(in the) afternoon	*ba^d iDohr*
(in the) evening	*il maghrib*
(at) night	*bilayl*

this morning	*inaharda iSobH*
this afternoon	*inaharda ba^d iDohr*
this evening	*inaharda il maghrib*

tomorrow morning	*bokra iSobH*
tomorrow afternoon	*bokra ba^d iDohr*
tomorrow evening	*bokra il maghrib*

yesterday morning	*imbariH iSobH*
yesterday afternoon	*imbariH ba^d iDohr*
yesterday evening	*imbariH il maghrib*

on Monday	*yowm il itnayn*
on Tuesdays	*kol yowm talaet*
every Wednesday	*kol yowm arba^a*

in August	*fi aghostos*
at the beginning of March	*awil maeris*

in the middle of June	*fi noS yonyo*
at the end of September	*fi akhir sebtambir*
during the summer	*fil Sayf*
two years ago	*min sanatayn*
in the nineties	*fil tes^aeenaet*
last Monday	*il itnayn ili faet*
last week	*il izboo^a ili faet*
last month	*ishahr ili faet*
last year	*isana ili faetit*
next Tuesday	*italaet ili gay*
next week	*il izboo^a ili gay*
next month	*ishahr ili gay*
next year	*isana igaya*
before Saturday	*abl yowm isabt*
after Tuesday	*ba^ad yowm italaet*
until/by Friday	*lighayit yowm igom^aa*
two days ago	*min yowmayn*
three days ago	*min talat tiyaem*
What day is it today?	*inaharda ay*
What is the date today?	*inaharda kaem fishahr*
When is your birthday?	*^aeed milaedak/milaedik imta*
On the first of January	*awil yanayer*
On Tuesday 10 May	*yowm italaet ^aashra mayo*
1993	*sanat alf tos^aomaya wi talaeta wi tes^aeen*
In the 15th century	*fil qarn il khamastashar*

The Muslim year

The Islamic calendar is a lunar one, and moves forward around eleven days in each 'Western' year. The year itself is dated from A.D. 580, and this means that, according to the Muslim calendar, 1993 for example falls half into the Islamic year 1413, and half into 1414. You may see the Islamic year written on documents (such as hotel registration forms), especially in the Gulf region.

The Islamic year is divided into twelve lunar months, as follows:

1st	*moHaram*	7th	*ragab*
2nd	*saffar*	8th	*sha^{a}baen*
3rd	*rabee^a ilawal*	9th	*ramadan*
4th	*rabee^a itaeni*	10th	*shawael*
5th	*gamadee ilawal*	11th	*zool qe^{a}da*
6th	*gamadee itaeni*	12th	*zool Haga*

TIME

one o'clock	*issa*ᵃ*a waHda*
two o'clock	*issa*ᵃ*a itnayn*
three o'clock	*issa*ᵃ*a talaeta*
quarter past . . .	*. . . wi rob*ᵃ
half past . . .	*. . . wi noS*
five past . . .	*. . . wi khamsa*
twenty past . . .	*. . . wi tilt*
twenty-five past . . .	*. . . wi noS ila khamsa*
quarter to . . .	*. . . ila rob*ᵃ
ten to . . .	*. . . ila* ᵃ*ashra*
twenty to . . .	*. . . ila tilt*
half past three	*talaeta wi noS*
half past seven	*saba*ᵃ*a wi noS*
five past nine	*tes*ᵃ*a wi khamsa*
quarter to five	*khamsa ila rob*ᵃ
ten to eleven	*Hidashar ila* ᵃ*ashra*
noon/midday	*iDohr*
midnight	*noS ilayl*
in the morning	*iSobH*
in the afternoon	*ba*ᵃ*d iDohr*
in the evening	*il maghrib*
a quarter of an hour	*rob*ᵃ *sa*ᵃ*a*
three quarters of an hour	*talatirba*ᵃ *sa*ᵃ*a*
half an hour	*noS sa*ᵃ*a*

The 24-hour clock is not generally used in the Arab world.

soon	*qareeban*
early	*badri*
late	*mit'akhar*
on time	*fi mi^aado*
half an hour ago	*min noS sa^aa*
in ten minutes' time	*kamaen ^aashar d'ayi'*
in a quarter of an hour	*kamaen rob^a sa^aa*
What time is it?	*issa^aa kaem*
It's . . .	*issa^aa . . .*
It's nine o'clock	*issa^aa tes^aa*
It's six o'clock	*issa^aa setta*
It's quarter past eight	*issa^aa tamanya wi rob^a*
(At) what time . . .?	*. . . issa^aa kaem*
At . . .	*issa^aa . . .*
At half past one	*issa^aa waHda wi noS*
At quarter to seven	*issa^aa sab^aa ila rob^a*
(At) exactly two o'clock	*issa^aa itnayn tamaeman*
About half past six	*Hawaeli setta wi noS*
Nearly quarter to five	*Hawaeli khamsa ila rob^a*

173

COUNTRIES AND NATIONALITIES

Country/Continent

Nationality & Adjective
(masculine/feminine)

Country/Continent		Nationality & Adjective (masculine/feminine)
Africa	*afriqya*	*afreeqee/afreeqaya*
Algeria	*il gaza'ir*	*gaza'iri/gaza'iraya*
America	*amreeka*	*amreeki/amreekaya*
Asia	*asya*	*asyawi/asyawaya*
Austria	*inemsa*	*nemsawi/nemsawaya*
Australia	*ostralya*	*ostorali/ostoralaya*
Bahrain	*il baHrayn*	*baHrani/baHranaya*
Belgium	*baljeeka*	*biljeeki/biljeekaya*
Canada	*kanada*	*kanadi/kanadaya*
China	*iSeen*	*Seeni/Sennaya*
Denmark	*idenmark*	*denmarki/denmarkaya*
Egypt	*maSr*	*maSri/maSraya*
England	*ingilterra*	*ingleezi/ingleezaya*
Europe	*orobba*	*orobbi/orobbaya*
Finland	*finlanda*	*finlandi/finlandaya*
France	*faransa*	*faransawi/faransawaya*
Germany	*almanya*	*almaeni/almanaya*
Gibraltar	*gabal Tari'*	*min gabal Tari'*
Great Britain	*briTanya il^{a}ozma*	*briTani/briTanaya*
Greece	*il yonaen*	*yonaeni/yonaenaya*
Holland	*holanda*	*holandi/holandaya*
India	*il hind*	*hindi/hindaya*
Iran	*iraan*	*iraani/iranaya*
Iraq	*il ^{a}iraq*	*^{a}iraqi/^{a}iraqaya*
Ireland	*ayrlanda*	*ayrlandi/ayrlandaya*
Israel	*isra'eel*	*isra'eeli/isra'eelaya*
Italy	*iTaliya*	*Tilyani/Tilyanaya*

Japan	*il yabaen*	*yabaeni/yabanaya*
Jordan	*ilordon*	*ordonni/ordonnaya*
Kuwait	*ikoweet*	*kweeti/kweetaya*
Lebanon	*libnaen*	*libnaeni/libnaenaya*
Libya	*libya*	*leebee/leebaya*
Malta	*malTa*	*malTi/malTaya*
Mauritania	*moritanya*	*moritaeni/moritaenaya*
Morocco	*il maghreb*	*maghrebi/maghrebaya*
New Zealand	*nyozeelanda*	*nyozeelandi/ nyozeelandaya*
Norway	*inorweeg*	*norweegi/norweegaya*
Oman	*ᵃoman*	*ᵃomani/ᵃomanaya*
Palestine	*filisTeen*	*filisTeeni/filisTeenaya*
Portugal	*il bortoghael*	*bortoghaeli/ bortoghaelaya*
Qatar	*qaTar*	*qaTari/qaTaraya*
Russia	*rosya*	*roosee/roosaya*
Saudi Arabia	*isoᵃodaya*	*soᵃoodi/soᵃoodaya*
Scotland	*skotlanda*	*iskotlandi/iskotlandaya*
Spain	*asbaniya*	*asbaeni/asbanaya*
Sudan	*isoodaen*	*soodaeni/soodanaya*
Sweden	*isoweed*	*soweedi/soweedaya*
Switzerland	*swisra*	*siwesri/siwesraya*
Syria	*sorya*	*sooree/sooraya*
Tunisia	*toonis*	*tonsi/tonsaya*
Turkey	*torkaya*	*torki/torkaya*
United Arab Emirates	*il imaraat il ᵃarabaya*	*min ilmaraat il ᵃarabaya*
United States of America	*il wilayaet il motaHida il amreekaya*	*amrikaeni/ amrikaenaya*
Wales	*waylz*	*min waylz*
Yemen	*il yaman*	*yamani/yamanaya*

PLACE NAMES

Abu Dhabi	*aboo Zabi*	أبوظبي
Aleppo	*Halab*	حلب
Alexandria	*iskinderayya*	الأسكندريه
Algiers	*algazaeir*	الجزائر
Amman	*ᵃamaen*	عمان
Cairo	*ilqahira*	القاهره
Casablanca	*idar ilbayDa*	الدار البيضاء
Damascus	*dimash'*	دمشق
Dubai	*doobay*	دبي
Fez	*faes*	فاس
Jeddah	*gadda*	جده
Luxor	*lo'Sor*	الأقصر
Karnak	*alkarnak*	الكرنك
Khartoum	*alkharToom*	الخرطوم
Marrakesh	*maraakish*	مراكش
Mecca	*makka*	مكه
Medina	*imadeena*	المدينه
Petra	*betra*	بترا
Riyadh	*ariyaaD*	الرياض
Suez	*isoways*	السويس
Tangier	*Tanga*	طنجه
Tripoli	*Tarablos*	طرابلس
Tunis	*toonis*	تونس
Valley of the Kings	*waedi imolooq*	وادى الملوك

GENERAL SIGNS AND NOTICES

إجذب	Pull
إحذر	Caution
إحذرالكلب	Beware of the dog
إدفع	Push
اسعافات أوليه	First aid
الدخول مجاناً	Admission free
أطرق الباب من فضلك	Please knock
الدورالأرضى	Ground floor
اوكازيون	Sale, For sale
بارد	Cold
بوليس	Police
بويه	Wet paint
جرس حريق	Fire alarm
حجرات للأيجار	Rooms to let
خدمات الزبائن	Customer service
خروج	Exit
خروج (طوارئ)	(Emergency) exit
خطر	Danger
خطرالموت	Danger of death
دخول	Entrance
دق الجرس من فضلك	Please ring
رجال	Gentlemen
ساخن	Hot
سلم كهر	Escalator
سيدات	Ladies
صراف	Cashier

ضريبه	Tax, VAT
طريق خاص	Private road
عاطل	Out of order
عرض مسائى	Late performance
فاضى	Free, vacant
عرض خاص	Special offer
للأيجار	To let, For hire
محجوز	Reserved
مرحباً	Welcome
مشغول	Engaged
مصعد	Lift
مغلق	Closed
مغلق بمناسبة الأعياد	Closed for holidays
مغلق بمناسبة الأجازة الرسميه	Closed on public holidays
مغلق طول اليوم	Closed all day
مفتوح	Open
مفتوح خلال الأسبوع	Open on weekdays
مكان للوقوف فقط	Standing room only
ممنوع	Forbidden, prohibited
ممنوع الأزعاج	Do not disturb
ممنوع التجاوز	No trespassing
ممنوع التدخين	No smoking
ممنوع الدخول	No entrance
ممنوع اللمس	Do not touch
ممنوع المرور للمشاه	No thoroughfare for pedestrians
منطقه عسكريه	Military zone
مياه غيرصالحه للشرب	Not drinking water
مياه صالحه للشرب	Drinking water

CONVERSION TABLES (approximate equivalents)

Linear measurements

centimetres	*santimetr*	سينتيمتر
metres	*metr*	متر
kilometres	*keeloometr*	كيلومتر

10 cm = 4 inches   1 inch = 2.45 cm
50 cm = 19.6 inches   1 foot = 30 cm
1 metre = 39.37 inches   1 yard = 0.91 m
(just over 1 yard)
100 metres = 110 yards
1 km = 0.62 miles   1 mile = 1.61 km

To convert: km to miles: divide by 8 and multiply by 5
             miles to km: divide by 5 and multiply by 8

Miles		Kilometres
0.6	1	1.6
1.2	2	3.2
1.9	3	4.8
2.5	4	6.4
3	5	8
6	10	16
12	20	32
19	30	48
25	40	64
31	50	80
62	100	161
68	110	177
75	120	193
81	130	209

Liquid measures

litre   *litr*   لتر

1 litre = 1.8 pints		1 pint = 0.57 litres
5 litres = 1.1 gallons		1 gallon = 4.55 litres

'A litre of water's a pint and three quarters'

Gallons		**Litres**
0.2	1	4.5
0.4	2	9
0.7	3	13.6
0.9	4	18
1.1	5	23
2.2	10	45.5

Weights

gram	*gram*	جرام
100 grams	*meet gram*	١٠٠ جرام
200 grams	*meetayn gram*	٢٠٠ جرام
kilo	*keeloo*	كيلو

100 g = 3.5 oz	1 oz = 28 g
200 g = 7 oz	$^{1}/_{4}$ lb = 113 g
$^{1}/_{2}$ kilo = 1.1 lb	$^{1}/_{2}$ lb = 227 g
1 kilo = 2.2 lb	1 lb = 454 g

Pounds		Kilos (Grams)
2.2	1	0.45 (450)
4.4	2	0.9 (900)
6.6	3	1.4 (1400)
8.8	4	1.8 (1800)
11	5	2.3 (2300)
22	10	4.5 (4500)

Area

The unit of area used in the Arabic-speaking world is the *fedaen*, which is slightly larger than an acre, or about half a hectare. In some countries, hectares are also used.

Hectares		Acres
0.4	1	2.5
2	5	12
4	10	25
10	50	124
40.5	100	247

Clothing and shoe sizes

Women's dresses and suits

UK	10	12	14	16	18	20
Arab world	36	38	40	42	44	46

Men's suits and coats

UK	36	38	40	42	44	46
Arab world	46	48	50	52	54	56

Men's shirts

UK	14	$14^1/_2$	15	$15^1/_2$	16	$16^1/_2$	17
Arab world	36	37	38	39	41	42	43

Shoes

UK	2	3	4	5	6	7	8	9	10	11
Arab world	35	36	37	38	39	41	42	43	44	45

Waist and chest measurements

inches	28	30	32	34	36	38	40	42	44	46	48	50
centimetres	71	76	81	87	91	97	102	107	112	117	122	127

Tyre pressures

lb/sq in	15	18	20	22	24	26	28	30	33	35
kg/sq cm	1.1	1.3	1.4	1.5	1.7	1.8	2.0	2.1	2.3	2.5

NATIONAL HOLIDAYS

(*see* Religion and culture, *page 8*)

Christian and Islamic feasts are celebrated at different times each year according to the Muslim (lunar) or Christian (Coptic) calendar.

The main religious holidays are:

Muslim

ªeed il fiTr	The Breakfast Feast (3 days, after Ramadan)
ªeed il aDHa	The Biram Feast (4 days)
il moolid il nabawi	The Prophet's Birthday (1 day)

The timing of all these feasts depends upon the sighting of the New Moon.

Christian

krismas	Christmas (25 December)
ras il sana	New Year (31 December)
krismas	Coptic Christmas (7 January)
ªeed il qlyama	Easter

Other days mark political and military achievements and each country will have its own particular public days of celebration or holiday. It is advisable to check with the relevant tourist office before planning a visit, to ensure that you do not arrive at a time when everything is closed!

USEFUL ADDRESSES

In the UK and Ireland

(Where no separate address is given, Ireland is accredited to the London embassies.)

Egypt

Egyptian Embassy
26 South Street, London W1 *Tel:* 071-499 2401

Eygptian Consulate (*for visas*)
2 Lowndes Street, London SW1 *Tel:* 071-235 9777

Egyptian Embassy
12 Clyde Road, Ballsbridge, Dublin *Tel:* 01 606 566

Egyptian Tourist Authority
168 Piccadilly, London W1 *Tel:* 071-493 5282

Jordan

Jordanian Embassy
6 Upper Phillimore Gardens, London W8 *Tel:* 071-937 3685

Tourist information on Jordan is supplied through:

Royal Jordanian Airlines
211 Regent Street, London W1 *Tel:* 071-437 9465

Morocco

Moroccan Embassy
49 Queensgate Gardens, London SW7 *Tel:* 071-581 5001

Moroccan Consulate
97 Praed Street, London W2 *Tel:* 071-724 0719

Ireland is accredited to the Moroccan Embassy in Brussels:
29 Boulevard St Michel, 1040 Brussels
Tel: 376 1100/5

Moroccan Tourist Office
174 Regent Street, London W1 *Tel:* 071-437 0073

Saudi Arabia

Saudi Arabian Embassy
15 Curzon Street, London W1 *Tel:* 071-917 3000

Bahrain

Bahraini Embassy
98 Gloucester Road, London SW7 *Tel:* 071-370 5132

Syria

Syrian Embassy
8 Belgrave Square, London W1 *Tel:* 071-245 9012

In the Arab world

Egypt

British Embassy
Ahmed Ragheb Street, Garden City, Cairo *Tel:* 02 354 0850

There are British consulates in Alexandria, Luxor, Suez and
Port Said.

There is no Irish Embassy in Egypt, only an honorary consul.
Find out details before travelling, since they are liable to change.

Egyptian Tourist Authority (*headquarters*)
Misr Travel Tower, Abbassia Square, Cairo *Tel:* 02 823510/
02 824858

Jordan

British Embassy
P.O.B. 87, Abdoun, Amman *Tel:* 06 823100

There is an Irish honorary consul in Amman. Check details before travel.

Tourist information is available from the Ministry of Tourism in Amman. *Tel:* 06 642311.

Morocco

British Embassy
17 Boulevard de la Tour, Hasan Rabat *Tel:* 0727 20905/6

There are also British Embassy representatives in Tangier, Casablanca and Agadir.

Morocco is accredited to the Irish Embassy in Paris:
Embassy of Ireland, 12 Avenue Foch, 75116 Paris
Tel: 45 00 20 87

Tourist Information Centre
22 Avenue d'Alger, Rabat *Tel:* 0773 0562

Saudi Arabia

British Embassy
P.O.B. 94351, Riyadh 11693 *Tel:* 01 488 0077

There is also a British consulate in Jeddah.

Irish Embassy
Diplomatic Quarter, Riyadh *Tel:* 01 488 2300

Bahrain

British Embassy
21 Government Avenue, Manama, Bahrain *Tel:* 534404

Bahrain is accredited to the Irish Embassy in Riyadh.

Syria

British Embassy
Quarter Malki, 11 Mohammad Kurd Ali Street, Imm Kotob,
Damascus *Tel:* 011 712561

There is also a British consulate in Aleppo.

Tourist information is available from Damascus airport, and
from the Ministry of Tourism, Damascus.

NUMBERS

0	*Sefr*	.
1	*waHid, waHda*	١
2	*itnayn*	٢
3	*talaeta*	٣
4	*arbaᵃa*	٤
5	*khamsa*	٥
6	*setta*	٦
7	*sabᵃa*	٧
8	*tamanya*	٨
9	*tesᵃa*	٩
10	*ᵃashra*	١٠
11	*Hidashar*	١١
12	*itnashar*	١٢
13	*talatashar*	١٣
14	*arbaᵃtashar*	١٤
15	*khamastashar*	١٥
16	*setashar*	١٦
17	*sabaᵃtashar*	١٧
18	*tamantashar*	١٨
19	*tesaᵃtashar*	١٩
20	*ᵃishreen*	٢٠
21	*waHid wi ᵃishreen*	٢١
22	*itnayn wi ᵃishreen*	٢٢
23 etc.	*talaeta wi ᵃishreen*	٢٣
30	*talaeteen*	٣٠
31	*waHid wi talaeteen*	٣١
32 etc.	*itnayn wi talaeteen*	٣٢
40	*arbᵃeen*	٤٠
50	*khamseen*	٥٠
60	*seteen*	٦٠
70	*sabᵃeen*	٧٠

80	*tamaneen*	٨٠
90	*tes^aeen*	٩٠
100	*maya*	١٠٠
101	*maya wi waHid*	١٠١
102 *etc.*	*maya wi itnayn*	١٠٢
150	*maya wi khamseen*	١٥٠
200	*mitayn*	٢٠٠
300	*toltomaya*	٣٠٠
400	*rob^aomaya*	٤٠٠
500	*khomsomaya*	٥٠٠
600	*sotomaya*	٦٠٠
700	*sob^aomaya*	٧٠٠
800	*tomnomaya*	٨٠٠
900	*tos^aomaya*	٩٠٠
1,000	*alf*	١٠٠٠
1,100 *etc.*	*alf wi maya*	١١٠٠
2,000	*alfayn*	٢٠٠٠
3,000	*talatalaef*	٣٠٠٠
4,000	*arba^atalaef*	٤٠٠٠
5,000	*khamastalaef*	٥٠٠٠
6,000	*setalaef*	٦٠٠٠
7,000	*saba^atalaef*	٧٠٠٠
8,000	*tamantalaef*	٨٠٠٠
9,000	*tesa^atalaef*	٩٠٠٠
100,000	*mit alf*	١٠٠٬٠٠٠
1,000,000	*miliown*	١٬٠٠٠٬٠٠٠
2,000,000	*itnayn miliown*	٢٬٠٠٠٬٠٠٠

The number one has two forms, for use with masculine and feminine nouns: *waHid* (m) and *waHda* (f).

Compound numbers in Arabic are written from left to right as in English. For example, 1993 = ١٩٩٣; 1414 = ١٤١٤.

● Years

1993	*alf wi tos^aomaya talaeta wi tes^aeen*
2000	*alfayn*

ENGLISH - ARABIC DICTIONARY

There is a list of car and bicycle parts on pages 46, parts of the body on page 148, and Menu reader on page 98; see also the lists on pages 168–176. Numbers are inside the front cover and on page 188.

Verbs are given in the third person singular (*m* and *f*). (*See* Basic grammar, *page 158*.)

A

about (*relating to*)	*ªan*	عن
(*approximately*)	*Hawaeli*	حوالى
above	*fo'*	فوق
abroad	*barra*	بره
abscess	*waram* (m)	ورم
accept: he/she accepts	*ye'bal* (m)/*te'bal* (f)	يقبل/ تقبل
accident	*Hadsa* (f)	حادثه
accommodation	*sakan* (m)	سكن
according to	*Hasab*	حسب
account (*bank; bill*)	*Hissaeb* (m)	حساب
accountant	*moHaesib* (m)/ *moHasba* (f)	محاسب/ محاسبه
ache	*wagaª* (m)	وجع
acid	*Haamid* (m)	حامض
across	*ªabr*	عبر
acrylic	*akrilik* (m)	اكريليك
act (*on stage*): he/she acts	*yemassel* (m)/ *temassel* (f)	يمثل/ تمثل
activity	*nashaat* (m)	نشاط

actor	*momassil* (m)	ممثل
actress	*momassilla* (f)	ممثله
adaptor (*electrical*)	*moHawil* (m)	محول
add (*count*): he/she adds	*ye^ad* (m)/*te^ad* (f)	يعد/ تعد
addicted	*modmin* (m)/ *modmina* (f)	مدمن/ مدمنه
address	*^aenwaen* (m)	عنوان
adhesive tape	*wara' lazza'* (m)	ورق لزاق
admission	*dekhool* (m)	دخول
admission charge	*tazkarit dekhool*	تزكرة دخول
adopted	*tabaenna* (m)/ *tabaennat* (f)	تبنى/ تبنت
adult	*raashid* (m)/ *rashida* (f)	رشيد/ رشيده
advance: in advance	*mo'addam: mo'addaman*	مقدم/ مقدماً
advanced (level)	*(mestawa) ^aaeli*	مستوى عالى
advertisement	*i^alaen* (m)	إعلان
advertising	*de^aaya* (f)	دعايه
aerial	*erial* (m)	إيريال
aeroplane	*Taiyaara* (f)	طياره
afford: I/we can't afford it	*mish 'addena*	مش قدنا
afraid: he/she is afraid	*khayef* (m)/*khayfa* (f)	خايف/ خايفه
after(wards)	*ba^adayn*	بعدين
afternoon	*ba^ad iDohr* (m)	بعدالظهر
aftershave	*ba^ad il Hela'a*	بعدالحلاقه
again	*taeni*	تانى
against	*Ded*	ضد
age	*^aomr* (m)	عمر
agency	*wikaela* (f)	وكاله
ago	*min*	من
a week ago	*min izboo^a*	من اسبوع

agree: he/she agrees	*yewafe'* (m)/	يوافق/ توافق
	tewafe' (f)	
I agree	*ana metefe'* (m)/	أنامتفق/ أنامتفقه
	ana metefa' (f)	
I don't agree	*ana mish mewafe'*	انامش موافق/
	(m)/*ana mish*	انامش موافقه
	mewaf'a (f)	
AIDS	*aidz* (m)	أيدز
air	*hawa* (m)	هواء
by air	*bil gaw*	بالجو
(by) air mail	*bareed gawi*	بريد جوى
air conditioning	*takyeef hawa* (m)	تكييف هواء
air force	*selaH eTayaran* (m)	سلاح الطيران
airline	*khaT gawi* (m)	خط جوى
airport	*maTaar* (m)	مطار
aisle	*Tor'a* (f)	طرقه
alarm	*inzaar* (m)	إنزار
alarm clock	*menabbeh* (m)	منبه
alcohol	*khamra* (f)	خمره
alcoholic (*content*)	*fi khamra*	فيه خمره
(*person*)	*khamorggi* (m)/	خمرجى/ خمرجيه
	khamorggaya (f)	
alive	*Hai* (m)/*Haiya* (f)	حى/ حيه
all	*kol*	كل
allergic (to)	*Hasassayya* (Ded)	حساسيه ضد
alley	*Hara* (f)	حاره
allow: he/she allows	*yesmaH* (m)/	يسمح/ تسمح
	tesmaH (f)	
(not) allowed	(*mish*) *masmooH*	(مش) مسموح
all right	*kwayyis* (m)/	كويس/ كويسه
	kwayissa (f)	
almond	*lowz* (pl)	لوز
alone	*lewaHdi*	لوحدى
also	*kamaen*	كمان
although	*belraghm min*	بالرغم من
always	*dayman*	دائما
am (*see* 'to be', *p. 165*)		

192

ambassador	*safeer* (m)/*safeera* (f)	سفير/ سفيره
ambition	*TomooH* (m)	طموح
ambitious	*TomooH* (m)/ *TamooHa* (f)	طموح/ طموحه
ambulance	*es^aaaf* (m)	إسعاف
among	*min Demn*	من ضمن
amount	*kemayya* (f)	كميه
amusement arcade	*Salit le^ab*	صالة لعب
amusement park	*malaehee* (pl)	ملاهى
anaesthetic	*beng* (m)	بنج
general anaesthetic	*beng ^aam*	بنج عام
and	*wa*	و
angry	*ghaDbaan* (m)/ *ghaDbaana* (f)	غضبان/ غضبانه
animal	*Hayaewaen* (m)	حيوان
anniversary	*zekra* (f) *sanawaya*	ذكرى سنويه
annoyed	*metdaye'* (m)/ *metday'a* (f)	متدايق/ متدايقه
anorak	*jaketta* (f)	جاكته
another (one)	*kamaen (waHid* (m)/ *waHda* (f))	كمان (واحد/ واحده)
answer	*gawaeb* (m)	جواب
answer: he/she answers	*yigaewib* (m)/ *tigaewib* (f)	يجاوب/ تجاوب
antibiotic	*moDaad Hayawee* (m)	مضاد حيوى
antique	*'adeem* (m)/ *'adeema* (f)	قديم/ قديمه
antiseptic	*mo^aaqam* (m)/ *mo^aaqama* (f)	معقم/ معقمه
anxious	*'al'aen* (m)/ *'al'aena* (f)	قلقان/ قلقانه
anyone	*ay Had*	أى حد
anything	*ay Haga*	أى حاجة
anything else?	*Haga tanya*	حاجه نانيه؟
anyway	*^aalla 'ay Haal*	على أى حال
anywhere	*ay makaen*	أى مكان
apart (from)	*biSarf inaZar (^aan)*	بصرف النظر (عن)

English	Transliteration	Arabic
apartment	*sha'a* (f)	شقه
aperitif	*fatH nefs* (m)	فتح نفس
appendicitis	*il moSran ela°war* (m)	المصران الأعور
apple	*tofaHa* (f)	تفاحه
appointment	*mi°aed* (m)	ميعاد
approximately	*Hawaeli*	حوالي
apricot	*mishmish* (m)	مشمش
Arab	*°arabi* (m)/	عربي/عربيه
	°arabaya (f)	
Arabic	*°arabi* (m)	عربي
arch	*qoos* (m)	قوس
archaeology	*°ilm il athaar* (m)	علم الآثار
architect	*mohandis me°maeri*	مهندس معماري/
	(m)/*mohandissa*	مهندسه معماريه
	me°maraya (f)	
are (see 'to be', p. 165)		
argument	*mona'sha* (f)	مناقشه
arm	*dera°* (m)	ذراع
army	*gaysh* (m)	جيش
around	*Hawalayn*	حول
arrange: he/she		
arranges		
(*appointment*)	*yewaDab* (m)/	يوضب/توضب
	tewaDab (f)	
(*flowers etc.*)	*yenassa'* (m)/	ينسق/تنسق
	tenassa' (f)	
arrivals	*woSool* (m)	وصول
arrive: he/she arrives	*waSal* (m)/*waSalit* (f)	وصول/وصلت
art	*faen* (m)	فن
fine arts	*faenoon*	فنون جميله
	gameela (pl)	
art gallery	*matHaf* (m)	متحف
artichoke	*kharshoof* (m)	خرشوف
article	*maqala* (f)	مقاله
artificial	*Senaa°i* (m)/	صناعي/صناعيه
	Senaa°iya (f)	
artist	*faennaen* (m)/	فنان/فنانه
	faennaena (f)	

artistic	*faenni* (m)/	فنى / فنيه
	faennaya (f)	
as (*like*)	*zai*	زى
(*while*)	*baynama*	بينما
ash	*Tafye* (f)	طفيه
ashtray	*Taffaya* (f)	طفايه
ask: he/she asks	*yes'al* (m)/*tes'al* (f)	يسأل / تسأل
aspirin	*asbereen* (m)	اسبرين
assistant (*in shop*)	*baya*ᵃ (m)/*baya*ᵃ*a* (f)	بياع / بياعه
asthma	*raboo* (m)	ربو
Aswan Dam	*isad il*ᵃ*aeli*	السد العالى
at	*fi*	فى
athletics	*gombaaZ* (m)	جمباز
atmosphere	*gaw* (m)	جو
attack: he/she	*yehgem* (m)/	يهجم / تهجم
attacks	*tehgem* (f)	
attendant (*garage*)	*baya*ᵃ (m)/*baya*ᵃ*a* (f)	بياع / بياعه
(*museum*)	*mowaZaf* (m)/	موظف / موظفه
	mowaZafa (f)	
attractive	*gaZaeb* (m)/	جذاب / جذابه
	gaZaeba (f)	
aubergine	*betingaen* (m)	باذنجان
auction	*maezaed* (m)	مزاد
aunt (*mother's side*)	*khaela* (f)	خاله
(*father's side*)	ᵃ*amma* (f)	عمه
author	*mo'allif* (m)/	مؤلف / مؤلفه
	mo'allifa (f)	
automatic	*tomateeki* (m)/	اوتوماتيكى /
	tomateekaya (f)	اوتوماتيكيه
autumn	*khareef* (m)	خريف
avenue	*share*ᵃ (m)	شارع
avocado	*avokaeta* (f)	افوكاته
avoid: he/she avoids	*yatagannab* (m)/	يتجنب / تتجنب
	tatagannab (f)	
away	*be*ᵃ*eed*	بعيد
... away (*distance*)	... *min hena*	من هنا
awful	*weHish* (m)/	وحش / وحشه
	weHsha (f)	

B

English	Transliteration	Arabic
baby	*baybi* (m)	بايبى
baby food	*akl* (m) *il baybi*	أكل البيبى
baby's bottle	*bazaezit* (f) *il baybi*	بزازيت البيبى
babysitter	*galeesit aTfaal* (f)	جليسةاطفال
back	*Dahr* (m)	ظهر
back: at the back (of)	*khalf*	خلف
backwards	*khalfi*	خلفى
bad	*weHish* (m)/ *weHsha* (f)	وحش / وحشه
bag	*shanTa* (f)	شنطة
baggage	*ᵃafsh* (pl)	عفش
baker's	*khabbaez* (m)	خباز
balcony	*balakowna* (f)	بلكونه
bald	*aSlaᵃ* (m)	أصلع
ball	*kora* (f)	كوره
ballet	*ra's il balay* (m)	رقص الباليه
ballpoint pen	*alam gaef* (m)	قلم جاف
banana	*mowza* (f)	موزه
band (*music*)	*fer'a* (f)	فرقه
bandage	*rabTa* (f)	ربطه
bank	*bank* (m)	بنك
bank (*i.e. public*) holiday	*'agaeza rasmaya* (f)	اجازه رسميه
bar	*baar* (m)	بار
barber	*Hallae'* (m)	حلاق
bargain	*lo'Ta* (f)	لقطه
bargain: he/she bargains	*yizaewid* (m)/ *tizaewid* (f)	يذايد/ تذايد
baseball	*bayzbowl* (m)	بايزبول
basement	*badrown* (m)	بدرون
basin	*HowD* (m)	حوض
basket	*sabat* (m)	سبت
basketball	*korit il salla*	كورة السلة
bath	*banyo* (m)	بانيو

English	Transliteration	Arabic
bathe: he/she bathes	*yestaHamma* (m)/ *testaHamma* (f)	يستحمى / تستحمى
bathing costume	*mayo* (m)	مايوه
bathroom	*Hammaem* (m)	حمام
battery	*baTarayya* (f)	بطاريه
bay	*sharm* (m)	شرم
bazaar	*sooq* (m)	سوق
be (see 'to be', p. 165)		
beach	*shaati'* (m)	شاطئ
beans (dried brown)	*fool* (m)	فول
(French/green)	*faSolya khaDra* (f)	فاصوليا خضراء
beard	*da'n* (f)	دقن
beautiful	*gameel* (m)/ *gameela* (f)	جميل / جميله
because	*bisabab*	بسبب
bed	*sereer* (m)	سرير
bedroom	*otil* (f) *nowm*	حجرة النوم
bee	*naHla* (f)	نحله
beef	*ba'ari* (f)	بقرى
beer	*beera* (f)	بيره
beetroot	*bangar* (m)	بنجر
before	*'abl*	قبل
begin: he/she begins	*yabda'* (m)/*tabda'* (f)	يبدأ / تبدأ
beginner	*mobtade'* (m)/ *mobtade'a* (f)	مبتدى / مبتدئه
beginning	*bidaya* (f)	بدايه
behind	*wara*	وراء
beige	*bayj*	بيج
believe: he/she believes	*yeSada'* (m)/ *teSada'* (f)	يصدق / تصدق
bell	*garas* (m)	جرس
below	*taHt*	تحت
belt	*Hizaem* (m)	حزام
bend	*monHana* (m)	منحنى
bend: he/she bends	*yetnee* (m)/*tetnee* (f)	يتنى / تتنى
bent	*matni* (m)/*matnaya* (f)	متنى / متنيه
berries	*toot* (pl)	توت
berth	*sereer* (m)	سرير

beside	*ganb*	جنب
besides	*bil eDaafa ila*	بالأضافة
best	*aHsan*	أحسن
better (than)	*aHsan (min)*	أحسن من
between	*bayn*	بين
beyond (*place*)	*ba^ad*	بعد
bib	*maryala* (f)	مريله
Bible	*ingeel* (m)	إنجيل
bicycle	*^aagala* (f)	عجله
big	*kibeer* (m)/	كبير / كبيره
	kibeera (f)	
bigger	*akbar*	أكبر
bill	*fatoora* (f)	فاتوره
bin (*rubbish*)	*SafeeHa* (f)	صفيحه
binoculars	*naDara* (f)	نضاره معظمه
	mo^aazzama	
biochemistry	*kemya Hayawaya* (f)	كيمياء حيويه
biology	*aHia'* (pl)	أحياء
bird	*^aaSfoora* (f)	عصفوره
birthday	*^aeed milaed* (m)	عيد ميلاد
biscuit	*baskaweet* (pl)	بسكويت
bishop	*osqof* (m)	أسقف
(a) bit	*showaya*	شويه
bite: he/she bites	*ye^aoD* (m)/*te'^aoD* (f)	يعض / تعض
bitter	*morr* (m)/*morra* (f)	مر / مره
black	*eswid* (m)/*sowda* (f)	أسود / سوده
black and white (*film*)	*abyaD wi eswid*	أبيض و أسود
black coffee	*'ahwa saeda*	قهوة ساده
blanket	*baTanaya* (f)	بطانيه
bleed: he/she bleeds	*yenzif* (m)/*tenzif* (f)	ينزف / تنزف
blister	*qorHa* (f)	قرحه
blocked	*masdood* (m)/	مسدود / مسدوده
	masdooda (f)	
blond(e)	*ash'ar* (m)/	اشقر / شقره
	sha'ara (f)	
blood	*dam* (m)	دم

blouse	bilooza (f)	بلوزه
blow: he/she blows	yenfokh (m)/ tonfokh (f)	ينفخ / تنفخ
blue	azra' (m)/zar'a (f)	ازرق / زرقاء
board: he/she boards (bus etc.)	yerkab (m)/terkab (f)	يركب / تركب
boarding card	biTa'it (f) isaffar	بطاقه السفر
boat	markib (f)	مركب
boat trip (by sea)	reHla baHaraya	رحله بحريه
(on river)	reHla nahraya	رحله نهريه
body	gesm (f)	جسم
bodyguard	Haris (m)	حارس
boil: he/she boils	yeghlee (m)/teghlee (f)	يغلي / تغلي
boiled egg	bayDa masloo'a (f)	بيضه مسلوقه
boiler	sakhaen (m)	سخان
bomb	kombela (f)	قنبله
bone	ªaDma (f)	عظمه
book	kitaeb (m)	كتاب
book: he/she books	yeHgiz (m)/ teHgiz (f)	يحجز / تحجز
booking	Hagz (m)	حجز
booking office	shibaek il Hagz (m)	شباك الحجز
booklet	kotayib (m)	كتيب
bookshop	maktaba (f)	مكتبه
boots	boot (m)	بوت
border (edge/ frontier)	Hedood (pl)	حدود
bored	zah'aen (m)/ zah'aena (f)	زهقان / زهقانه
boring	momil (m)/ momila (f)	ممل / مممله
boss	irayyis (m)/ irayissa (f)	الريس / الريسه
both	ilitneen	الأتنين
bottle	izaeza (f)	قزازه
bottle opener	fataeHa (f)	فتاحه
bottom	'a°ª (m)	قاع

bow (*ship*)	*moqademit il markib* (f)	مقدمة المركب
(*knot*)	*babyowna* (f)	بابيونه
bowl	*Taba'* (m) *ghaweet*	طبق غويط
box	*aelba* (f)	علبه
box office	*shibaek* (m) *il Hagz*	شباك الحجز
boy	*walad* (m)	ولد
boyfriend	*boyfrend* (m)	بوى فريند
bra	*sotyaen* (m)	سوتيان
bracelet	*isswera* (f)	إسوره
braces	*Hammaela* (f)	حماله
brain	*aa'l* (m)	عقل
branch (*of tree*)	*fara* (m)	فرع
brand	*marka* (f)	ماركه
brandy	*brandi* (f)	براندى
brass	*naHaes* (m)	نحاس
brave	*shogaea* (m)/ *shogaeaa* (f)	شجاع/ شجاعه
bread	*aaysh* (pl)	عيش
Arabic	*aaysh baladi*	عيش بلدى
bread shop	*khabbaez* (m)	خباز
break: he/she breaks	*yeksar* (m)/*teksar* (f)	يكسر/ تكسر
breakdown	*qoTl* (m)	عطل
breakfast	*fiTaar* (m)	أنطار
breast	*Sedr* (m)	صدر
breathe: he/she breathes	*yetanafis* (m)/ *tetanafis* (f)	يتنفس/ تتنفس
bride	*aaroosa* (f)	عروسه
bridegroom	*aarees* (m)	عريس
bridge	*kobri* (m)	كوبرى
briefcase	*shanTa* (f)	شنطة
bright (*colour*)	*faeteH*	فاتح
(*light*)	*baree'*	بريق
bring: he/she brings	*yegeeb* (m)/*tegeeb* (f)	يجيب/ تجيب
British	*briTani* (m)/ *briTanaya* (f)	بريطانى/ بريطانيه

broad	*^aareeD* (m)/	عريض/عريضه
	^aareeDa (f)	
brochure	*katalowg* (m)	كتالوج
broken	*maksoor* (m)/	مكسور/مكسوره
	maksoora (f)	
bronchitis	*iltihaeb re'awi* (m)	إلتهاب رئوي
bronze	*bronz* (m)	برونز
brooch	*browsh* (m)	بروش
brother	*'akh* (m)	أخ
my brother	*akhooya* (m)	اخويا
brother-in-law	*neseeb* (m)	نسيب
my brother-in-law	*neseebi* (m)	نسيبي
brown	*bonni*	بني
brown sugar	*sokkar* (m) *aSfar*	سكر اصفر
bruise	*khadsh* (m)	خدش
brush	*forsha* (f)	فرشه
bucket	*gardal* (m)	جردل
buffet	*boofay* (m)	بوفيه
build: he/she builds	*yebni* (m)/*tebni* (f)	يبني/تبني
builder	*^aamil bonna* (m)	عامل بناء
building	*mabna* (m)	مبنى
bulb (*light*)	*lamba* (f)	لمبه
bull	*towr* (m)	ثور
bumper	*ekSidaam* (m)	إكصدام
burn	*Har'* (m)	حرق
burn: he/she burns	*yeHra'* (m)/*teHra'* (f)	يحرق/تحرق
burnt	*maHroo'* (m)/	محروق/محروقه
	maHroo'a (f)	
bus	*otobees* (m)	اوتوبيس
by bus	*bil otobees*	بالأوتوبيس
bus-driver	*sawa'* (m) *ilotobees*	سواق الأوتوبيس
bus station, stop	*maHaTit ilotobees*	محطة الاوتوبيس
business	*ma'mooraya* (f)	مأموريه
business trip	*reHlit a^amael* (f)	رحلة أعمال
on business	*fi ma'mooraya*	في مأموريه
businessman	*ragil a^amael* (m)	رجل اعمال
businesswoman	*sayidit a^amael* (f)	سيدة اعمال

business studies	*idarit aᵃmael*	إدارة أعمال
busy	*mashghool* (m)/ *mashghoola* (f)	مشغول/ مشغوله
but	*laekin*	لكن
butane gas	*botagaez* (m)	بوتاجاز
butcher's	*gazzaar* (m)	جزار
butter	*zebda* (f)	زبده
butterfly	*faraasha* (f)	فراشه
button	*zooraar* (m)	زرار
buy: he/she buys	*yeshteri* (m)/ *teshteri* (f)	يشتري/ تشتري
by (*author*)	*ta'leef*	تأليف
(*train, bus etc.*)	*bil*	بال

C

cabbage	*koronb* (f pl)	كرنب
cabin	*kabeena* (f)	كابينه
cable car	*metro moᵃallaq*	مترو معلق
café	*'ahwa* (pl)	قهوه
cake	*kayka* (pl)	كيكه
cake shop	*Halawaenni* (m)	حلواني
calculator	*kalkoolaytor* (m)	كالكوليتر
call (*telephone*)	*mokalma* (f)	مكالمه
call: he/she calls	*yinaedee* (m)/ *tinaedee* (f)	ينادي/ تنادي
I am called	*ismi*	إسمي
calm	*haedi* (m)/*hadya* (f)	هادئ/ هادئه
camel	*gamal* (m & f)	جمل
camera	*kamira* (f)	كاميرا
camomile tea	*sheeH* (m)	شيح
campbed	*sereer khayma* (m)	سرير خيمه
camping	*yeᵃaskar* (m)	يعسكر
campsite	*moᵃaskar* (m)	معسكر

can: he/she can		
(is able to)	ye'dar (m)/te'dar (f)	يقدر / تقدر
(knows how to)	ye^araf (m)/te^araf (f)	يعرف / تعرف
I could	a'dar (m & f)	أقدر
can (tin)	^aelba (f)	علبه
can opener	fataHit il ^aelab (f)	فتاحة العلب
cancel: he/she cancels	yelghee (m)/telghee (f)	يلغى / تلغى
cancellation	elgha' (m)	إلغاء
cancer	saraTaan (m)	سرطان
candle	sham^aa (f)	شمعه
canoe	'aerib (m)	قارب
capital (city)	^aaSima (f)	عاصمه
captain	kaptin (m)	كابتن
car	^aarabaya (f), saiyaara (f)	عربيه/ سياره
by car	bil ^aarabaya	بالعربيه
car hire	saiyaraat lil iygar (pl)	سيارات للإيجار
car park	maw'af saiyaraat (m)	موقف سيارات
caravan	karavan (m)	كارافان
(of camels)	qafilat gimael	قافلة جمال
caravan site	mo^aaskar karavanaat	معسكر كارافانات
cardigan	jaketta (f)	جاكته
care: I don't care	walla yehemennee	ولا يهمنى
take care	khod baelak (m)/ khodi baelik (f)	خد بالك/ خدى بالك
careful	^aalla mahlak (m)/ mahlik (f)	على مَهلك/ مهلِك
careless	mohmil (m)/ mohmila (f)	مهمل/ مهمله
carpenter	naggar (m)	نجار
carpet	seggaeda (f)	سجاده
carriage (railway)	^aarabaya (f)	عربيه
carrier bag	shanTa (f)	شنطه
carrots	gazar (pl)	جزر

carry: he/she carries	*yesheel* (m)/*tesheel* (f)	يشيل/ تشيل
car wash	*ghaseel* (m) *saiyaraat*	غسيل سيارات
case: in case	*fi haalit*	فى حالة
cash	*kash* (m)	كاش
cash: he/she cashes	*yeSrif* (m)/*teSrif* (f)	يصرف/ تصرف
cash desk	*maktaeb* (m) *iSaraaf*	مكتب الصراف
cassette	*kassett* (m)	كاسيت
castle	*'alªa* (f)	قلعه
cat	*'ot* (m)/*'otta* (f)	قط/ قطه
catalogue	*katalowg* (m)	كتالوج
catch: he/she catches		
(*train/bus; cold*)	*yakhod* (m)/*takhod* (f)	ياخد/ تاخد
(*ball*)	*yemsik* (m)/ *temsik* (f)	يمسك/ تمسك
cathedral	*katedr'aya* (f)	كاتدرائيه
Catholic	*katoleekee* (m)/ *katoleekaya* (f)	كاثوليكى/ كاثوليكيه
cauliflower	*'arnabeeT* (pl)	قرنبيط
cause: he/she causes	*yesabib* (m)/*tisabib* (f)	يسبب/ تسبب
caution	*HaZar* (m)	حذر
cave	*kahf* (m)	كهف
ceiling	*sa'f* (m)	سقف
celery	*karafs* (pl)	كرفس
cellar	*badrown* (m)	بدرون
cemetery	*'araafa* (f)	قرافه
centimetre	*santimetr* (m)	سنتيمتر
central	*markazi*	مركزى
central heating	*tadfe'a markazaya* (f)	تدفئه مركزيه
centre	*markaz* (m)	مركز
century	*qarn* (m)	قرن
cereal (*crops*)	*Hoboob* (pl)	حبوب
certain	*moHadad*	محدد
certainly	*belta'keed*	بالتأكيد
certificate	*shahaeda* (f)	شهاده
chain	*selsela* (f)	سلسله
chair	*korsi* (m)	كرسى
chalet	*shalay* (m)	شاليه

champagne	shambanya (f)	شامبانيا
change (*small coins*)	fakka (pl)	فكه
change: he/she changes	yeghaiyyar (m)/ teghaiyyar (f)	يغير/ تغير
changing room	Hammaem (m)	حمام
chapel	keneesa (f)	كنيسه
charcoal	faHm (pl)	فحم
charge	ogra (f)	أجره
charge: he/she charges	yeHaesib (m)/ teHaesib (f)	يحاسب/ تحاسب
cheap	rekheeS (m)/ rekheeSa (f)	رخيص/ رخيصة
check: he/she checks	yata'kad (m)/ tata'kad (f)	يتأكد/ تتأكد
check-in (desk)	maktaeb il tasgeel (m)	مكتب التسجيل
cheek	khad (m)	خد
cheeky	sha'i (m)/sha'aya (f)	شقى/ شقيه
cheers!	fi seHetak (m)/ fi seHetik (f)/ fi seHetkom (pl)	فى صحتك/ فى صحتك/ فى صحتكم
cheese	gebna (f)	جبنه
chef	Tabbakh (m)/ Tabbakha (f)	طباخ/ طباخه
chemist	agzagi (m)	أجزجى
chemist's shop	agzakhaena (f)	أجزخانه
chemistry	kemya (f)	كيمياء
cheque	sheek (m)	شيك
cherries	kerayz (pl)	كريز
chess	shaTarang (m)	شطرنج
chewing gum	lebaena (f)	لبان
chicken	faerkha (f)/ firaekh (pl)	فرخه
chickenpox	gowdayri (m)	جديرى
child	Tefl (m)/Tefla (f)	طفل/ طفله
children	aTfaal	أطفال
chimney	madkhana (f)	مدخنه
china	Seenee (pl)	صينى

chips	*baTaaTis miHammar* (pl)	بطاطس محمّر
chocolate	*shokolaata* (f)	شيكولاته
choose: he/she chooses	*yekhtaar* (m)/ *tekhtaar* (f)	يختار/ تختار
chop (*lamb*)	*riyash (Daani)* (f)	ريش (ضاني)
Christian	*maseeHee* (m)/ *maseeHaya* (f)	مسيحى/ مسيحيه
Christmas	*krismas* (m)	كريسماس
Christmas Eve	*liltil ikrismas* (f)	ليلةالكريسماس
church	*keneesa* (f)	كنيسه
cigar	*sigaar* (m)	سيجار
cigarette	*sigaara* (f)	سيجاره
cigarette papers	*wara' sagayyer* (pl)	ورق سجاير
cinema	*sinema* (f)	سينما
cinnamon	*'erfa* (f)	قرفه
circle	*dayra* (f)	دائره
circus	*sirk* (m)	سرك
city	*madeena* (f)	مدينه
civil servant	*mowaZaf* (m)/ *mowaZafit Hokooma*	موظف/ موظفه حكومه
class	*faSl* (m)	فصل
classical music	*mazeeka klassiki* (f)	مزيكه كلاسيك
claustrophobia	*klostrofobya* (f)	كلوستروفوبيا
clean: he/she cleans	*yenaDaf* (m)/ *tenaDaf* (f)	ينظف/ تنظف
clean	*neDeef* (m)/ *neDeefa* (f)	نظيف/ نظيفه
clear	*waaDiH* (m)/ *waDHa* (f)	واضح/ واضحه
clerk	*mowaZaf* (m)/ *mowaZafa* (f)	موظف/ موظفه
clever	*shaaTir* (m)/ *shaaTra* (f)	شاطر/ شاطره
cliff	*Sakhara* (f)	صخره
climate	*gaw* (m)	الجو/ طقس

English	Transliteration	Arabic
climb: he/she climbs	*yatasala'* (m)/ *tatasala'* (f)	يتسلق / تتسلق
climber	*motasali'* (m)/ *motasali'a* (f)	متسلق / متسلقة
climbing	*tasalo'* (m)	تسلق
clinic	*ªeyaeda* (f)	عياده
cloakroom	*Hammaem* (m)	حمام
clock	*saªa* (f)	ساعه
close (by)	*orayyib*	قريب
close to	*orayyib min*	قريب من
close: he/she closes	*ye'fil* (m)/*te'fil* (f)	يقفل / تقفل
closed	*ma'fool* (m)/ *ma'foola* (f)	مقفول / مقفوله
cloth	*o'maesh* (f)	قماش
clothes	*hedoom* (pl)	هدوم
clothes peg(s)	*mashbak* (s)/ *mashaabik* (pl)	مشبك / مشابك
cloud	*siHaebba* (f)	سحابه
cloudy (*weather*)	*meghayyim*	الجو مغيم
club (*society*)	*naedi* (m)	نادى
coach (*bus*)	*otobees* (m)	اوتوبيس
(*railway*)	*ªarabayit sekka Hadeed* (f)	عربية سكة حديد
coal	*faHm* (pl)	فحم
coarse	*khishin* (m)/ *khishna* (f)	خشن / خشنه
coast	*shaaTi'* (m)	شاطئ
coat	*balToo* (m)	بالطو
coat-hanger	*shamaªit* (f) *hidoom*	شماعة هدوم
cocktail	*koktayl* (m)	كوكتيل
code (*telephone*)	*nemrit ilkowd* (f)	نمرة الكود
coffee	*'ahwa* (f)	قهوه
coin	*'ersh* (m)	قرش
cold	*baerid* (m)/*barda* (f)	بارد / بارده
and/I have a cold	*ªandi bard* (m)	عندى برد
collar	*yaeªa* (f)	ياقه
colleague	*zimeel* (m)/*zimeela* (f)	زميل / زميله

207

collect: he/she collects	*yelem* (m)/*tilem* (f)	يلم / تلم
collection	*magmoo^aa* (f)	مجموعه
(*post*)	*gam^a il bareed*	جمع البريد
college	*kollaya* (f)	كليه
colour	*lown* (m)	لون
colour blind	*^aama alwaen* (m & f)	عماء ألوان
comb	*meshT* (m)	مشط
come: he/she comes	*gay* (m)/*gaya* (f)	جاى
he/she comes back	*yerga^a* (m)/ *terga^a* (f)	يرجع / ترجع
he/she comes in	*yedkhol* (m)/ *tedkhol* (f)	يدخل / تدخل
come in!	*'edkhol* (to m)/ *'edkholi* (to f)	إدخل / إدخلي
comedy	*komidia* (f)	كوميديا
comfortable	*moreeH* (m)/ *moreeHa* (f)	مريح / مريحه
comic (*magazine*)	*megallit karikatir* (f)	مجله كاريكاتير
(*funny*)	*moDhik* (m)/ *moDhika* (f)	مضحك / مضحكه
commercial	*togaeri* (m)/ *togaeraya* (f)	تجارى / تجاريه
common	*ma^aroof* (m)/	معروف / معروفه
(*well-known*)	*ma^aroofa* (f)	
(*shared*)	*moshtarak* (m)/ *moshtaraka* (f)	مشترك / مشتركه
(Holy) Communion	*^aasha' rabaennee* (m)	عشاء ربانى
communism	*shoyoo^aaya* (f)	شيوعيه
compact disc	*seedee* (f)	سى دى
company (*firm*)	*shirka* (f)	شركه
compared with	*bil moqarnna li*	بالقارنه
compartment	*diwaen* (m)	ديوان
compass	*bargal* (m)	برجل
complain: he/she complains	*yeshteki* (m)/ *teshteki* (f)	يشتكى / تشتكى
complaint	*shakwa* (f)	شكوه

complete	*kaemil* (m)/*kamla* (f)	كامل / كامله
complicated	*mi^a'ad* (m)/ *mi^a'ada* (f)	معقد / معقده
composer	*mo'alif moseeqee* (m)/ *mo'alifa moseeqaya* (f)	مؤلف موسيقى / مؤلفه موسيقيه
compulsory	*igbaeri* (m)/ *igbaeraya* (f)	إجبارى / إجباريه
computer	*kombyootaar* (m)	كومبيوتر
operator	^a*amil* (m)/^a*amila* (f) *kombyootaar*	عامل / عامله كومبيوتر
programmer	*mo^aid baramig kombyootaar* (m)	معد برامج كومبيوتر
studies	*deraasit il kombyootaar*	دراسة الكومبيوتر
concert	*Hafla moseeqaya* (f)	حفله موسيقيه
concert hall	*Saalit il Hafalaet* (f)	صالة الحفلات
concussion	*irtigaeg fil mokh* (m)	إرتجاج فى المخ
condition	*Hala* (f)	حاله
condom	*kabboot* (m)	كبوت
conference	*mo'tamar* (m)	مؤتمر
confirm	*yo'akid* (m)/ *to'akid* (f)	يؤكد / تؤكد
conscious	*wa^aee* (m)/*wa^aya* (f)	داعى / داعية
conservation	*il moHafzaH* (f)	المحافظة
conservative	*moHaafiZ* (m)/ *moHaafZa* (f)	محافظ / محافظه
constipation	*imsaek* (m)	إمساك
consul	*'onsol* (m & f)	قنصل
consulate	*'onsolaya* (f)	قنصليه
consultant	*mostashaar* (m)/ *mostashaara* (f)	مستشار / مستشاره
contact lens	^a*adasa lasqa* (f)/ ^a*adasaet lasqa* (pl)	عدسه لاصقه / عدسات لاصقه
contact lens cleaner	*monazef il* ^a*adasaet*	منظف العدسات
continent	*qarra* (f)	قاره

contraceptive	*man^a il Haml* (m)	منع الحمل
contract	*kontraatoo* (m), *^{a}aqd* (m)	كونتراتو/ عقد
control (*passport*)	*gawazaet* (pl)	جوازات
convenient	*monaesib* (m)/ *monasba* (f)	مناسب/ مناسبه
convent	*dayr il rahibaet* (m)	دير الراهبات
cook	*Tabbakh* (m)/ *Tabbakha* (f)	طباخ/ طباخه
cook: he/she cooks	*yaTbookh* (m)/ *toTbookh* (f)	يطبخ/ تطبخ
cooked	*maTbookh* (m)/ *maTbookha* (f & pl)	مطبوخ/ مطبوخه
cooker	*botagaez* (m)	بوتاجاز
cool	*baerid* (m)/ *barda* (f)	بارد
cool box	*^{a}elbit talg* (f)	علبة ثلج
copper	*naHaes* (m)	نحاس
copy	*noskha* (f)	نسخه
copy: he/she copies	*yen'el* (m)/ *ten'el* (f)	ينقل/ تنقل
cork	*fella* (f)	فله
corkscrew	*fataeHit il azayiz* (f)	فتاحة زجاجات
corner	*rokna* (f)	ركنه
correct	*SaaHeeH* (m)/ *SaaHeeHa* (f)	صحيح/ صحيحه
corridor	*Tor'a* (f)	طرقه
cosmetic	*saaT-Hi* (m)/ *SaaT-Haya* (f)	سطحى/ سطحيه
cosmetics	*makyaj* (pl)	ميكياج
cost	*takleffa* (f)	تكلفه
cost: it costs	*yetkallif* (m)/ *tetkallif* (f)	يتكلف/ تتكلف
cot	*sereer aTfaal* (m)	سرير أطفال
cottage	*kookh* (m)	كوخ
cotton	*'otn* (pl)	قطن
cotton wool	*'otna* (f)	قطنه
cough	*koHa* (f)	كحه

English	Transliteration	Arabic
cough: he/she coughs	*yekoH* (m)/*tekoH* (f)	يكح / تكح
could (*see* 'can')		
count: he/she counts	*ye**id* (m)/*te**id* (f)	يعد / تعد
counter (*shop*)	*maktaeb il biy* (m)	مكتب البيع
country (*nation*)	*balaed* (f)	بلد
country(side)	*reef* (m)	ريف
in the country	*fil reef*	فى الريف
couple (*pair*)	*zowg* (pl)	زوج
courgettes	*kowsa* (pl)	كوسة
course (*lessons*)	*kors* (m)	كورس
court (*law*)	*maHkama* (f)	محكمة
(*tennis etc.*)	*mal**ab* (m)	ملعب
cousin: my cousin		
father's brother's son	*ibn* *amee*	ابن عمى
father's brother's daughter	*bint* *amee*	بنت عمى
father's sister's son	*ibn* *ameti*	ابن عمتى
father's sister's daughter	*bint* *ameti*	بنت عمتى
mother's brother's son	*ibn khaeli*	ابن خالى
mother's brother's daughter	*bint khaeli*	بنت خالى
mother's sister's son	*ibn khaelti*	ابن خالتى
mother's sister's daughter	*bint khaelti*	بنت خالتى
cover	*ghaTa* (m)	غطاء
cow	*ba'ara* (f)	بقرة
crab	*kaboorya* (f)	كابوريا
cramp	*kramp* (m)	كرامب
crayons	*qalam alwaen* (m)	قلم الوان
crazy	*magnoon* (m)/ *magnoona* (f)	مجنون

cream (*food*)	*kreem* (m)	كريم
(*lotion*)	*kreem* (m)	كريم
(*colour*)	*kraym* (m)/*krayma* (f)	كريم/كريمة
cream cheese	*gebna bil krema* (f)	جبنه بالكريمه
credit card	*karnay i'timaen* (m)	كارنيه إمتحان
cricket	*krikit* (m)	كريكيت
crisps	*baTaaTis miHammar* (pl)	بطاطس محمر
crescent	*hilael* (m)	هلال
Red Crescent	*il hilael laHmar* (m)	الهلال الأحمر
cross	*Saaleeb*	صليب
Red Cross	*iSaaleeb laHmar* (m)	الصليب لأحمر
cross: he/she crosses (*border*)	*ye^adee* (m)/ *te^adee* (f)	يعدى/ثعدى
crossing (*sea*)	*^oboor* (m)	عبور
crossroads	*takaato^* (m)	تقاطع
crowd	*ziHam* (m)	زحام
crowded	*mazHoom* (m & f)	مزحوم
crown	*taeg* (m)	تاج
cruise (*at sea*)	*reHla baHaraya*	رحله بحريه
(*on river*)	*reHla nahraya*	رحله نهريه
crutches	*^okaez* (m)	عكاز
cry: he/she is crying	*ye^aiyat* (m)/ *te^aiyat* (f)	يعيط/تعيط
crystal	*kristael* (m)	كريستال
cucumber	*khiyaar* (m)	خيار
cuff	*eswerra* (f)	إسوره
cup	*fingaen* (m)	فنجان
cupboard	*doolaab* (m)	دولاب
cure (*remedy*)	*^elaeg* (m)	علاج
cure: he/she cures	*ye^alig* (m)/*te^alig* (f)	يعالج/تعالج
curly	*memawig* (m & f)	مموج
current (*electricity*)	*tayaar* (m)	تيار
curtain	*sitaara* (f)	ستاره
curve	*monHana* (m)	منحنى
cushion	*makhadda* (f)	مخده

customs	*gomrok* (m)	جمرك
cut	*'aT'a* (m)	قطع
cut: he/she cuts	*ye'Ta'a* (m)/*te'Ta'a* (f)	يقطع / تقطع
I've cut myself	*'awart nafsi*	عورت نفسى
cycling	*rekoob il daragaat* (m pl)	ركوب الدراجات
cyclist	*raekib il daraga* (m)	راكب الدراجه
cylinder (*car*)	*soltanayya* (f)	سلطانيه
(*gas*)	*amboobit il botagaez* (f)	أمبوبةالبوتاجاز
cystitis	*iltihaeb* (m) *imasaena*	التهاب المثانه

D

daily	*yowmi*	يومى
damage	*kasr* (m)	كسر
damage: he/she damages	*kassar* (m)/*kassarit* (f)	كسر / كسرت
damp	*mablool* (m)/ *mabloola* (f)	مبلول / مبلوله
dance	*ra'S* (m)	رقص
dance: he/she dances	*yor'oS* (m)/*tor'oS* (f)	يرقص / ترقص
danger	*khaTar* (m)	خطر
dangerous	*khaTeer* (m)/ *khaTeera* (f)	خطير / خطيره
dark	*Dalma* (f)	ظلمه
(*colour*)	*ghaemi'* (m)/ *ghami'a* (f)	غامق / غامقه
darling	*Habeebee* (m)/ *Habibti* (f)	حبيبى / حبيبتى
data (*information*)	*ma'loomaet* (pl)	معلومات
date (*day*)	*taereekh* (m)	تاريخ
(*fruit*)	*balaH* (pl)	بلح
daughter	*ibna* (f)	ابنه
my daughter	*binti* (f)	بنتى
daughter-in-law	*miraat il ibn* (f)	مرات الأبن

213

day	*yowm* (m)	يوم
day after tomorrow	*ba*ᵃ*d bokra*	بعد بكره
day before yesterday	*awil imbariH*	اول إمبارح
dead: he/she is dead	*maeyit* (m)/ *maeyita* (f)	ميت/ ميته
Dead Sea	*ibaHr ilmayit*	البحر الميت
deaf	*'aTrash* (m)/ *Tarsha* (f)	أطرش/ طرشه
dealer	*baya*ᵃ (m) *baya*ᵃ*a* (f)	بياع/ بياعه
dear (*precious*) (*expensive*)	*aezeez* (m) *aezeeza* (f) *ghaelee* (m)/ *ghalya* (f)	عزيز/ عزيزه غالي/ غاليه
death	*mowt* (m)	موت
debt	*dayn* (m)	دين
decaffeinated coffee	*'ahwa min ghayr kafyeen* (f)	قهوه من غير كافين
decide: he/she decides	*qarrar* (m)/*qararat* (f)	قرر/ قررت
deck	*dek* (m)	دك
deckchair	*shez long* (m)	شيز لونج
declare: he/she declares	*yeSaraH* (m)/ *teSaraH* (f)	يصرح/ تصرح
deep	*ghaweeT* (m & f)	غويط
deer	*ghazael* (m)	غزال
defect (*fault*)	*ᵃayb* (m)	عيب
defective	*bayiZ* (m)/*bayZa* (f)	بايظ/ بايظه
definitely	*mo'akad*	مؤكد
defrost	*yesayaH* (m)/ *tesayaH* (f)	يسيح/ تسيح
degree	*daraga* (f)	درجه
delay	*ta'kheer* (m)	تأخير
delicate	*ra'ee'* (m)/*ra'ee'a* (f)	رقيق/ رقيقه
delicious	*lazeez* (m)/*lazeeza* (f)	لذيذ/ لذيذه
deliver: he/she delivers	*yessaelim* (m)/ *tessaelim* (f)	يسلم/ تسلم
delivery	*istilaem* (m)	استلام

214

English	Transliteration	Arabic
demonstration	moZahra (f)	مظاهره
denim	denim (m)	دنم
dental	sinaen (pl)	سنان
dentist	doktowr sinaen (m)/	دكتور/ سينان
	doktowrit sinaen (f)	دكتورة سينان
dentures	sinaen Sina°aya (pl)	سنان صناعه
deodorant	Ded el°ara' (m)	ضدالعرق
depart: he/she departs	yesaefir (m)/ tisaefir (f)	يسافر / تسافر
department	qism (m)	قسم
department store	soopar market (m)	سوبر ماركت
departure	saffar (m)	سفر
departure lounge	Salit il saffar (m)	صالةالسفر
deposit	mo'addam (m)	مقدم
describe: he/she describes	yowSif (m)/towSif (f)	يوصف/ توصف
description	waSf (m)	وصف
desert	SaHara (f)	صحراء
design	TaSmeem (m)	تصميم
design: he/she designs	yeSamim (m)/ tiSamim (f)	يصمم/تصمم
designer	moSamim (m)/ moSamaema (f)	مصمم/ مصممه
dessert	Helw (m)	حلو
destination	nihaeyit il saffar (m)	نهايةالسفر
details	tafaSeel (pl)	تفاصيل
detergent	monaZif (m)	منظف
develop: he/she develops	yeTawar (m)/ teTawar (f)	يتطور/ تتطور
diabetes	sokkar (m)	سكر
diabetic: he is diabetic	°andoo sokkar	عنده سكر
she is diabetic	°andaha sokkar	عندها سكر
dial: he/she dials	yoTlob (m)/toTlob (f)	يطلب/ تطلب
dialling code	nemrit ilkowd (f)	نمرة الكود
diamond	maesa (f)	ماسه
diarrhoea	is-hael (m)	إسهال
diary	mozakkaraat (pl)	مزكرات

dice	*Zahr* (pl)	زهر
dictator	*diktatoor* (m)/ *diktatoora* (f)	دكتاتور/ دكتاتوره
dictionary	*qamoos* (m)	قاموس
die: he/she dies	*yemoot* (m)/*timoot* (f)	يموت/ تموت
. . . died	. . . *maet* (m)/ *maetit* (f)	. . . مات/ ماتت
diesel	*deezil* (m)	ديزل
diet	*rezheem* (m)	رجيم
different	*mokhtilif* (m)/ *mokhtilifa* (f)	مختلف/ مختلفه
difficult	*Sa^ab* (m)/*Sa^aba* (f)	صعب/ صعبه
dining-room	*otil akl* (f)	اودة السفره
dinner	*^aasha* (m)	عشاء
dinner jacket	*takseedo* (m)	تاكسيدو
diplomat	*diblomaesee* (m)/ *diblomaesaya* (f)	دبلوماسي/ دبلوماسيه
direct (*route*)	*dairekt* or *mobaeshaer*	دايركت/ مباشر
direction	*itigae* (m)	إتجاه
director	*ra'ees* (m)/*ra'eesa* (f)	رئيس/ رئيسه
directory (*telephone*)	*daleel* (m)	دليل
dirty	*wesikh* (m)/*weskha* (f)	وسخ/ وسخه
disabled	*mo^aawaq* (m)/ *mo^aawaqa* (f)	معوق/ معوقه
disappointed (*upset*)	*za^alaen* (m)/ *za^alaena* (f)	زعلان/ زعلانه
disc (*record*)	*isTiwaana* (f)	إسطوانه
(*token*)	*feesha* (f)	فيشه
disc jockey	*disk jokkey* (m)	ديسك جوكي
disco(thèque)	*disko* (m)	ديسكو
discount	*Takhfeed* (m)	تخفيض
dish	*Taba'* (m)	طبق
dishwasher	*ghasaelit* (f) *il itba'*	غسالة/ لأطباق
disinfectant	*moTahir* (m)	مطهر
dislocated	*yekhla^a* (m)/ *tekhla^a* (f)	يخلع/ تخلع

disposable	*mostahlak* (m)/	مستهلك/ مستهلكه
	mostahlaka (f)	
distance	*masaefa* (f)	مسافه
distilled water	*maiya ma'aTara* (f)	مياه مقطره
district (*of country*)	*moqaT'a* (f)	مقاطعه
(*of town*)	*DaHaya* (f)	ضاحيه
dive: he/she dives	*yeghooS* (m)/	يغوص/ تغوص
	teghooS (f)	
diversion	*taHweela* (f)	تحويله
diving	*ghawaSan* (m)	غوصان
diving-board	*minaSit* (f) *ghaTs*	منصة غطس
divorced	*meTala'* (m)/	مطلق/ مطلقه
	meTala'a (f)	
dizzy	*daeyikh* (m)/	دايخ/ دايخه
	daeyikha (f)	
do: he/she does	*ye'mil* (m)/	يعمل/ تعمل
	te'mil (f)	
done	*'amal* (m)/	عمل/ عملت
	'amalit (f)	
dock	*meena* (f)	ميناء
doctor	*doktowr* (m)/	دكتور/ دكتوره
	doktowra (f)	
documents	*mostanadaet* (pl)	مستندات
dog	*kalb* (m)/*kalba* (f)	كلب/ كلبه
doll	*'aroossa* (f)	عروسه
dollars	*dollaraat* (pl)	دولارات
dome	*'obba* (f)	قبه
dominoes	*domino* (m)	دومينو
donkey	*Homar* (m)/	حمار/ حماره
	Homara (f)	
door	*baeb (m)*	باب
double	*dobl*	دوبل
double bed	*sereer* (m) *dobl*	سرير دوبل
dough	*'ageena* (f)	عجينه
down	*taHt*	تحت
downstairs	*taHt*	تحت
drain	*magaree* (pl)	مجارى

drama	*drama* (f)	دراما
draught (*air*)	*Taiyaar* (m)	تيار
draw: he/she draws	*yersim* (m)/*tersim* (f)	يرسم/ترسم
drawer	*dorg* (m)	درج
drawing	*rasm* (m)	رسم
drawing-pin	*dabboos* (m)	دبوس
dreadful	*weHish* (m)/ *weHsha* (f)	وحش/وحشه
dream	*Helm* (m)	حلم
dress	*foostaen* (m)	فستان
dress: he/she gets dressed	*yelbis* (m)/*telbis* (f)	يلبس/تلبس
dressing (*medical*)	*gheyaar* (m)	غيار
(*salad*)	*Sows* (m)	صوص
drink	*mashroob* (m)	مشروب
drink: it drinks	*yishrab* (m)/*tishrab* (f)	يشرب/تشرب
drip: it drips	*yena'aT* (m)/ *tena'aT* (f)	ينقط/تنقط
drive: he/she drives	*yesoo'* (m)/*tesoo'* (f)	يسوق/تسوق
driver	*sawae'* (m)/*sawae'a* (f)	سواق/سواقه
driving licence	*rokhSa* (f)	رخصه
drown: he/she drowns	*yeghra'* (m)/ *teghra'* (f)	يغرق/تغرق
drug(s)	*mokhaddar* (s)/ *mokhaddaraat* (pl)	مخدر/مخدرات
drug addict	*modmin* (m)/ *modmina* (f)	مدمن/مدمنه
drum	*Tabla* (f)	طبله
drunk	*sakraan* (m)/ *sakraana* (f)	سكران/سكرانه
dry	*naeshif* (m)/ *naeshfa* (f)	ناشف/ناشفه
(*wine*)	*draiy*	دراي
dry-cleaning	*tanZeef* *alal naeshif*	تنظيف على الناشف
dubbed	*doblaej* (m)	دوبلاج
duck	*baTa* (f)	بطه
dull (*weather*)	*weHish* (m)	وحش
dumb	*akhras* (m)/*kharsa* (f)	أخرس/خرسه

218

dummy (imitation)	ta'leed (m)	تقليد
(baby's)	bazaeza (f)	بزازه
during	khilael	خلال
dust	toraab (pl)	تراب
dustbin	safeeHit izibaela (f)	صفيحةالزباله
dusty	motrib (m & f)	مترب
duty (tax)	Dareeba (f)	ضريبه
duty-free (market)	(il soo') il Horra (f)	السوق الحره
duvet	liHaef (m)	لحاف

E

each (one)	kol (waHid) (m)/	كل واحد/كل واحده
	kol (waHda) (f)	
ear(s)	wedn (f)/widaen (pl)	ودن/ويدان
earache	wagaᵃ (m) fil wedn	وجع فى الودن
eardrops	'atra lil wedn (f)	قطره للودن
early	badri	بدرى
earlier than	badri ᵃan	بدرى عن
earn: he/she earns	yeksaeb (m)/	يكسب/ تكسب
	teksaeb (f)	
earrings	Hel'aen (pl)	حلقان
earth (soil)	il torba (f)	التربه
(world)	il arD (f)	الأرض
earthquake	zilzael (m)	زلزال
east	shar' (m)	شرق
eastern	shar'ee	شرقى
Easter	ᵃeed il qiyama	عبدالقيامه
easy	sahl (m)/sahla (f)	سهل/ سهله
eat: he/she eats	yaekol (m)/taekol (f)	يأكل/ تاكل
economical	iqtiSaadi (m)/	إقتصادى/ إقتصاديه
	iqtiSaadaya (f)	
economy	iqtiSaad (m)	إقتصاد
edible	yettaekil (m)/	يتاكل/ تتاكل
	tettaekil (f)	
egg	hayDa (f)/bayD (pl)	بيضه/ بيض

219

either: either one	*'ay*	أى
either . . . or . . .	*ya . . . 'aw . . .*	يا . . . أو . . .
elastic	*astik* (m)	استيك
elections	*intikhabaet* (pl)	انتخابات
electric	*kahrobae'ee* (m)/ *kahrobae'aya* (f)	كهربائى/ كهربائيه
electrician	*kahrabae'ee* (m)	كهربائى
electricity	*kahraba* (f)	كهرباء
electronic	*iliktrowni* (m)/ *iliktrownaya* (f)	الكترونى/ الكترونيه
else: anything else?	*ay khedma*	أى خدمة؟
embark: he/she embarks	*yabda'* (m)/*tabda'* (f)	يبدأ/ تبدأ
embarrassing	*yeksif* (m)/*teksif* (f)	يكسف/ تكسف
embassy	*sifaara* (f)	سفاره
emergency	*Tawari'* (pl)	طوارئ
emergency exit	*baeb* (m) *il tawari'*	باب الطوارئ
emergency telephone	*tilifown* (m) *il Tawari'*	تليفون الطوارئ
empty	*faaDi* (m)/*faDya* (f)	فاضى/ فاضيه
empty: he/she empties	*yefaDi* (m)/*tefaDi* (f)	يفضى/ تفضى
enamel	*Tilae'* (m)	طلاء
end	*nehaya* (f)	نهايه
end: he/she ends	*yekhallaS* (m)/ *tekhallaS* (f)	يخلص/ تخلص
energetic	*nasheeT* (m)/ *nasheeTa* (f)	نشيط/ نشيطه
energy	*nashaaT* (m)	نشاط
engaged (*to be married*)	*makhToob* (m)/ *makhTooba* (f)	مخطوب/ مخطوبه
(*occupied*)	*mashghool* (m)/ *mashghoola* (f)	مشغول/ مشغوله
engine	*maTowr* (m)	ماتور
engineer	*mohandis* (m)/ *mohandissa* (f)	مهندس/ مهندسه
engineering	*handassa* (f)	هندسه

English	Transliteration	Arabic
England	*ingilterra* (f)	إنجلترا
English	*ingleezi* (m)/ *ingleezaya* (f)	انجليزي/ انجليزيه
enjoy: he/she enjoys	*yetmatta^a* (m)/ *tetmatta^a* (f)	يتمتع/ تتمتع
enough	*kifaeya*	كفايه
is that enough?	*kifaeya kida*	كفايه كده؟
enter: he/she enters	*yedkhol* (m)/ *tedkhol* (f)	يدخل/ تدخل
entertainment	*taslaya* (f)	تسليه
enthusiastic	*motaHamis* (m)/ *motaHamissa* (f)	متحمس/ متحمسه
entrance	*madkhael* (m)	مدخل
envelope	*maZroof* (m)	مظروف
environment	*beey'a* (f)	بيئه
equal	*motasaewee* (m)/ *motasaewaya* (f)	متساوي/ متساويه
equipment	*^aedda* (f)	عده
escalator	*sellim* (m) *kahraba*	سلم كهرباء
especially	*bizzaet*	بالذات
essential	*Daroori* (m)/ *Daroraya* (f)	ضروري/ ضروريه
estate	*^aiqaar* (m)	عقار
estate agent	*simsaar* (m)/ *simsaara* (f)	سمسار/ سمساره
evaporated milk	*laban* (m) *nesla*	لبن نسله
even (*including*)	*Hatta*	حتى
(*not odd*)	*zowgi*	زوجي
evening	*masae'* (m)	مساء
every	*kol*	كل
everyone	*kol waHid* (m)/ *kol waHda* (f)	كل واحد/ كل واحده
everything	*koli shay'*	كل شئ
everywhere	*koli makaen*	كل مكان
exact	*mazboot*	مظبوط
exactly	*biZabT*	بالظبط
examination	*imtiHan* (m)	امتحان

example	*masal* (m)	مثل
for example	*masalan*	مثلًا
excellent	*momtaez* (m)/ *momtaeza* (f)	ممتاز/ممتازه
except	*illa*	إلا
excess luggage	*wazn* (m) *ziyaeda*	وزن زياده
exchange: he/she exchanges	*yeyghaiyyar* *ᵃomla* (m)/ *tighaiyyar* *ᵃomla* (f)	يغير عمله/ تغير عمله
exchange rate	*nesbit* (f) *il taghyeer*	نسبة التغير
excited, exciting	*moseer* (m)/ *moseera* (f)	مثير/مثيره
excursion	*reHla* (f)	رحله
excuse me (*sorry*)	*aesif* (to m)/ *asfa* (to f)	آسف/أسفه
(*to attract attention*)	*ᵃan iznak* (to m)/ *ᵃan iznik* (to f)	عن إذنك/ عن إذنك
executive	*idaeri* (m)/ *idaeraya* (f)	إداري/إداريه
exercise	*tamreen* (n)	تمرين
exhibition	*maᵃraD* (m)	معرض
exit	*khoroog* (m)	خروج
expect: he/she expects	*montazir* (m)/ *montazira* (f)	منتظر/منتظره
expensive	*ghaeli* (m)/*ghalya* (f)	غالي/غاليه
experience	*khebra* (f)	خبره
expert	*khabeer* (m)/ *khabeera* (f)	خبير/خبيره
explain: he/she explains	*yeshraH* (m)/ *teshraH* (f)	يشرح/تشرح
explosion	*infigaar* (m)	انفجار
export	*taSdeer* (m)	تصدير
export: he/she exports	*yeSaddar* (m)/ *teSaddar* (f)	يصدر/تصدر
express (*service*)	*mistaᵃgil* (m)/ *mistaᵃgila* (f)	مستعجل/ مستعجله
(*train*)	*sareeᵃ* (m)	سريع
extension (*to visa*)	*tamdeed* (m)	تمديد

extra (spare)	iDaafi (m)/iDafaya (f)	إضافي/إضافيه
eye(s)	ᵃayn (f)/ᵃayoon (pl)	عين/عيون
eyebrow	Hagib (m)	حاجب
eyebrow pencil	'alam (m) Hawagib	قلم حاجب
eyelash	remsh (m)/	رمش/رموش
	remoosh (pl)	
eyeliner	'alam (m) remoosh	قلم رموش
eyeshadow	Zil (m) ᵃayoon	ظل عيون

F

fabric	'omaesh (m)	قماش
a piece of fabric	Hetit 'omaesha (f)	حتة قماشه
face	wesh (m)	وش
face cream	kreem (m) lil wesh	كريم الوجه
face powder	bodra (f) lil wesh	بودره الوجه
facilities	tas-heelaet (pl)	تسهيلات
fact	waqeᵃ (m)	واقع
in fact	fil waqeᵃ	في الواقع
factory	maSnaᵃ (m)	مصنع
failure	fashal (m)	فشل
faint: he/she faints	oghma ᵃalay (m)/	أغمي عليه/
	oghma ᵃalayha (f)	أغمى عليها
fair (haired)	blond (m)/	بلوند/بلوندايه
	blondaya (f)	
(weather)	kwayyis	كويس
fair	maᵃraD (m)	معرض
trade fair	maᵃraD (m) togaeri	معرض تجاري
faith	eemaen (m)	إيمان
fake	mezawar (m)/	مذور/مذوره
	mezawara (f)	
fall (down/over):	yo'aᵃ (m)/to'aᵃ (f)	يقع/تقع
he/she falls		
false	falSo	فالصو
false teeth	sinaen (pl) falSo	سنان فالصو
familiar	maᵃroof (m)/	معروف/معروفه
	maᵃroofa (f)	

English	Transliteration	Arabic
family	*ªa'ila* (f)	عائله
famous	*mashhoor* (m)/	مشهور/ مشهوره
	mashhoora (f)	
fan (*air*)	*marwaHa* (f)	مروحه
(*supporter*)	*moshaggeª* (m & f)/	مشجع/
	moshaggeªeen (pl)	مشجعين
fantastic	*modhish* (m)/	مدهش/ مدهشه
	modhisha (f)	
far (*away*)	*beªeed* (m)/*beªeeda* (f)	بعيد/ بعيده
is it far?	*beªeed*	بعيد؟
as far as I know	*ªala Hasab ªelmi*	على حسب علمي
fare	*ogra* (f)	أجره
farm	*mazraªa* (f)	مزرعه
farmer	*mozaereª* (m)	مزارع
fashion	*mowda* (f)	موده
fashionable	*mowda* (m & f)	موده
fast	*sareeª* (m)/*sareeªa* (f)	سريع/ سريعه
fat (*adj*)	*tekheen* (m)/	تخين/ تخينه
	tekheena (f)	
fat (*n*)	*tokhn* (m)	تخن
fatal	*momeet* (m)/	مميت/ مميته
	momeeta (f)	
father	*'ab* (m)	أب
my father	*'abooya* (m)	أبويا
father-in-law	*Hama* (m)	حماه
my father-in-law	*Hamaeya* (m)	حمايا
fault	*ghalaT* (m)	غلط
it's not my fault	*mish ghalTiti*	مش غلطتي
faulty	*bayiZ* (m)/*bayZa* (f)	بايظ/ بايظه
favourite	*mofaDal* (m)/	مفضل/ مفضله
	mofaDala (f)	
fax	*faks* (m)	فاكس
feather	*reesha* (f)	ريشه
fed up	*zahªaen* (m)/	زهقان/ زهقانه
	zahªaena (f)	
fee	*ogra* (f)	احره
feed: he/she feeds	*yeªakil* (m)/*teªakil* (f)	ياكل/ تاكل
she breastfeeds	*bitraDaª* (f)	بترضع

feel: he/she feels		يحس / تحس
(touch)	*yeHess* (m)/*teHess* (f)	
(emotion)	*yash^aor* (m)/	يشعر / تشعر
	tash^aor (f)	
I don't feel well	*ana ta^abaen* (m)/	انا تعبان / تعبانه
	ta^abaena (f)	
female	*onsa* (f)	انثى
feminine	*Hareemee* (f)	حريمى
fence	*soor* (m)	سور
ferry	*markib* (m)	مركب
festival	*mahragaen* (m)	مهرجان
fetch: he/she fetches	*yegeeb* (m)/*tegeeb* (f)	يجيب / تجيب
fever	*Harara* (f)	حراره
a few	*'aleel*	قليل
fiancé(e)	*khaTeeb* (m)/	خطيب / خطيبه
	khaTeeba (f)	
fibres	*alyaef* (pl)	الياف
field	*ghayT* (m)	غيط
figs	*teen* (pl)	تين
fight: he/she fights	*yiHareb* (m)/	يحارب / تحارب
	tiHareb (f)	
file (documents)	*mallaf* (m)	ملف
(nail, DIY)	*mabraD* (m)	مبرد
fill (in): he/she fills	*yemla* (m)/*temla* (f)	يملأ / تملأ
filling (dental, pie	*Hashw* (m)	حشو
etc.)		
film	*film* (m)	فيلم
filter	*filtar* (m)	فلتر
finance: he/she	*yimawel* (m)/	يمول / تمول
finances	*timawel* (f)	
financial	*maeli* (m)/*maeliya* (f)	مالى / ماليه
find: he/she finds	*yelae'ee* (m)/	يلاقي / تلاقي
	telae'ee (f)	
fine (OK)	*kwayyis* (m)/	كويس / كويسه
	kwayIssa (f)	
(weather)	*kwayyis*	كويس
(fabric)	*qayyim* (m)/	قيم / قيمه
	qayyima (f)	

fine (*penalty*)	*gharama* (f)	غرامه
finger	*Soba*[a] (m)	صباع
finish: he/she finishes	*yekhallaS* (m)/ *tekhallaS* (f)	يخلص/ تخلص
fire	*Haree'a* (f)	حريقه
fire brigade	*maTaefi* (pl)	مطافئ
fire extinguisher	*Tafaiyit* (f) *Haree'a*	طفاية حريقه
firewood	*khashab* (pl) *lil Har'*	خشب للحرق
fireworks	*Sawareekh* (pl)	صواريخ
firm (*adj*)	*gaemid* (m)/ *gamda* (f)	جامد/ جامده
firm (*n*)	*shirka* (f)	شركه
first	*awil* (m)/ *awila* (f)	اول/ اوله
first aid	*is*[a]*aef* (m) *awalee*	اسعاف أولى
first-aid kit	*Sandoo'il is*[a]*aef* (m)	صندوق لأسعاف
fish	*samak* (pl)	سمك
fish/go fishing: he/she fishes	*yiSTaad* (m)/ *tiSTaad* (f)	يصطاد/ تصطاد
fishing	*Sayd samak* (m)	صيد سمك
fishing rod	*sinnara* (f)	سناره
fishmonger's	*samaek* (m)	سماك
fit (*healthy*)	*laye' Tebayan* (m)/ *laye'a Tebayan* (f)	لائق طبياً/ لائقه طبياً
fit: it fits me	*ma'aaesi*	مقاسى
this doesn't fit me	*mish ma'aaesi*	مش مقاسى
fitting room	*'odit* (m) *il borowva*	حجره البروفه
fix: he/she fixes	*yeSalaH* (m)/ *teSalaH* (f)	يصلح/ تصلح
fizzy	*fawaar* (m)/ *fawaara* (f)	فوار/ فواره
flag	*[a]alam* (m)	علم
flash	*baree'* (m)	بريق
flashbulb	*flaesh* (m)	فلاش
flat (*apartment*)	*sha'a* (f)	شقه
flat (*level*)	*motasaewee* (m)/ *motasawya* (f)	متساوى/ متساويه
flat battery	*baTarayya* (f) *faDya*	بطاريه فاضيه

flavour	*ta^am* (m)	طعم
flaw	*ghalaT* (pl)	غلط
flea	*barghoot* (m)	برغوت
flight	*reHla* (f)	رحله
flight bag	*shanTit* (f) *isaffar*	شنطة السفر
flood	*fayaDan* (pl)	فيضان
floor	*arD* (m)	أرض
on the first floor	*fil dowr il awil*	فى الدور الأول
on the ground floor	*fil dowr il arDee*	فى الدور الأرضى
flour	*de'ee'* (pl)	دقيق
flower	*warda* (f)	ورده
flu	*anfilwanza* (f)	انفلونزا
fluent	*Taleeq* (m)/	طليق/ طليقه
	Taleeqa (f)	
fluently	*biTaala'a*	بطلاقة
fluid (*n*)	*sae'il* (m)	سائل
fly	*dibaena* (f)	دبانه
fly spray	*rashaashit* (f)	رشاشة الدبان
	iddibaen	
fly: he/she flies	*yeTeer* (m)/*teTeer* (f)	يطير/ تطير
fog	*Dabaab* (pl)	ضباب
foil	*wara'* (pl)	ورق المونيوم
	alamonyom	
folding (*e.g. chair*)	*yeTaba'* (m)/	يطبق/ تطبق
	teTaba' (f)	
folk music	*mazeeka* (f) *baladi*	مزيكه بلدى
follow: he/she follows	*yetba^a* (m)/*tetba^a* (f)	يتبع/ تتبع
following (*next*)	*molHa'*	ملحق
food	*akl* (m)	أكل
food poisoning	*tasamom* (m)	تسمم
foot	*qaddam* (m)	قدم
on foot	*mashi*	مشى
football	*korit il qaddam*	كرة القدم
footpath	*Taree'* (m)	طريق
for	*li*	لى

forbidden	*mamnoo^a* (m)/ *mamnoo^a a* (f)	ممنوع/ممنوعه
foreign, foreigner	*agnabi* (m)/ *agnabaya* (f)	اجنبي/اجنبيه
forest	*ghaeba* (f)	غابه
forget: he/she forgets	*yensa* (m)/*tensa* (f)	ينسى/تنسى
forgetfulness	*naesaeyaen* (m)	نسيان
forgive: he/she forgives	*yisaemeH* (m)/ *tisaemeH* (f)	يسامح/تسامح
fork	*showka* (f)	شوكه
form (*document*)	*Talab* (m)	طلب
fortnight	*izboo^ayn* (m)	اسبوعين
forward (*direction*)	*motaqadim*	متقدم
fountain	*nafoora* (f)	نافوره
foyer	*Sala* (f)	صاله
fracture	*kasr* (m)	كسر
frankly	*biSaraHa*	بصراحه
freckles	*namash* (pl)	نمش
free (*of charge*) (*available, unoccupied*)	*bibalaesh* (m & f) *faaDi* (m)/ *faDya* (f)	بلاش فاضي/فاضيه
freedom	*Horayya* (f)	حريه
freeze (*food*): he/she freezes	*yetalig* (m)/*tetalig* (f)	يتلج/تتلج
freezer	*freezar* (m)	فريزر
frequently	*keteer*	كتير
fresh	*TaaZa*	طازه
fridge	*talaega* (f)	ثلاجة
fried	*miHammar* (m)/ *miHammara* (f)	محمر/محمره
friend	*SaHib* (m)/*SaHba* (f)	صاحب/صاحبه
frightened	*khayef* (m)/*khayfa* (f)	خايف/خايفه
fringe (*hair*)	*'ossa* (f)	قصه
frog	*DofDa^a* (f)	ضفدعة
from	*min*	من

front	moqaddema (f)	مقدمه
in front of	'oddaem	قدام
front door	madkhal (m)	مدخل
frontier	gabha (f)	جبهه
frost	Saqee[a] (m)	صقيع
frozen (food)	metalig (m)/ metaliga (f)	مثلج/ مثلجه
fruit	fak-ha (pl)	فاكهة
fruit shop	fakahaeni (m)	فكهاني
fry: he/she fries	yiHammar (m)/ tiHammar (f)	يحمر/ تحمر
frying pan	Taasa (f)	طاسه
fuel	benzeen (m)	بنزين
full	malyaen (m)/ malyaena (f)	مليان/ مليانه
full board	fool bord	فول بورد
full up	komplay	كومبليه
fun: he/she has fun	yestamta[a] (m)/ testamta[a] (f)	يستمتع/ تستمتع
funeral	ganaeza (f)	جنازه
funfair	malaehee (pl)	ملاهى
funny (amusing)	moDHik (m)/ moDHika (f)	مضحك/ مضحكه
(peculiar)	ghareeb (m)/ ghareeba (f)	غريب/ غريبه
fur	farw (pl)	فرو
furniture	[a]afsh (pl)	عفش
further on	ab[a]ad	ابعد
fuse	Samaam (m)	صمام
fusebox	[a]elbit (f) iSamamaat	علبة الصمامات

G

gallery	*ma*^a*raD* (m)	معرض
gambling	*'omaar* (m)	قمار
game (*match*)	*matsh* (m)	ماتش
gangway	*madkhal* (m)	مدخل
garage (*for storage*)	*garaj* (m)	جراج
(*for repairs*)	*warsha* (pl)	ورشه
garden	*ginayna* (f)	جنينه
gardener	*ganaynee* (m)	جناينى
garlic	*towm* (m)	ثوم
gas	*botagaez* (m)	بوتاجاز
gas bottle, refill	*amboobit* (f) *botagaez*	انبوبة بوتاجاز
gastritis	*iltihaeb* (m) *ma*^a*awi*	إلتهاب معوى
gate	*bawaeba* (f)	بوابه
general	^a*amm*	عام
generally, in general	^a*omoomaen*	عموماً
generous	*kareem* (m)/ *kareema* (f)	كريم / كريمه
gentle	*ra'ee'* (m)/*ra'ee'a* (f)	رقيق / رقيقه
gentleman/men (*gents*)	*jentilmaen*	جنتلمان
genuine	*'aSeel* (m)/*'aSeela* (f)	أصيل / اصيله
geography	*goghrafya* (f)	جغرافيا
get: he/she gets (*receives*)	*yestelim* (m)/ *testelim* (f)	يستلم / تستلم
he/she gets off (*e.g. bus*)	*yenzil* (m)/*tenzil* (f)	ينزل / تنزل
he/she gets on (*e.g. bus*)	*yerkaeb* (m)/ *terkaeb* (f)	يركب / تركب
gift	*hidaya* (f)	هديه
gin	*jin* (m)	جن
gin and tonic	*jin wi tonik*	جن و تونيك
girl	*bint* (f)	بنت
girlfriend	*gerlfrend* (f)	صديقه
give: he/she gives	*yedi* (m)/*tedi* (f)	يعطى / تعطى

English	Transliteration	Arabic
glass (*for drinking*)	*kobbaya* (f)	كوب
(*substance*)	*izaez* (m)	زجاج
glasses (*spectacles*)	*naDara* (f)	نظاره
gloves	*gowantee* (m)	جوانتى
glue	*Samgh* (m)	صمغ
go: he/she goes	*yerowH* (m)/	يروح / تروح
	terowH (f)	
he/she goes away	*yessaefir* (m)/	يسافر / تسافر
	tissaefir (f)	
go away!	*imshi*	امشى !
he/she goes down	*yinzil* (m)/*tinzil* (f)	ينزل / تنزل
he/she goes in	*yedkhol* (m)/	يدخل / تدخل
	tedkhol (f)	
he/she goes out	*yekhrog* (m)/	يخرج / تخرج
	tokhrog (f)	
he/she goes up	*yeTlaᵃ* (m)/	يطلع / تطلع
	teTlaᵃ (f)	
let's go!	*yalla*	يالله
goal	*gown* (m)	جول
goat	*meᵃza* (f)	معزه
God	*alla*	الله
gold	*dahab* (m)	ذهب
golf	*golf* (m)	جولف
golf clubs	*maDrab* (m) *golf*	مضرب جولف
golf course	*malᵃab* (m) *golf*	ملعب جولف
good	*kwayyis* (m)/	كويس / كويسه
	kwayissa (f)	
good day	*nahaarak saᵃeed* (m)/	نهارك سعيد
	nahaarik saᵃeed (f)	نهارك سعيد
good morning	*SabaH il kheer*	صباح الخير
good evening	*misa' il kheer*	مساء الخير
good night	*tiSbaH* (to m)/	تصبح /
	tiSbaHi (to f)/	تصبحى /
	tiSbaHoo (to pl)	تصبحو
	ᵃala kheer	على خير
goodbye	*maᵃassalaema*	مع السلامه

goods	*boDaaªa* (pl)	بضاعه
government	*Hokooma* (f)	حكومه
gram	*graam* (m)	جرام
grammar	*qawaªid* (pl)	قواعد
grandchildren	*aHfaed* (pl)	احفاد
granddaughter	*Hafeeda* (f)	حفيده
grandfather	*ged* (m)	جد
my grandfather	*geddi* (m)	جدى
grandmother	*geda* (f)	جده
my grandmother	*gedetti* (f)	جدتى
grandson	*Hafeed* (m)	حفيد
grandstand	*minaSa* (f)	منصه
grapes	*ªenab* (pl)	عنب
grapefruit	*graypfroot* (m)	جرايب فروت
grass	*zarªa* (pl)	زرع
grateful: I am	*shakir faDlak* (to m)/	شاكر فضلك/
grateful	*shakir faDlik* (to f)	شاكر فضلك
greasy	*mizayit* (m & f)	مزيت
great!	*ªazeem*	عظيم
green	*'akhDar* (m)/	أخضر/خضراء
	khaDra (f)	
greengrocer's	*khoDari* (m)	خضرى
greet: he/she greets	*yessalim* (m)/	يسلم/ تسلم
	tessalim (f)	
grey	*romaadee* (m & f)	رمادى
grilled	*mashwi* (m)/	مشوى/مشويه
	mashwaya (f)	
grocer's	*ba'ael* (m)	بقال
ground	*arD* (f)	ارض
ground floor	*il dowr* (m) *il arDi*	الدورالأرضى
group	*magmooªa* (f)	مجموعه
grow (*cultivate*):	*yezraª* (m)/	يزرع/ تزرع
he/she grows	*tezraª* (f)	
guarantee	*Damaan* (m)	ضمان
guard (*on train*)	*Haeris* (m)	حارس

guest	*Dayf* (m)/*Dayfa* (f)	ضيف / ضيفه
(in hotel)	*zeboon* (m)/	زبون / زبونه
	zeboona (f)	
guest house	*bansyown* (m)	بنسيون
guide	*morshid* (m)/	مرشد / مرشده
	morshida (f)	
guided tour	*ziyara* (f) *maᵃa*	زياره مع مرشد
	morshid	
guidebook	*daleel* (m)	دليل
guilty	*moznib* (m)/	مذنب / مذنبه
	mozniba (f)	
guitar	*geeTar* (m)	جيتار
Gulf	*ilkhaleeg*	الخليج
gun	*bondoᵃaya* (f)	بندقيه
guy rope	*Habl* (m)	حبل
gymnastics	*gombaaz* (m)	جباز

H

habit	*ᵃada* (f)	عاده
hair	*shaᵃr* (pl)	شعر
hairbrush	*forsha* (f)	فرشه
haircut	*Hilaᵃa* (f)	حلاقه
hairdresser	*Hallaᵃ* (m)	حلاق
hairdrier	*seshwaar* (m)	سشوار
hairgrip	*bensa* (f)	بنسه
hairspray	*bakhaekhit* (f) *shaᵃr*	بخاخة شعر
half	*noS*	نصف
half board	*hafbord*	هاف بورد
half price	*noS tazkara* (f)	نصف تزكره
half fare	*noS itaman*	نصف الثمن
half-hour/half an hour	*noSissaᵃa*	نصف ساعه
half past . . .	*. . . wi noS*	. . . و نصف
(see Time, p. 172)		

hall (*in house*)	**Saalla** (f)	صاله
(*concert*)	**qa^aa** (f)	قاعه
ham	**jambon** (m)	جامبون
hamburger	**hamborger** (m)	همبورجر
hammer	**shakoosh** (m)	شاكوش
hand	**yad** (f)	يد
hand cream	**kreem aydayn**	كريم اليد
hand luggage	**shonaaT yad**	شنط يد
hand-made	**yadawi** (m)/ **yadawaya** (f)	يدوى/ يدويه
handbag	**shanTit** (f) **yad**	شنطة يد
handicapped	**mo^aawaq** (m)/ **mo^aawaqa** (f)	معوق/ معوقه
handkerchief	**mandeel** (m)	منديل
handle	**yad** (f)	يد
hang up: he/she hangs up	**ye^aala'** (m)/**te^aala'** (f)	يعلق/ تعلق
happen: it happens	**HaSal** (m)/ **HaSalat** (f)	حصل/ حصلت
happy	**mabsooT** (m)/ **mabsooTa** (f)	مبسوط/ مبسوطه
harbour	**meena** (f)	ميناء
hard	**gaemid** (m)/ **gaemda** (f)	جامد/ جامده
(*difficult*)	**Sa^ab** (m)/**Sa^aba** (f)	صعب/ صعبه
hat	**bornaeTa** (f)	برنيطه/ قبعه
hate: he/she hates	**yekra** (m)/**tekra** (f)	يكره/ تكره
have: he/she has	**^aando** (m)/ **^aandaha** (f)	عنده/ عندها
(*see p. 166*)		
I have	**^aandi**	عندى
I have with me	**ma^aaya**	معايا
hay	**'ash** (pl)	قش
hay fever	**Hasasaya** (f)	حساسيه
hazelnut	**bondo'** (m)	بندق
he (*see* Basic grammar, *p. 161*)	**howa**	هو

234

head	*raas* (m)	رأس
(*boss*)	*rayis* (m)/*rayisa* (f)	رئيس / رئيسه
headache	*Soda*[a] (m)	صداع
headphone	*samae*[a]*a* (f)	سماعه
heal: he/she heals	*yekhafif* (m)/	يخفف / تخفف
	tekhafif (f)	
health	*SeHa* (f)	صحة
health foods	*akl* (m) *SeHi*	أكل صحي
healthy, in good health	*seHa kwayissa*	صحة كويسه
hear: he/she hears	*yesma*[a] (m)/*tesma*[a] (f)	يسمع / تسمع
hearing (*facility*)	*sama*[a] (m)	سماع
hearing aid	*samae*[a]*a* (f)	سماعه
heart	*'alb* (m)	قلب
heart attack	*sakta* (f) *'albaya*	سكته قلبيه
heat	*Harara* (f)	حراره
heater	*dafaya* (f)	دفايه
heating	*tadfe'a* (f)	تدفئه
heaven	*ganna* (f)	جنه
heavy	*ti'eel* (m)/*ti'eela* (f)	ثقيل / ثقيله
heel	*ka*[a]*b* (m)	كعب
height	*Tool* (m)	طول
helicopter	*helikoptar* (f)	هليوكوبتر
hell	*gohannam* (f)	جهنم
hello	*ahlan*	أهلا
helmet	*khowza* (f)	خوزه
help	*mosa*[a]*da* (f)	مساعده
help!	*ilHa'ooni*	إلحقوني!
help: he/she helps	*yisa*[a]*id* (m)/*tisa*[a]*id* (f)	يساعد / تساعد
her (*pronoun*)	*haya*	هي
(*adj.*) (*see* Basic grammar, *p. 160*)		
herb	*nabaeti* (m)	نباتي
herbal tea	*shay a*[a]*shaeb*	شاي أعشاب
here	*hena*	هنا
here is . . .	*aho* . . .	أهو . . .
hiccups	*zoghoTa* (f)	زغطه
high	[a]*ali* (m)/[a]*alya* (f)	عالي / عاليه
high chair	*korsi* (m) [a]*ali*	كرسي عالي

English	Transliteration	Arabic
hijack: he/she hijacks	yekhTaf (m)/ tekhTaf (f)	يخطف / تخطف
hill	rabwa (f)	ربوه
him (see p. 161)		
hire: he/she hires	ye'aggar (m)/te'aggar (f)	يأجر / تأجر
his (see p. 160)		
history	tareekh (m)	تاريخ
hit: he/she hits	yeDrab (m)/teDrab (f)	يضرب / تضرب
hobby	howaya (f)	هوايه
hold: he/she holds	yemsik (m)/temsik (f)	يمسك / تمسك
hole	khorm (m)	خرم
holidays	'agaeza (f)	أجازه
on holiday	fi 'agaeza	في أجازه
holy	moqadas (m)/ moqadassa (f)	مقدس / مقدسه
home	bayt (m)	بيت
at home	fil bayt	في البيت
home address	ªenwaen (m) il bayt	عنوان البيت
he/she goes home	yerawaH (m)/ terawaH (f)	يروح / تروح
homosexual	shaez (m) ginsayan	شاذ جنسياً
honest	'ameen (m)/ 'ameena (f)	أمين / أمينه
honeymoon	shahr ªassal (m)	شهر عسل
hope: he/she hopes	yatamanna (m)/ tatamanna (f)	يتمنى / تتمنى
I hope so	atamanna	أتمنى
horrible	faZeeª (m)/ faZeeªa (f)	فظيع / فظيعه
horse	HoSaan (m)	حصان
hose	kharToom (m)	خرطوم
hospital	mostashfa (f)	مستشفى
host	imoDeef (m)	المضيف
hot (temperature)	Har (m & f)	حر
(spicy)	Harra' (m)/ Harra'a (f)	حراق / حراقه

hotel	*hotayl* (m)	هوتيل
hour	*sa^aa* (f)	ساعه
half-hour	*noSissa^aa*	نصف ساعه
house	*bayt* (m)	بيت
housewife	*sit* (f) *bayt*	ست بيت
housework	*shoghl* (m) *il bayt*	شغل البيت
hovercraft	*hoverkraft*	هوفركرافت
how	*izzay*	إزاى
how long/many/ much?	*'ad ay*	قدايه؟
how much does it/do they cost?	*bikaem*	بكام؟
human	*insaeni* (m)/ *insaenaya* (f)	إنسانى/ إنسانيه
human being	*insaen* (m)/ *insaena* (f)	إنسان/ إنسانه
hungry	*ga^aaen* (m)/ *ga^aaena* (f)	جعان/ جعانه
hunt: he/she hunts	*yeSTaad* (m)/ *teSTaad* (f)	يصطاد/ تصطاد
hunting	*Sayd* (m)	صيد
hurry: he/she is in a hurry	*mista^agil* (m)/ *mista^agila* (f)	مستعجل/ مستعجله
hurt: he/she hurts	*yegraH* (m)/*tegraH* (f)	يجرح/ تجرح
it hurts	*biyewga^a* (m)/ *bitewga^a* (f)	بيوجع/ بتوجع
husband	*gowz* (m)	جوز
hut	*kookh* (m)	كوخ
hydrofoil	*haydrowfoyl* (m)	هيدروفويل

I (*see* Basic grammar, *p. 161*)	*ana*	أنا
ice	*talg* (m)	ثلج
ice-cream	*'ays kreem* (m)	أيس كريم

icy	*mitalig* (m)/ *mitaliga* (f)	مثلج/ مثلجه
(*weather*)	*sa'e^a*	ساقع
idea	*fikra* (f)	فكره
if	*izza*	إذا
ill	*^aayaen* (m)/ *^aayaena* (f)	عيان/ عيانه
illness	*maraD* (m)	مرض
imagination	*khayael* (m)	خيال
imagine: he/she imagines	*yetkhayael* (m)/ *tetkhayael* (f)	يتخيل/ تتخيل
immediately	*Hallan*	حالاً
immersion heater	*sakhaen* (m)	سخان
impatient	*ma^aendoosh Sabr* (m)/ *ma^aendahaesh Sabr* (f)	معندوش صبر/ معندهاش صبر
important	*mohim* (m)/ *mohima* (f)	مهم/ مهمه
impossible	*mostaHeel* (m)/ *mostaHeela* (f)	مستحيل/ مستحيله
impressive	*modhish* (m)/ *modhisha* (f)	مدهش/ مدهشه
in	*fi*	في
included	*min Demn*	من ضمن
income	*dakhl* (m)	دخل
indeed	*Tab^aan*	طبعا
independent	*mostaqil* (m)/ *mostaqila* (f)	مستقل/ مستقله
indigestion	*soo' haDm* (m)	سوء هضم
indoors	*gowa*	جوا
industrial	*Sinaa^ai* (m)/ *Sinaa^aiya* (f)	صناعي/ صناعيه
industry	*Sinaa^aa* (f)	صناعه
infected	*melawath* (m)/ *melawatha* (f)	ملوث/ ملوثه
infection	*^aadwa* (f)	عدوى

238

infectious	mo^adee (m)/ mo^adaya (f)	معدى/معديه
inflamed	moltahib (m)/ moltahiba (f)	ملتهب/ملتهبه
inflammation	iltihaeb (m)	إلتهاب
influenza	infilwanza (f)	انفلونزا
informal	ghayr rasmee (m)/ ghayr rasmaya (f)	غير رسمى/ غير رسميه
information	ma^aloomaet (pl)	معلومات
information desk/office	maktaeb il isti^alamaet	مكتب استعلامات
injection	Ho'na (f)	حقنه
injure: he/she injures	yegraH (m)/tegraH (f)	يجرح/تجرح
injured	itgaraH (m)/ itgaraHit (f)	المجرح/المجرحت
injury	garH (m)	جرح
ink	Hebr (m)	حبر
inner	dakhili (m)/ dakhilaya (f)	داخلى/داخليه
innocent	baree' (m)/baree'a (f)	برى ء/بريئه
insect	Hashara (f)	حشره
insect bite	^aaDit Hashara	عضة حشره
insect repellent	Ded il Hasharaat	ضدالحشرات
inside	gowa	جوا
insist	yeSamim (m)/ tiSamim (f)	يصمم/تصمم
inspector	mofatish (m)/ mofatisha (f)	مفتش/مفتشه
instant coffee	neskafay (f)	نسكافيه
instead of	badal min	بدل من
instructor	moddarris (m)/ moddarissa (f)	مدرس/مدرسه
insulin	insooleen (m)	إنسولين
insult	ihaena (f)	إهانه
insurance	ta'meen (pl)	تأمين
insurance certificate	shahaedit (f) ta'meen	شهاده تأمين

239

insure: he/she insures	*ye'amin* (m)/ *te'amin* (f)	يأمن/ تأمن
insured	*mo'amin* (m)/ *mo'amina* (f)	مؤمن/ مؤمنه
intelligent	*nabee* (m)/*nabeeha* (f)	نبيه/ نبيهه
interested, interesting	*moseer lil ihtimam*	مثيرللاهتمام
interior	*dakhili* (m)	داخلي
intermediate	*metawasiT* (m)/ *metawasiTa* (f)	متوسط/ متوسطه
international	*dawli* (m)/*dawlaya* (f)	دولي/ دوليه
interpret: he/she interprets	*yetargim* (m)/ *tetargim* (f)	يترجم/ تترجم
interpreter	*motargim* (m)/ *motargima* (f)	مترجم/ مترجمه
interval (*theatre etc.*)	*istiraHa* (f)	إستراحه
interview	*moqabla* (f)	مقابله
into	*fi*	في
introduce: he/she introduces	*ye'adim* (m)/ *te'adim* (f)	يقدم/ تقدم
invitation	*da^awa* (f)	دعوه
invite: he/she invites	*yad^o* (m)/*tad^ee* (f)	يدعو/ تدعى
iodine	*iodeen* (pl)	ايودين
Ireland	*ayrlanda* (f)	ايرلندا
Irish	*ayrlandi* (m)/ *ayrlandaya* (f)	ايرلندي/ ايرلنديه
iron (*metal*)	*Hadeed* (pl)	حديد
(*for clothes*)	*makwa* (f)	مكوه
iron: he/she irons	*yekwi* (m)/*tekwi* (f)	يكوى/ تكوى
person who irons clothes	*makwagi* (m)	مكوجى
is (*see* 'to be', *p. 165*)		
is there . . .?	*fi . . .*	في . . . ؟
Islam	*islaem* (m)	أسلام
Islamic	*Islaemi* (m)/ *islaemaya* (f)	اسلامى/ اسلاميه
island	*gizeera* (f)	جزيره
it (*see* Basic grammar, *p. 161*)		

itch   *harsha* (f)   هرشه
its (*see* Basic grammar, *p. 160*)

J

jacket	*jaketta* (f)	جاكته
jam	*mirabba* (f)	مربى
jar	*barTamaan* (m)	برطمان
jazz	*mazeeka gaez* (m)	موسيقى الجاز
jeans	*jeenz* (pl)	جينز
jelly (*food*)	*jellee* (m)	جلى
jellyfish	*qandeel il baHr* (m)	قنديل البحر
Jesus Christ	*il maseeH* (m)	المسيح
jetty	*marsa* (f)	مرسى
jeweller's	*gawahirgi* (m)	جواهرجى
Jewish	*yahoodee* (m)/	يهودى/ يهوديه
	yahoodaya (f)	
job	*wazeefa* (f)	وظيفه
jog: he/she jogs	*yegri* (m)/*tegri* (f)	يجرى/ تجرى
jogging	*gari* (m)	جرى
joke	*nokta* (f)	نكته
journalist	*SaHafi* (m)/	صحفى/ صحفيه
	SaHafaya (f)	
journey	*reHla* (f)	رحله
judge	*qaadi* (m)	قاضى
jug	*shafsha'* (m)	شفشق
juice	*ªaSeer* (m)	عصير
jump: he/she jumps	*yenoT* (m)/*tenoT* (f)	ينط/ تنط
jumper	*bolovar* (m)	بلوفر
junction	*moltaqa* (f)	ملتقى
just (*only*)	*bas*	بس

K

keep: he/she keeps	*yaHtafiZ* (m)/	يحتفظ/ تحتفظ
	taHtafiZ (f)	

kettle	*barraad* (m)	براد
key	*moftaeH* (m)	مفتاح
key ring	*midaiyit* (f) *mafateeH*	ميدالية مقاتيح
kidney	*kelwa* (f) / *kalaewi* (pl)	كلية / كلاوى
kill: he/she kills	*yeqtil* (m) / *teqtil* (f)	يقتل / تقتل
kilo(gram)	*keeloo* (m)	كيلو
kilometre	*keelomitr* (m)	كيلومتر
kind (*sort*)	*now*^a (m)	نوع
(*generous*)	*kareem* (m) / *kareema* (f)	كريم / كريمه
king	*malik* (m)	ملك
kiss	*bosa* (f)	بوسه
kiss: he/she kisses	*yiboos* (m) / *tiboos* (f)	يبوس / تبوس
kitchen	*maTbakh* (m)	مطبخ
knickers	*libaes* (m)	لباس
knife	*sikkeena* (f)	سكينه
knitting	*tereeko* (m)	تريكو
knitting needle	*ibrit* (f) *tereeko*	إبرة تريكو
knock (*on door*): he/she knocks	*yekhabat* (m) / *tekhabat* (f)	يخبط / تخبط
knot	*^aoqda* (f)	عقده
know: he/she knows	*ye^araf* (m) / *te^araf* (f)	يعرف / تعرف
as far as I know	*^aala Hasab ^aelmi*	على حسب علمى
Koran	*qor'an* (m)	قرأن

L

label	*tikit* (m)	تيكت
lace	*dantayl* (f)	دانتيل
ladder	*sellem* (m)	سلم
lady	*sayeda* (f)	سيده
ladies	*sayedaet* (pl)	سيدات
lager	*beera* (f)	بيره
lake	*boHira* (f)	بحيره
lamb (*animal*)	*kharoof* (m)	خروف
(*meat*)	*Daani* (m)	ضانى

lamp	*lamba* (f)	لمبه
lamp post	*ᵃamood noor* (m)	عمود نور
land	*arD* (f)	أرض
land: he/she lands	*yahbaat* (m)/ *tahbaat* (f)	يهبط/ تهبط
landing (*house*)	*dowr* (m)	دور
(*plane*)	*hoobooT* (m)	هبوط
landlady	*SaHbit ilbayt* (f)	صاحبةالبيت
landlord	*SaHb ilbayt* (m)	صاحب البيت
lane (*country road*)	*Taree'* (m)	طريق
language	*logha* (f)	لغة
large	*Dakhm* (m)/ *Dakhma* (f)	ضخم/ ضخمه
last	*akheer* (m)/ *akheera* (f)	أخير/ أخيره
last: he/she lasts	*yastaghriq* (m)/ *tastaghriq* (f)	يستغرق/ تستغرق
late: (it is) late	*metᵃakhar*	متأخر
later	*baᵃdayn*	بعدين
laugh	*DeHk*	ضحك
laugh: he/she laughs	*yeDHak* (m)/ *teDHak* (f)	يضحك/ تضحك
launderette	*ghassaela* (f)	غساله
laundry	*ghaseel* (pl)	غسيل
law	*qanoon* (m)	قانون
lawyer	*moHaemi* (m)/ *moHaemaya* (f)	محامى/ محاميه
laxative	*mosahil* (m)	مسهل
lazy	*kaslaen* (m)/ *kaslaena* (f)	كسلان/ كسلانه
lead (*metal*)	*roSaaS* (pl)	رصاص
lead-free	*min ghayr roSaaS*	من غير رصاص
lead: he/she leads	*yaqood* (m)/ *taqood* (f)	يقود/ تقود
leaf	*wara'a* (f)	ورقه
leaflet	*manshoor* (m)	منشور

English	Transliteration	Arabic
lean: he/she leans (out)	*yanHani* (m)/ *tanHani* (f)	ينحني/ تنحني
learn: he/she learns	*yet ªalim* (m)/ *tet ªalim* (f)	يتعلم/ تتعلم
learner	*mota ªalim* (m)/ *mota ªalima* (f)	متعلم/ متعلمه
least: at least	*ªalalaqal*	على الأقل
leather	*geld* (m)	جلد
leave: he/she leaves (*message etc.*)	*yeseeb* (m)/*teseeb* (f)	يسيب/ تسيب
(*goes away*)	*yemshi* (m)/ *temshi* (f)	يمشى/ تمشى
lecturer	*moHaaDir* (m)/ *moHaaDira* (f)	محاضر/ محاضره
left	*shimael*	شمال
left-handed	*ashwal* (m)/ *showla* (f)	أشول/ شوله
leg	*regl* (m)	رجل
legal	*qanooni* (m)/ *qanoonaya* (f)	قانونى/ قانونيه
lemon	*lamoona* (f)/ *lamoon* (pl)	ليمونه/ ليمون
lemonade	*lamonaeta* (f)	ليموناده
lend: he/she lends	*yisallif* (m)/*tisallif* (f)	يسلف/ تسلف
length	*Tool* (m)	طول
lens (*camera*)	*ªadasa* (f)	عدسه
lentils	*ªats* (pl)	عدس
lesbian	*shaeZa ginsayan* (f)	شاذه جنسياً
less	*a'al*	أقل
lesson	*dars* (m)	درس
let: he/she lets (*allows*)	*yesmaH* (m)/ *tesmaH* (f)	يسمح/ تسمح
(*rents*)	*ye'agar* (m)/ *te'agar* (f)	يأجر/ تأجر
letter	*gawaeb* (m)	جواب
letterbox	*Sandoo' bareed* (m)	صندوق بريد

244

lettuce	*khas* (m)	خس
leukaemia	*saraTaan* (m) *fil dam*	سرطان في الدم
level (*height, standard*)	*mistawa* (m)	مستوى
level (*flat*)	*misaTaH* (m)/ *misaTaHa* (f)	مسطح / مسطحه
level crossing	*ᵃoboor* (m) *sekka Hadeed*	عبور سكه حديد
library	*maktabba* (f)	مكتبه
licence (*driving etc.*)	*rokhSa* (f)	رخصه
lid	*ghaTa* (m)	غطاء
lie down: he/she lies down	*yastalqi* (m)/ *tastalqi* (f)	يستلقى / تستلقى
life	*Haiyae* (f)	حياه
lifebelt	*Toq nagae* (m)	طوق نجاه
lifeboat	*qarib nagae* (m)	قارب نجاه
lifeguard	*ᵃamil inqaaZ* (m)	عامل إنقاذ
lifejacket	*towb nagae* (m)	ثوب نجاه
lift	*asanser* (m)	اسانسير
light (*n*)	*noor* (m)	نور
light bulb	*lamba* (f)	لمبه
light (*coloured*)	*faetiH* (m)/*fatHa* (f)	فاتح / فاتحه
(*weight*)	*khafeef* (m)/ *khafeefa* (f)	خفيف / خفيفه
light: he/she lights (*fire*)	*yewalaᵃ* (m)/ *tewalaᵃ* (f)	يولع / تولع
lighter (*cigarette*)	*walaᵃa* (f)	ولاعه
lighter fuel	*botagaez* (m)	بوتاجاز
lightning	*bar'* (m)	برق
like (*similar to*)	*zay*	زى
like this/that	*zay da* (m)	زى ده
what is . . . like?	*. . . zaya ay*	. . . زى إيه؟
like: he/she likes	*biHeb* (m)/*bitHeb* (f)	بيحب / بتحب
I like it	*ᵃagebni*	عاجبنى
likely	*gayiz*	جائز
limited	*maHdood* (m)/ *maHdooda* (f)	محدود / محدوده

245

line	*khaT* (m)	خط
lion	*asad* (m)	أسد
lioness	*labwa* (f)	لبوه
lip	*sheffa* (f)	شفه
lipstick	*'alam* (m) *rooj*	قلم روج
liqueur	*likayr* (m)	ليكير
liquid	*sae'il* (m)	سائل
list	*lista* (f)	لسته
listen: he/she listens (to)	*yesma^a* (m)/*tesma^a* (f)	يسمع / تسمع
litre	*litr* (m)	لتر
litter	*zibaela* (pl)	زباله
little	*Soghayar* (m)/ *Soghayara* (f)	صغير/ صغيره
little: a little	*showaya*	شويه
live: he/she lives	*ye^aeesh* (m)/ *te^aeesh* (f)	يعيش / تعيش
liver	*kibda* (f)	كبده
living-room	*antray* (m)	انتريه
loaf	*regheef* (m)	رغيف
local	*maHaeli* (m)/ *maHalaya* (f)	محلي/ محليه
lock	*terbaes* (m)	ترباس
lock: he/she locks	*yetarbis* (m)/ *tetarbis* (f)	يتربس / تتربس
London	*landan* (f)	لندن
lonely	*waHeed* (m)/ *waHeeda* (f)	وحيد/وحيده
long	*Taweel* (m)/ *Taweela* (f)	طويل/ طويله
long-distance call	*masafa* (f) *Taweela*	مسافه طويله
look: he/she looks (at)	*yeboS* (^a*ala*) (m)/ *teboS* (^a*ala*) (f)	يبص/ تبص
he/she looks after	*yakhod baeloo* (m)/ *takhod balha* (f)	بأخذ باله تأخذ بالها
he/she looks for	*yedawar ^aala* (m)/ *tedawar ^aala* (f)	يدورعلى/ تدورعلى

English	Transliteration	Arabic
he/she looks like	*yeshbih* (m)/ *teshbih* (f)	يشبه / تشبه
loose (*clothes*)	*khafeef* (m)/ *khafeefa* (f)	خفيف / خفيفه
lorry	*looree* (m)	لورى
lorry-driver	*sawa' looree* (m)	سواق لورى
lose: he/she loses	*yafqod* (m)/ *tafqod* (f)	يفقد / تفقد
. . . is lost (see p. 155)	. . . *Da*ª	ضاع . . .
lost property (office)	(*maktaeb*) (m) *il mafqoodaet*	مكتب المفقودات
a lot (of)	*kiteer* (m)/ *kiteera* (f)	كتير / كتيره
lotion	*kreem* (m)	كريم
lottery	*lotaraya* (f)	لوتاريه
loud	*Sowt* ª*alee* (m & f)	صوت عالى
lounge (*airport*)	*Saala* (f)	صاله
(*hotel*)	*Salown* (m)	صالون
love	*Hob* (m)	حب
love: he/she loves	*yiHeb* (m)/*tiHeb* (f)	يحب / تحب
lovely	*Helw* (m)/*Helwa* (f)	حلو / حلوه
low	*waaTi* (m)/*waTya* (f)	واطى / واطيه
lower	*awTa*	أوطى
lozenge (for throat)	*basteel* (m) (*lil zowr*)	باستيل (للزور)
lucky	*maHZooZ* (m)/ *maHZooZa* (f)	محظوظ / محظوظه
luggage	*shonaaT* (pl)	شنط
luggage allowance	*ishonaaT il masmooH biha*	الشنط المسموح بها
lump	*kotla* (f)	كتله
(*swelling*)	*waram* (f)	ورم
lunch	*ghadda* (f)	غذاء

M

English	Transliteration	Arabic
machine	*makanna* (f)	ماكينه
machinist	*mikaneekee* (m)/ *mikaneekaya* (f)	ميكانيكى / ميكانيكيه

mad	*magnoon* (m)/ *magnoona* (f)	مجنون/ مجنونه
madam	*madaem* (f)	مدام
magazine	*megalla* (f)	مجله
mail	*bareed* (m)	بريد
main	*asaesee* (m)/ *asasaya* (f)	أساسى/ أساسيه
make (*car etc.*)	*marka* (f)	ماركه
make: he/she makes	*ye^amil* (m)/*te^amil* (f)	يعمل/ تعمل
make-up	*makyaj* (m)	ماكياج
male	*zakar* (m)	ذكر
man	*ragil* (m)	راجل
manager	*modeer* (m)/*modeera* (f)	مدير/ مديره
managing director	*modeer ^aam* (m & f)	مديرعام
many	*kiteer*	كثير
not many	*mish kiteer*	مش كثير
map	*khareeTa* (f)	خريطه
marble	*rokhaem* (m)	رخام
margarine	*margareen* (m)	مارجرين
market	*sooq* (m)	سوق
married	*metgawiz* (m)/ *metgawiza* (f)	متجوز/ متجوزه
marry: he/she gets married	*yetgawiz* (m)/ *tetgawiz* (f)	يتجوز/ تتجوز
mascara	*maskara* (f)	مسكره
masculine	*zakar* (m)	ذكر
mask (*for protection*)	*qinae^a* (m)	قناع
mass (*church*)	*qodas* (m)	قداس
match (*game*)	*matsh* (m)	ماتش
matches	*kabreet* (pl)	كبريت
material (*cloth*)	*o'maesh* (pl)	قماش
mathematics	*riyaDa* (f)	رياضه
matter: it doesn't matter	*mish mohim*	مش مهم
what's the matter?	*fi ay*	فى ايه؟
mattress	*martaba* (f)	مرتبه
air mattress	*martabit hawa*	مرتبة هواء

248

mature (*cheese etc.*)	*qadeem* (m)/ *qadeema* (f)	قديم/قديمه
mayonnaise	*mayonayz* (m)	مايونيز
me (*see* Basic grammar, *p. 161*)	*ana*	أنا
with me	*ma^aaya*	معايا
meadow	*mar^aa* (m)	مرعى
meal	*akla* (f)	أكله
mean: what does this mean?	*ya^anee ay*	يعنى أيه؟
meanwhile	*baynama*	بينما
measles	*HaSba* (f)	حصبه
German measles	*HaSba almaeni*	حصبه ألمانى
measure: he/she measures	*ye'ees* (m)/*te'ees* (f)	يقيس/تقيس
measurement	*ma'aaes* (m)	مقاس
meat	*laHma* (f)	لحمه
cold meats	*laHm baerid* (pl)	لحم بارد
mechanic	*mikaneekee* (m)/ *mikaneekaya* (f)	ميكانكى/ميكانيكيه
medical	*Tebbee* (m)/ *Tebbaya* (f)	طبى/طبيه
medicine	*dawa* (f)	دواء
Mediterranean sea	*ibaHr ilabyaD ilmitawassiT*	البحر الأبيض المتوسط
medium	*noS noS*	نص نص
(*steak*)	*noSi siwa*	نصف سواء
medium dry (*wine*)	*medyam*	مديم
meet: he/she meets	*ye'abil* (m)/*te'abil* (f)	يقابل/تقابل
meeting (*accidental*)	*moqabla* (f)	مقابله
(*business*)	*igtimae^a* (m)	أجتماع
melon	*shamaema* (f)	شمامه
watermelon	*baTeekha* (f)	بطيخه
member	*^aodw* (m & f)	عضو
men	*rigaela* (pl)	رجاله
mend: he/she mends	*yeSallaH* (m)/ *tiSallaH* (f)	يصلح/تصلح

menu	*menyoo* (m)	منيو
message	*risaela* (f)	رساله
metal	*ma°adan* (m)	معدن
meter	*°adaed* (m)	عداد
metre	*metr* (m)	متر
microwave oven	*maikrowayv* (m)	مايكرو وايڤ
midday	*iDohraya* (f)	الظهريه
middle	*mitawassiT* (m)/	متوسط/ متوسطه
	mitawassiTa (f)	
middle-aged	*fi montaSaf*	فى منتصف العمر
	il °omr	
midnight	*fi noS ilayl*	فى نصف الليل
migraine	*meegrayn* (m)	ميجراين
mild	*khafeef* (m)/	خفيف/ خفيفه
	khafeefa (f)	
mile	*meel* (m)	ميل
milk	*laban* (m)	لبن
milkshake	*milkshayk (m)*	ميلك شيك
mill	*TaHoona* (f)	طاحونه
mince	*laHma*	لحمه مفرومه
	mafrooma (m)	
mind: do you mind	*°andak* (to m)/	عندك/ عندك
(if) . . .?	*°andik* (to f)	مانع . . .؟
	maeni° . . .	
I don't mind	*ma°andeesh maeni°*	معنديش مانع
minibus	*minibas* (m)	مينى باس
minister	*wazeer* (m)/	وزير/ وزيره
	wazeera (f)	
minute (*time*)	*de'e'a* (f)/*da'ayi'* (pl)	دقيقه/ دقائق
mirror	*miraya* (f)	مرءاه
Miss	*aenisa* (f)	أنسه
miss: he/she misses		
(*bus etc.*)	*faetoo* (m)/*fat-ha* (f)	فاته/ فاتها
(*nostalgia*)	*waHshoo* (m)/	واحشو/ واحشها
	waHesh-ha (f)	
mist	*Dabaab* (m)	ضباب

250

mistake	*ghalTa* (f)	غلطه
he/she is mistaken	*ghalTaan* (m)/	غلطان/غلطانه
	ghalTaana (f)	
mixed	*khalaT* (m)/	خلط/خلط
	khalaTit (f)	
mixture	*makhlooT* (pl)	مخلوط
model	*modayl* (f)	موديل
modern	*modaern* (m & f)	مودرن
moisturiser	*kraym* (m) *moraTib*	كريم مرطب
monastery	*dayr* (m)	دير
money	*filoos* (pl)	فلوس
month	*shahr* (m)	شهر
monument	*naSb tizkaeri* (m)	نصب تزكارى
moon	*'amar* (m)	قمر
moped	*fesba* (f)	فسبه
more	*aktar*	اكثر
no more	*kifaeya*	كفايه
morning	*SabaH* (m)	صباح
mortgage	*rahn* (m)	رهن
mosque	*game^a* (m)	جامع
mosquitoes	*namoos* (pl)	ناموس
mosquito net	*namoosaya* (f)	ناموسيه
most (of)	*mo^aZam*	معظم
mother	*'om* (f)	أم
mother-in-law	*Hama* (f)	حماه
my mother-in-law	*Hamaeti* (f)	حماتى
motor	*maTowr* (m)	موتور
motorbike	*motosekl* (m)	موتوسيكل
motorboat	*lansh* (m)	لنش
motor racing	*saba'* (m) *saiyaraat*	سباق سيارات
motorway	*otostraad* (m)	أوتوستراد
mountain	*gabal* (m)	جبل
mountaineering	*tasaloq il gibael*	تسلق الجبال
mouse	*far* (m)	فأر
moustache	*shanab* (m)	شنب
mouth	*bo'* (m)	بق
move: he/she moves	*ye^aazil* (m)/*te^aazil* (f)	يعزل/تعزل

Mr	*isayed*	السيد
Mrs	*isayeda*	السيده
much	*kiteer*	كتير
not much	*mish kiteer*	مش كثير
mug	*fingaen* (m)	فنجان
mullah (*Muslim religious leader*)	*shaykh* (m)	شيخ/ إمام
murder	*qatl* (m)	قتل
museum	*matHaf* (m)	متحف
music	*mazeeka* (f)	مزيكه
musical	*mosiqi* (m)/ *mosiqaya* (f)	موسيقى/ موسيقيه
musician	*molaHin* (m)/ *molaHina* (f)	ملحن/ ملحنه
Muslim	*moslim* (m)/ *moslima* (f)	مسلم/ مسلمه
must: you must . . .	*laezim* . . .	لازم . . .
mustard	*mostarda* (f)	مستارده
my (*see* Basic grammar, p. 160)		
mystery	*loghz* (m)	لغز

N

nail (*DIY*)	*mosmaar* (m)	مسمار
(*finger/toe*)	*Dofr* (m)	ظفر
nail clippers/scissors	*maqaS* (m) *Dawafir*	مقص أظافر
nail file	*mabraD* (m) *Dawafir*	مبرض أظافر
nail polish	*maniker* (m)	مانيكير
naked	*ᵃeryaen* (m)/ *ᵃeryaena* (f)	عريان/ عريانه
name	*ism* (m)	أسم
my name is . . .	*ismi* . . .	أسمى . . .
what is your name?	*ismak ay* (to m)/ *ismik ay* (to f)	اسمك ايه/ اسمك ايه
napkin	*mandeel* (m)	منديل

nappies	*gheyar* (pl) *lil baybee*	غبار للبايبي
narrow	*Daiya'* (m)/*Daiya'a* (f)	ضيق/ ضيقه
national	*qawmee* (m)/ *qawmaya* (f)	قومى/ قوميه
nationality	*ginsaya* (f)	جنسيه
natural	*Tabee^aee* (m)/ *Tabee^aaya* (f)	طبيعى/ طبيعيه
naturally	*Tabee^aee*	طبيعى
naughty	*sha'ee* (m)/*sha'aya* (f)	شقى/ شقيه
navy	*baHaraya* (f)	بحريه
navy blue	*azra'* (m)/*zar'a* (f)	أزرق/ زرقاء
near (to)	*orayyib* (*min*)	قريب (من)
nearby	*orayyib* (m)/ *orayyiba* (f)	قريب/ قريبه
nearest	*a'rab*	أقرب
nearly	*t'areeban*	تقريباً
necessary	*Darooree* (m)/ *Daroraya*	ضرورى/ ضروريه
it is necessary	*laezim*	لازم
necklace	*^aoqd* (m)	عقد
need: he/she needs	*meHtaeg* (m)/ *meHtaega* (f)	محتاج/ محتاجه
needle	*ebra* (f)	إبره
negative (*photo*)	*negateef* (m)	نيجاتيف
neighbour	*gaar* (m)/*gaara* (f)	جار/ جاره
neither . . . nor	*la . . . walla*	لا . . . ولا
nephew (*brother's son*)	*ibn akhooya*	إبن أخويا
(*sister's son*)	*ibn okhti* (m)	أبن أختى
nervous	*metnarviz* (m)/ *metnarviza* (f)	متنرفز/ متنرفزه
net	*shabaka* (f)	شبكه
never	*abadan*	أبداً
new	*gideed* (m)/*gideeda* (f)	جديد/ جديده
New Year	*^aam gideed*	عام جديد
news	*akhbaar* (pl)	أخبار

newspaper	*gornaal* (m)	جرنال
newspaper kiosk	*koshk* (m) *igaraiyid*	كشك الجرائد
next	*baᵃd* (m & f)	بعد
next to	*ganb*	جنب
nice (*person*)	*Zareef* (m)/*Zareefa* (f)	ظريف/ ظريفه
(*thing*)	*Helw* (m)/*Helwa* (f)	حلو/ حلوه
niece (*brother's daughter*)	*bint akhooya*	بنت أخويا
(*sister's daughter*)	*bint okhti*	بنت أختى
night	*layl* (m)	ليل
nightclub	*nayt klab* (m)	نايت كلوب
nightdress	*'ameeS* (m) *nowm*	قميص نوم
no	*la'a*	لأ
nobody	*mafeesh Had*	مفيش أحد
noise	*dawsha* (f)	دوشه
noisy (*person*)	*dawshagi* (m)/ *dawshagaya* (f)	دوشجى/ دوشجيه
(*place, thing*)	*dawsha* (m & f)	دوشه
non-alcoholic	*bidoon khamra*	بدون خمر
non-smoking	*mafeesh tadkheen*	مفيش تدخين
none	*wala waHid* (m)/ *wala waHda* (f)	ولا واحد/ولا واحده
normal	*ᵃaedee* (m)/ *ᵃaedaya* (f)	عادى/عاديه
normally	*ᵃadatan*	عادة
north	*shamael*	شمال
nose	*manakheer* (f)	مناخير
nosebleed	*nazeef aenfi* (m)	نزيف أنفى
nostril	*fatHit* (m) *il aenf*	فتحة الأنف
not	*la*	لا
note (*bank*)	*bankenowt* (m)	بنكنوت
notepad	*daftar* (m)	دفتر
nothing (else)	*wala Haga (tanya)*	ولا حاجة (تانيه)
now	*delwa'ti*	دلوقتى
nowhere	*wala makaen*	ولا مكان
nuclear	*Zarree* (m)/*Zarraya* (f)	ذرى/ ذريه
nuclear power	*il Taqa* (f) *iZarraya*	الطاقة الذريه

number	**nemra** (f)	نمره
nurse	**momarriD** (m)/ **momariDa** (f)	ممرض/ ممرضه
nut (*DIY*)	**Samoola** (f)	صاموله
nuts	**mikassaraat** (pl)	مكسرات
nylon	**naylon** (m & f)	نايلون

O

oasis	**waeHa** (f)	واحه
oar	**migdaef** (m)	مجداف
object	**shay'** (m)	شيء
obvious	**waaDiH** (m)/ **waDHa** (f)	واضح/ واضحه
occasionally	**aHyaenan**	أحياناً
occupied (*toilet*)	**mashghool** (m)/ **mashghoola** (f)	مشغول/ مسغوله
odd (*strange*)	**ghareeb** (m)/ **ghareeba** (f)	غريب/ غريبه
(*not even*)	**fardi** (m)/**fardaya** (f)	فردي/ فرديه
of course	**Tab²an**	طبعا
off (*power*)	**maTfi** (m)	مطفأ
offended	**it-haen** (m)/**it-haenit** (f)	إتهان/ اتهانت
offer	**²arD** (m)	عرض
special offer	**arD khaaS**	عرض خاص
office	**maktaeb** (m)	مكتب
officer (*police etc.*)	**zaabit** (m)/**zabta** (f)	ضابط/ ضابطه
official	**rasmi** (m)/**rasmaya** (f)	رسمي/ رسميه
often	**ghaliban**	غالبا
how often?	**kaem marra**	كم مره؟
oil	**zayt** (m)	زيت
OK	**owkay**	اوكي
old (*people*)	**²agooz** (m)/**²agooza** (f)	عجوز/ عجوزه
(*places, things*)	**qadeem** (m)/ **qadeema** (f)	

(*places, things*)	*qadeem* (m)/ *qadeema* (f)	قديم/قديمه
how old are you?	^a*andak kaem sana* (to m)/ ^a*andik kaem sana* (to f)	عندَك كام سنه؟/ عندِك كام سنه؟
how old is he/ she/it?	^a*andoo* (m)/ ^a*andaha* (f) *kaem sana*	عنده/عندها كام سنه؟
I am . . . years old	*ana* ^a*andi . . . sana*	انا عندى . . . سنه
old-fashioned	*da'a qadeema*	دقه قديمه
olive	*zatoon* (pl)	زيتون
olive oil	*zayt* (m) *zatoon*	زيت زيتون
on	^a*ala*	على
(*light etc.*)	*miwalla*^a (m)/ *miwalla*^a*a* (f)	مولع/مولعه
once	*marra*	مره
onion	*baSala* (f)/*baSal* (pl)	بصله/بصل
only	*bas*	بس
open	*maftooH* (m)/ *maftooHa* (f)	مفتوح/مفتوحه
open: he/she opens	*yeftaH* (m)/*teftaH* (f)	يفتح/تفتح
opera	*obra* (f)	اوبرا
operation	^a*amalaya* (f)	عمليه
opinion: in my opinion	*fi ra'yi*	فى رأى
opposite	*Ded*	ضد
opposite the house	*oddaem ilbayt*	امام البيت
optician	*naddaraati* (m)	نظاراتى
optional	*ikhtiyaeri* (m)/ *ikhtiyaeraya* (f)	أختيارى/أختياريه
or	*aw*	أو
orange (*fruit*)	*borto'an*	برتقال
(*colour*)	*borto'aeni*	برتقالى
order: he/she orders	*yoTlob* (m)/*toTlob* (f)	يطلب/تطلب
ordinary	^a*aedi* (m)/^a*aedaya* (f)	عادى/عاديه
organise: he/she organises	*yenaZam* (m)/ *tenaZam* (f)	ينظم/تنظم

English	Transliteration	Arabic
painting (*art*)	*rasm* (m)	رسم
pair	*gowz*	جوز
palace	*'asr* (m)	قصر
pale	*shaHib* (m)/ *shaHba* (f)	شاحب/ شاحبه
palm tree	*nakhla* (f)	نخله
pants (*men's underwear*)	*libaes* (m)	لباس
paper	*wara'a* (f)	ورقه
paper clip	*dabboos* (m)	دبوس
paraffin	*gaez* (m)	جاز
paralysed	*mashlool* (m)/ *mashloola* (f)	مشلول/ مشلوله
parcel	*Tard* (m)	طرد
pardon?	*^aan iznak* (to m)/ *^aan iznik* (to f)	عن إذنك؟/ عن إذنك؟
parents	*ahl* (pl)	أهل
park	*ginayna* (f)	جنينه
park: he/she parks	*yerkin* (m)/*terkin* (f)	يركن/ تركن
parking	*raekn* (m)	ركن
car park	*maw'aef* (m) *saiyaraat*	موقف سيارات
no parking	*mamnoo^a il intiZaar*	ممنوع الأنتظار
parking meter	*^aadaed il intiZaar*	عداد الأنتظار
parliament	*barlamaen* (m)	برلمان
part	*goz'* (m)	جزء
parting (*hair*)	*far'* (m)	فرق
(*farewell*)	*wadae^a* (m)	وداع
partly	*goz'ayan*	جزئيا
partner	*shereek* (m)/ *shereeka* (f)	شريك/ شريكه
party	*Hafla* (f)	حفله
pass (*permit*)	*izn* (m)	إذن
pass (*on road*): he/she passes	*ye^aadi* (m)/*te^aadi* (f)	يعدى/ تعدى
passenger	*raekib* (m)/*raekiba* (f)	راكب/ راكبه

original	*gideed* (m)/*gideeda* (f)	جديد/ جديده
other	*akhar* (m)/*okhra* (f)	خر/ اخرى
others	*il akhareen*	الأخرين
our (*see* Basic grammar, *p. 160*)		
out (*of . . .*)	*khaerig (il . . .)*	خارج (ال . . .)
outdoor	*barra*	بره
over	*fow'*	فوق
overcast (*weather*)	*ma'loob*	مقلوب
overcoat	*balToo* (m)	بالطو
overtake: he/she overtakes	*yesba'* (m)/*tesba'* (f)	يسبق/ تسبق
owe: he/she owes	*mitdayin* (m)/ *mitdayna* (f)	متداين/ متداينه
I owe you . . .	*ana mitdayin . . .*	انا متداين . . .
own: he/she owns	*yemlik* (m)/*temlik* (f)	يملك/ تملك
owner (*of . . .*)	*SaHib (il . . .)*	صاحب (ال . . .)

P

package tour	*reHla* (f) *shamila*	رحله شامله
packet	*bako* (m)	باكو
paddle (*canoeing*)	*migdaef* (m)	مجداف
padlock	*terbaes* (m)	ترباس
page	*SafHa* (f)	صفحه
pain	*waga^a* (m)	وجع
painful	*biyewga^a* (m)/ *bitewga^a* (f)	بيوجع/ بتوجع
painkiller	*DeD ilalam* (m)	ضد الألم
paint	*booya* (f)	بويه
paint: he/she paints		
(*pictures*)	*yersim* (m)/*tersim* (f)	يرسم/ ترسم
(*walls*)	*yebayaD* (m)/ *tebayaD* (f)	يبيض/ تبيض
painter (*artist*)	*rassaem* (m)/ *rassaema* (f)	رسامه
(*artisan*)	*bohyagi* (m)/ *bohyagaya* (f)	بوهيجى/ بوهيجيه

passion	*aTifa* (f)	عاطفه
passport	*basbor* (m)	باسبور
passport control	*gawazaet* (pl)	جوازات
past	*maaDee*	ماضى
in the past	*fil maaDee*	فى الماضى
pasta	*makarowna* (f)	مكرونه
pastille	*bastilla* (f)	باستله
pastry	*ageena* (f)	عجينه
path	*Taree'* (m)	طريق
patient (*hospital*)	*mareeD* (m)/ *mareeDa* (f)	مريض/ مريضه
pattern (*template*)	*batrown* (m)	باترون
pavement	*raSeef* (m)	رصيف
pay: he/she pays	*yedfa* (m)/*tedfa* (f)	يدفع/ تدفع
peas	*bisella* (pl)	بسله
peace	*salaem* (m)	سلام
peach	*khowkh* (m)	خوخ
peanut	*sodaeni* (m)	سودانى
pear	*kommitra* (f)	كمثرى
pedal	*gadown* (m)	جدون
pedal-boat	*'aerib* (m) *bi gadown*	قارب بالجادون
pedestrian	*moshaeh* (pl)	مشاه
pedestrian crossing	*oboor* (m) *ilmoshaeh*	عبورالمشاه
peel: he/she peels	*ye'ashar* (m)/ *te'ashar* (f)	يقشر/ تقشر
peg	*mashbak* (m)	مشبك
pen	*'alam* (m)	قلم
pencil	*'alam roSaaS* (m)	قلم رصاص
pencil sharpener	*barraya* (f)	برايه
penfriend	*moraasil* (m)/ *morasla* (f)	مراسل/ مراسله
penicillin	*bansileen* (m)	بنسلين
penknife	*maTwa* (f)	مطوه
pension	*ma*aesh* (m)	معاش
pensioner	*ala il ma*aesh*	على المعاش
people	*naes* (pl)	ناس

English	Transliteration	Arabic
pepper	*filfil* (m)	فلفل
green pepper	*filfil akhDar*	فلفل أخضر
red pepper	*filfil aHmar*	فلفل أحمر
peppermint	*ne^ana^a* (m)	نعناع
per	*fi*	فى
per hour	*fi sa^aa*	فى ساعه
per week	*filizboo^a*	فى الأسبوع
perfect	*tamaem* (m & f)	تمام
performance	*^aarD* (m)	عرض
perfume	*barfaen* (m)	برفان
perhaps	*yemkin*	يمكن
period (*menstrual*)	*^aaeda* (f) *shahraya*	عاده شهريه
period pains	*alaem* (pl) *il ^aaeda ishahraya*	الام العاده الشهريه
perm	*barmanant* (m)	برماننت
permit	*izn* (m)	إذن
work permit	*izn ^aamal*	إذن عمل
permit: he/she permits	*yesmaH* (m)/ *tesmaH* (f)	يسمح/ تسمح
person	*shakhS* (m)	شخص
personal	*shakhSee* (m)/ *shakhSaya* (f)	شخصى/ شخصيه
personal stereo	*wokman* (m)	واكمان
petrol	*banzeen* (m)	بنزين
petrol can	*^aelbit* (f) *banzeen*	علبة بنزين
petrol station	*maHaTit* (f) *banzeen*	محطة بنزين
petticoat	*'ameeS* (m) *Hareemi*	قميص حريمى
pharaoh	*far^aown* (m)	فرعون
philosophy	*falsafa* (f)	فلسفه
photocopy	*Soora* (f)	صوره
photocopy: he/she photocopies	*yeSawar* (m)/ *tiSawar* (f)	يصور/ تصور
photo(graph)	*Soora* (f)	صوره
photographer	*miSawaraati* (m)/ *miSawarataya* (f)	مصوراتى/ مصوارتيه
photography	*taSweer* (m)	تصوير
phrase book	*kitaeb* (m) *^aibaraat*	كتاب عبارات

physics	*Tabee^aa* (f)	طبيعه
piano	*biano* (m)	بيانو
pick: he/she picks *(chooses)*	*yekhtar* (m)/ *tekhtar* (f)	يختار / تختار
(flowers etc.)	*yo'tof* (m)/ *to'tof* (f)	يقطف / تقطف
pick up *(fetch):* he/she picks up	*yegeeb* (m)/*tegeeb* (f)	يجيب / تجيب
picnic	*nozha* (f)	نزهه
picture	*Soora* (f)	صوره
piece	*goz'* (m)	جزء
pier	*raSeef* (m)	رصيف
pierced	*makhroom* (m)/ *makhrooma* (f)	مخروم / مخرومه
pig	*khanzeer* (m)	خنزير
pigeon	*Hamaem* (m)	حمام
pills	*Hoboob* (pl)	حبوب
(contraceptive)	*Hoboob man^a ilHaml*	حبوب منع الحمل
pillow	*makhadda* (f)	مخده
pillowcase	*kees* (m) *makhadda*	كيس مخده
pilot	*Taiyaar* (m)	طيار
pilot light	*^aayn* (f)	عين
pin	*daboos* (m)	دبوس
pineapple	*ananaes* (m)	اناناس
pink	*bamba* (f)	بمبه
pipe *(smoking)*	*beeba* (f)	بيبه
(drain)	*masoora* (f)	ماسوره
place	*makaen* (m)	مكان
plain	*saeda*	ساده
plan *(of town etc.)*	*khareeTa* (f)	خريطه
plane	*Taiyaara* (f)	طياره
plant	*nabaet* (pl)	نبات
plaster *(sticking)*	*blaster* (m)	بلستر
plastic	*blastik* (m)	بلاستيك
plastic bag	*shanTa* (f) *blastik*	شنطه بلاستيك
plate	*Taba'* (m)	طبق
platform	*raSeef* (m)	رصيف

play (theatre)	masraHaya (f)	مسرحيه
play: he/she plays		
(instrument, sport)	yel^aab (m)/tel^aab (f)	يلعب/ تلعب
(record/tape/CD)	yedawar (m)/ tidawar (f)	يدور/ تدور
pleasant	Zareef (m)/Zareefa (f)	ظريف/ ظريفه
please	min faDlak (to m)/ min faDlik (to f)	من فضلك/ من فضلك
pleased	sa^aeed (m)/ sa^aeeda (f)	سعيد/ سعيده
plenty (of)	kiteer (m)/kiteera (f)	كثير/ كثيره
pliers	kammaesha (f)	كماشه
plimsolls	gazma (f) kawetch	جزمه كاوتش
plug (bath)	sadaeda (f)	سداده
(electrical)	kobs (m)	كبس
plumber	sabaek (m)	سباك
pneumonia	iltihaeb (m) re'awi	إلتهاب رئوى
pocket	gayb (m)	جيب
point	no'ta (f)	نقطه
poison	sem (m)	سم
poisonous	masmoom (m)/ masmooma (f)	مسموم/ مسمومه
pole	qotb (m)	قطب
police	bolees (pl)	بوليس
police car	^aarabayit (f) ibolees	عربيه البوليس
police station	maHaTit (f) ibolees	محطة البوليس
polish (for shoes etc.)	dahaen (m)	دهان
polite	mo'addab (m)/ mo'addaba (f)	مؤدب/ مؤدبه
political, politician	siyaesi (m)/siyasaya (f)	سياسى/ سياسيه
politics	siyaesa (f)	سياسه
polluted	molawas (m)/ molawasa (f)	ملوث/ ملوثه
pollution	talawos (m)	تلوث
pool (swimming)	Hammaem SibaHa (m)	حمام سباحه
poor	fa'eer (m)/fa'eera (f)	فقير/ فقيره
pop (music)	bob (m)	بوب

English	Transliteration	Arabic
Pope	*il baaba* (m)	البابا
popular	*sha*ᵃ*bi* (m)/ *sha*ᵃ*baya* (f)	شعبى/ شعبيه
pork	*khanzeer* (m)	خنزير
port	*meena* (f)	ميناء
porter	*shayael* (m)	شيال
porthole	*shibbaek* (m) *fil 'aerib*	شباك فى القارب
portion	*goz'* (m)	جزء
portrait	*Soora* (f)	صوره
positive (*sure*)	*mo'akad* (m)/ *mo'akada* (f)	مؤكد/ مؤكده
(*photo*)	*positeef* (m)	بوزيتيف
possible	*momkin*	ممكن
as soon as possible	*fawran*	فوراً
possibly	*gayiz*	جائز
post (*mail*)	*bareed* (m)	صندوق بريد
post: he/she posts	*yeb*ᵃ*at* (m)/*teb*ᵃ*at* (f)	يبعث/ تبعث
postbox	*Sandoo'* (m) *bareed*	صندوق بريد
postcard	*kart* (m)	كارت
poster	*Soora* (f)	صوره
postman	*bosTagi* (m)	بوسطجى
post office	*bosTa* (f)	بوسطه
postpone: he/she postpones	*ye'agil* (m)/*te'agil* (f)	يؤجل/ تؤجل
pot (*for cooking*)	*Halla* (f)	حله
potato	*baTaTis* (pl)	بطاطس
pottery	*khazaf* (m)	خزف
potty (*child's*)	*asraya* (f)	قصريه
pound (*money*)	*ginay* (m)	جنيه
(*sterling*)	*isterleenee*	أسترلينى
pour: he/she pours	*yedlo'* (m)/*tedlo'* (f)	يدلق/ تدلق
powder	*bodra* (f)	بوده
talcum powder	*bodrit* (f) *talg*	بودرة ثلج
powdered milk	*bodrit* (f) *laban*	بودرة لبن
power (*electricity*)	*kahraba* (f)	كهرباء
power cut	*'aT*ᵃ (m) *ikahraba*	قطع الكهرباء
pram	ᵃ*arabayit* (f) *aTfaal*	عربية أطفال

prefer: he/she prefers	*yefaDal* (m)/ *tefaDal* (f)	يفضل / تفضل
pregnant	*Haemil* (f)	حامل
prepare: he/she prepares	*yegahiz* (m)/ *tegahiz* (f)	يجهز / تجهز
prescription	*roshetta* (f)	روشته
present (*gift*)	*hidaya* (f)	هديه
president	*raiyyis* (m)/ *raiyissa* (f)	رئيس / رئيسه
press (*newspapers*) press office	*SaHaefa* (f) *il maktaeb* (m) *iSaHafi*	صحيفه المكتب الصحفي
pretty	*gameel* (m)/ *gameela* (f)	جميل / جميله
price	*taman* (m)	ثمن
priest	*'asees* (m)	قسيس
prime minister	*ra'ees* (m) *il wizaara*	رئيس الوزراه
primus stove	*baboor* (m) *gaez*	بابورجاز
prince	*'ameer* (m)	أمير
princess	*'ameera* (f)	أميره
print (*photo*)	*Soora* (f)	صوره
print: he/she prints	*yeTba*ᵃ (m)/*teTba*ᵃ (f)	يطبع / تطبع
prison	*segn* (m)	سجن
private	*shakhSee* (m)/ *shakhSaya* (f)	شخصى / شخصيه
prize	*gayza* (f)	جائزه
probably	*gayiz*	جائز
problem	*moshkila* (f)	مشكله
producer (*TV, theatre etc.*)	*montig* (m)/ *montiga* (f)	منتج / منتجه
profession	*mehna* (f)	مهنه
professor	*ostaez* (m)/*ostaeza* (f)	أستاذ / أستاذه
profit	*maksab* (m)	مكسب
programme	*birnaemig* (m)	برنامج
prohibited	*mamnoo*ᵃ (m)/ *mamnoo*ᵃa (f)	ممنوع / ممنوعه
promise: he/she promises	*yew*ᵃid (m)/*tew*ᵃid (f)	يوعد / توعد

pronounce: he/she pronounces	*yestahagga* (m)/ *tistahagga* (f)	يستهجنْ/ تستهجنْ
how do you pronounce this?	*istahagga di*	استهجنْ دى؟
proper	*maZbooT* (m)/ *maZbooTa* (f)	مظبوط/ مظبوطه
property (*land*)	*melk* (m)	ملك
prophet	*rasool* (m)	رسول
Protestant	*brotostant* (m)/ *brotostantaya* (f)	بروتستنت/ بروتستنتيه
public (*n*)	*isha*ᵃ*b* (pl)	الشعب
(*adj*)	ᵃ*aem* (m)/ᵃ*aema* (f)	عام/ عامه
public holiday	*'agaeza* (f) *rasmaya*	اجازه رسميه
public relations	ᵃ*ilaqat* ᵃ*aema*	علاقات عامه
pull: he/she pulls	*yished* (m)/*tished* (f)	يشد/ تشد
pulses (*food*)	*boqool* (pl)	بقول
pump up: he/she pumps up	*yenfokh* (m)/ *tenfokh* (f)	ينفخ/ تنفخ
puncture	*khorm* (m)	خرم
pure	*na'ee* (m)/*na'aya* (f)	نقى/ نقيه
purple	*orgwaeni* (m)/ *orgwanaya* (f)	اورجوانى/ اورجوانيه
purse	*kees* (m)	كيس
push: he/she pushes	*yezo'* (m)/*tezo'* (f)	يزق/ تزق
push-chair	ᵃ*arabayit* (f) *aTfaal*	عربية أطفال
put: he/she puts	*yeHoT* (m)/*teHoT* (f)	يحط/ نحط
pyjamas	*bijaema* (f)	بيجاما
pyramid	*haram* (m)/*ahraam* (pl)	هرم/ أهرام

265

Q

quality	*qeema* (f)	قيمه
quantity	*kemayya* (f)	كميه
quarter	*rob*ᵃ (m)	ربع
quay	*raSeef* (m)	رصيف
queen	*malika* (f)	ملكه
question	*soo'ael* (m)	سؤال

English	Transliteration	Arabic
queue	*Taboor* (m)	طابور
quick	*saree{a}* (m)/*saree{a}a* (f)	سريع / سريعه
quickly	*bisor{a}a*	بسرعه
quiet	*haedi* (m)/*hadya* (f)	هادئ / هادئه
quite	*'awi*	قوى
Qu'ran (Koran)	*qor'an* (m)	قرآن

R

English	Transliteration	Arabic
rabbi	*Hakhaem* (m)	حاخام
rabbit	*arnab* (m)	أرنب
rabies	*maraD* (m) *ikalb*	مرض الكلب
racecourse	*saba'* (m)	سباق
racing (*horse*)	*saba'* (m) *il khayl*	سباق الخيل
(*motor*)	*saba'* (m) *saiyaraat*	سباق سيارات
racket (*tennis etc.*)	*maDrab* (m)	مضرب
radiator	*radyater* (m)	رادياتير
radio	*radyo* (m)	راديو
radioactive	*ish{a}ae{a}i* (m)	إشعاعى
radio station	*maHaTit* (f) *radyo*	محطة راديو
railway	*sekka* (f) *Hadeed*	سكه حديد
railway station	*maHaTit* (f) *sekka Hadeed*	محطة سكه حديد
rain	*maTara* (f)	مطر
rain: it's raining	*bitmaTar*	تمطر
raincoat	*balToo* (m) *maTar*	بالطو مطر
rape	*ightiSaab* (m)	إغتصاب
rare	*naedir* (m)/*nadra* (f)	نادر / نادره
(*steak*)	*nay fi nay*	نئ فى نئ
rash (*on skin*)	*TafH* (m) *geldi*	طفح جلدى
raspberries	*toot* (pl)	توت
rat	*far* (m)	فأر
rate (*speed*)	*nesbit* (f) *isor{a}a*	نسبة السرعه
(*tariff*)	*nesbit* (f) *itaman*	نسبة الثمن
raw	*nay* (m)/*naya* (f)	نئ / نيئه
razor (blade)	*moos* (m)	موس

266

English	Transliteration	Arabic
reach: he/she reaches	yewSal (m)/tewSal (f)	يصل/ تصل
read: he/she reads	ye'ra (m)/te'ra (f)	يقرأ/ تقرأ
reading	'iraya (f)	قراءة
ready	gaehiz (m)/gahza (f)	جاهز/ جاهزه
real (authentic)	aSlee (m)/aSlaya (f)	أصلى/ أصليه
really	Ha'ee'ee	حقيقى
rear	khalfi (m)/ khalfaya (f)	خلفى/ خلفيه
reason (cause) (rationality)	sabab (m) ªa'lee	سبب عقلى
receipt	waSl (m)	وصل
receiver (telephone)	samaeªa (f)	سماعه
reception	istikbael (m)	إستقبال
receptionist	mowaZafit (f) ilistikbael	موظفة أستقبال
recipe	Taree'a (f)	طريقة
recognise: he/she recognises	yataªarraf (m)/ tataªarraf (f)	يتعرف/ تتعرف
recommend: he/she recommends	yewaSee (m)/ tewaSee (f)	يوصى/ توصى
record	segil (m)	سجل
record: he/she records	yesagil (m)/tesagil (f)	يسجل/ تسجل
record-player	steryo (m)	ستريو
recover: he/she recovers	yekhif (m)/tekhif (f)	يخف/ تخف
red	aHmar (m)/Hamra (f)	أحمر/ حمراء
Red Crescent	il hilael laHmar (m)	الهلال الأحمر
Red Cross	iSaaleeb laHmar	الصليب الأحمر
Red Sea	ibaHr ilaHmar	البحر الأحمر
reduction	tawfeer (m)	توفير
refill (gas)	amboobit (f) botagaez	انبوبة بوتاجاز
refrigerator	talaega (f)	ثلاجه
refugee	laegi' (m)/laegi'a (f)	لاجئ/ لاجئه
refund	istirdued (m)	استرداد
refund: he/she refunds	yesterid (m)/ testerid (f)	يسترد/ تسترد
region	manTi'a (f)	منطقه

register: he/she registers	*yesagil* (m)/*tesagil* (f)	يسجل/تسجل
registration	*tasgeel* (m)	تسجيل
registration number	*raqam* (m) *itasgeel*	رقم التسجيل
relation	*'areebee* (m)/*'aribti* (f)	قريبي/قريتي
religion	*deen* (m)	دين
remain: he/she remains	*yestana* (m)/ *testana* (f)	يستنى/تستنى
remember: he/she remembers	*yeftekir* (m)/ *teftekir* (f)	يفتكر/تفتكر
remove: he/she removes	*yen'il* (m)/*ten'il* (f)	ينقل/تنقل
rent	*iygaar* (m)	إيجار
rent: he/she rents	*ye'aggar* (m)/*te'aggar* (f)	يأجر/تأجر
repair: he/she repairs	*yeSalaH* (m)/ *teSalaH* (f)	يصلح/تصلح
repeat: he/she repeats	*yekarar* (m)/ *tekarar* (f)	يكرر/تكرر
reply	*rad* (m)	رد
reply: he/she replies	*yerod* (m)/*terod* (f)	يرد/ترد
report	*taqreer* (m)	تقرير
report: he/she reports	*yokhbir* (m)/ *tokhbir* (f)	يخبر/تخبر
rescue: he/she rescues	*yenqiz* (m)/*tenqiz* (f)	ينقذ/تنقذ
reservation	*Hagz* (m)	حجز
reserve: he/she reserves	*yeHgiz* (m)/*teHgiz* (f)	يحجز/تحجز
reserved	*maHgooz* (m)/ *maHgooza* (f)	محجوز/محجوزه
responsible	*mas'ool* (m)/ *mas'oola* (f)	مسؤول/مسؤوله
rest: he/she rests	*yerayaH* (m)/ *terayaH* (f)	يريح/تريح
restaurant	*maT^aam* (m)	مطعم
restaurant-car	*^aarabayit* (f) *il 'akl*	عربة الأكل
result	*nateega* (f)	نتيجه

retired	ªalal maªaesh (m & f)	على المعاش
return (*ticket*)	raiyiH gay	رايح جاي
return: he/she returns	yergaª (m)/tergaª (f)	يرجع / ترجع
reverse: he/she reverses	yaªkis (m)/taªkis (f)	يعكس / تعكس
rheumatism	romatizm (m)	روماتيزم
ribbon	shereeT (m)	شريط
rice	roz (m)	ارز
rich	ghanni (m)/ ghannaya (f)	غني / غنيه
ride (*horse, bicycle etc.*): he/she rides	yerkab (m)/terkab (f)	يركب / تركب
right	SaHeeH (m)/ SaHeeHa (f)	صحيح / صحيحه
right (*place*)	yemeen	يمين
on the right	ªalal yemeen	على اليمين
ring (*jewellery*)	khaetim (m)	خاتم
ripe	reTib (m)/reTba (f)	رطب / رطبه
river	nahr (m)	نهر
River Nile	nahr ineel	نهر النيل
road	Taree' (m)	طريق
roadworks	ashghael (pl) Toro'	اشغال طرق
roast	fil forn	فى الفرن
rob: he/she robs	yesra' (m)/tesra' (f)	يسرق / تسرق
robbery	ser'a (f)	سرقه
roof	SoT-H (m)	سطح
room	'owda (f)	حجره
(*space*)	makaen (m)	مكان
rope	Habl (m)	حبل
rose	zahra (f)	زهره
rotten	bayiZ (m)/bayZa (f)	بايظ / بايظه
rough (*surface*)	kheshin (m)/ kheshna (f)	خشن / خشنه
(*sea*)	haHr (m) hayig	بحر هائج
round	midawar (m)/ midawara (f)	مدور / مدوره
roundabout (*road*)	dawaraan (m)	دوران

row (*theatre etc.*)	*Saf* (m)	صف
row: he/she rows (*boat*)	*ye'adif* (m)/*te'adif* (f)	يقدف / تقدف
rowing boat	*'aerib ta'deef* (m)	قارب تجديف
royal	*malaki* (m)/ *malakaya* (f)	ملكى / ملكيه
rubber	*kawetch* (m)	كاوتش
rubber band	*astik* (m)	استك
rubbish	*zibaela* (f)	زباله
rucksack	*shanTit* (f) *Dahr*	شنطه
rude	*'aleel il'adab* (m)/ *'aleelit il'adab* (f)	قليل الأدب قليلةالأدب
ruins	*aTlal* (pl)	أطلال
ruler (*for measuring*)	*masTara* (f)	مسطره
rum	*rom* (m)	روم
run: he/she runs	*yegree* (m)/*tegree* (f)	يجرى / تجرى
rush hour	*sa*^{a}*it* (f) *ilziHaem*	ساعةالزحام
rusty	*meSadi* (m)/ *meSadaya* (f)	مصدى / مصدنه

270

S

sad	*Hazeen* (m)/ *Hazeena* (f)	حزين / حزينه
safe (*strongbox*)	*khazna* (f)	خزنه
safe (*adj*)	*'amaen* (m)/ *'amaena* (f)	أمان / أمانه
safety pin	*daboos mashbak* (m)	دبوس مشبك
sail	*shira*^{a} (m)	شراع
sail: he/she sails	*yibHar* (m)/*tibHar* (f)	يبحر / تبحر
sailing	*ibHaar* (m)	إبحار
sailing boat	*markib* (f) *shira*^{a}*aya*	مركب شراعيه
sailor	*baHaar* (m)	بحار
saint	*qedees* (m)	قديس
salad	*salaTa* (m)	سلطه
salami	*salaemi* (m)	سلامى
sale	*okasyown* (m)	اوكازيون

sales representative	*baya^a* (m)/*baya^a a* (f)	بياع / بياعه
salmon	*salamon* (m)	سلمون
salt	*malH* (m)	ملح
salty	*maeliH* (m)/*malHa* (f)	مالح / مالحه
same	*shaba*	شبه
sample	*^ayenna* (f)	عينه
sand	*raml* (m)	رمل
sandals	*Sandal* (m)	صندل
sandwich	*sandawich* (m)	سندونش
toasted sandwich	*towst* (m)	توست
sandy	*ramli* (m)/*ramlaya* (f)	رملي / رمليه
sanitary towels	*fowaT SiHaya* (pl)	فوط صحيه
sauce	*SawS* (m)	صوص
saucepan	*kasarolla* (f)	كسروله
saucer	*Taba'* (m)	طبق
sauna	*sowna* (f)	سونا
sausage	*sego'* (m)	سجق
save: he/she saves		
(*money etc.*)	*yeHawish* (m)/ *teHawish* (f)	يحوش / تحوش
(*rescue*)	*yenqiZ* (m)/ *tenqiZ* (f)	ينقذ / تنقذ
say: he/she says	*ye'ool* (m)/*te'ool* (f)	يقول / تقول
scald	*yeHra'* (m)/*teHra'* (f)	يحرق / تحرق
scales	*meeZaen* (pl)	ميزان
scarf (*ladies'*)	*isharb* (f)	إيشارب
(*woolly*)	*kofaya* (m)	كوفيه
scene	*manZar* (m)	منظر
scenery	*mashaehid* (pl)	مشاهد
scent	*reeHa* (f)	ريحه
school	*madrasa* (f)	مدرسه
science	*^iloom* (pl)	علوم
scientist	*^aelim* (m)/*^aelma* (f)	عالم / عالمه
scissors	*ma'aS* (m)	مقص
scooter	*skootar* (f)	سكوتر
score	*nateega* (f)	نتيجه
what's the score?	*ayhil nateega*	ايه النتيجه؟
Scotland	*skotlanda* (f)	سكوتلندا

Scottish	*skotlandi* (m)/ *skotlandaya* (f)	إسكوتلندى/ إسكوتلنديه
scratch	*khadsh* (m)	خدش
scratch: he/she scratches	*yehrosh* (m)/ *tehrosh* (f)	يهرش/ تهرش
screen (*partition*) (*cinema, TV etc.*)	*sitara* (f) *shaesha* (f)	ستاره شاشه
screw	*mosmar alawowz* (m)	مسمار قلاووز
screwdriver	*mifak* (m)	مفك
scuba-diving	*ghaTs* (m) *ªameeq*	غطس عميق
sculpture	*naHt* (m)	نحت
sea	*baHr* (m)	بحر
seasick	*dawar* (m) *ibaHr*	دوارالبحر
season	*moosim* (m)	موسم
season ticket	*karnay* (m)	كارنيه
seat	*korsi* (m)	كرسى
seatbelt	*Hizaem* (m) *ikorsi*	حزام الكرسى
second	*taeni*	تانى
second (*time period*)	*sanya* (f)	ثانيه
secret (*n*) (*adj*)	*ser* (m) *serri* (m)/*seraya* (f)	سر سرى/ سريه
secretary	*sekerter* (m)/ *sekertera* (f)	سكرتير/ سكرتيره
section	*qesm* (m)	قسم
see: he/she sees	*yeshoof* (m)/ *teshoof* (f)	يشوف/ تشوف
seem: he/she seems	*yabdoo* (m)/ *tabdoo* (f)	يبدو/ تبدو
it seems to me . . .	*yabdoo li* . . .	يبدولى . . .
self-service	*ikhdim nafsak* (for m)/*ikhdimi nafsik* (for f)	أخدم نفسك/ اخدم نفسك
sell: he/she sells	*yebeeª* (m)/*tebeeª* (f)	يبيع/ تبيع
send: he/she sends	*yebªat* (m)/*tebªat* (f)	يبعت/ تبعت
senior citizen	*kibeer fissaen* (m)/ *kibeera fissaen* (f)	كبير فى السن/ كبيره فى السن
sensible	*ªa'il* (m)/*ªa'la* (f)	عاقل/ عاقله
sentence	*gomla* (f)	جمله

separate(d)	*monfaSil* (m)/ *monfaSila* (f)	منفصل / متفصله
septic tank	tank (m) *il magaeri*	تنك مجاری
serious	*razeen* (m)/*razeena* (f)	رزين / رزينه
serve: he/she serves	*yekhdim* (m)/ *tekhdim* (f)	يخدم / تخدم
service (*church*)	*qidaes* (m)	قداس
service charge	*Dareebit* (f) *khedma*	ضريبة خدمه
set (*collection*)	*Ta'm* (m)	طقم
several	*ªedat*	عدة
sew: he/she sews	*yekhaiyaT* (m)/ *tekhaiyaT* (f)	يخيط / تخيط
sewing	*khiyaaTa* (f)	خياطه
sex	*gens* (m)	جنس
shade (*not sun*)	*Zel* (m)	ظل
shampoo	*shamboo* (m)	شامبو
sharp	*Haed* (m)/*Haeda* (f)	حاد / حاده
(*pain*)	*shideed* (m)/ *shideeda* (f)	شديد / شديده
shave: he/she shaves	*yeHla'* (m)/*teHla'* (f)	يحلق / تحلق
shaving cream/foam	*kraym Hila'a* (m)	كريم حلاقه
she (*see p. 158*)	*haya* (f)	هی
sheep	*kharoof* (m)	خروف
sheet (*bed*)	*milaya* (f)	ملاه
(*paper*)	*wara'a* (f)	ورقه
sheikh	*shaykh* (m)/ *shaykha* (f)	شيخ / شيخه
shelf	*raf* (m)	رف
shell (*egg*)	*ishr* (f) *bayDa*	قشر بيض
(*nut*)	*ishr* (f) *sodaeni*	قشر سودانی
(*sea*)	*Sadafa* (f)	صدفه
shellfish	*Haiyawanaet Sadafaya* (pl)	حيوانات صدفيه
shelter	*malga'* (m)	ملجأ
sherry	*sheri* (m)	شری
shiny	*laemiª* (m)/*lamªa* (f)	لامع / لامعه
ship	*markib* (f)	مركب
shirt	*'ameeS* (m)	قميص

English	Transliteration	Arabic
shock (*electric*)	*Sadma* (f) *kahrobae'aya*	صدمه كهربائيه
(*emotional*)	*Sadma* (f) *ªatifaya*	صدمه عاطفيه
shocked	*maSdoom* (m)/ *maSdooma* (f)	مصدوم/ مصدومه
shoe	*gazma* (f)	جزمه
shoelace	*robaaT* (f) *il gazma*	رباط الجزمه
shoe polish	*warneesh* (m) *il gezam*	ورنيش الجزم
shoe repairer's	*gazmagi* (m)	جزمجي
shoe shop	*maHal* (m) *aHzaya*	محل احذيه
shop	*maHal* (m)	محل
shop assistant	*bayaª* (m)/*bayaªa* (f)	بياع/ بياعه
shopping: he/she goes shopping	*yeroH* (m)/ *teroH* (f) *isoo'*	يروح/ تروح السوق
shopping centre	*markaz* (m) *togaeri*	مركز تجاري
short	*osaiyar* (m)/ *osaiyara* (f)	قصير/ قصيره
shorts	*short* (m)	شورت
shout: he/she shouts	*yezaªa'* (m)/ *tezaªa'* (f)	يزعق/ تزعق
show	*ªarD* (m)	عرض
show: he/she shows	*yeªriD* (m)/*teªriD* (f)	يعرض/ تعرض
shower	*dosh* (m)	دوش
shrink: he/she shrinks	*yekesh* (m)/*tekesh* (f)	يكش/ تكش
shrunk	*kash* (m)/*kashit* (f)	كش/ كشت
shut	*ma'fool* (m)/ *ma'foola* (f)	مقفول/ مقفوله
shutter	*sheesh* (m)	شيش
sick (*ill*)	*ªayaen* (m)/ *ªayaena* (f)	عيان/ عيانه
I feel sick	*ªayiz* (m)/*ªayza* (f) *astafragh*	عايز/ عايزه استفرغ
side	*ganb* (m)	جنب
sieve	*mankhol* (m)	منخل
sight	*naZar* (m)	نظر

sightseeing: he/she goes sightseeing	*yetfarag* (m)/*titfarag* (f) *ªala il maªaelim*	يتفرج / تتفرج على المعالم
sign	*loHit* (f) *iªlaenaet*	لوحة / إعلانات
sign: he/she signs	*yemDi* (m)/*temDi* (f)	يمضى / تمضى
signal	*ishaara* (f)	إشاره
signature	*imDa* (f)	إمضاء
silent	*saekit* (m)/*sakta* (f)	ساكت / ساكته
silk	*Hareer* (m)	حرير
silver	*faDDa* (f)	فضه
similar	*shebh*	شبه
simple	*baseeT* (m)/ *baseeTa* (f)	بسيط / بسيطه
since	*min*	من
sing: he/she sings	*yeghanni* (m)/ *teghanni* (f)	يغنى / تغنى
single (*room*)	*mofrad* (m)	مفرد
(*ticket*)	*raiyiH*	رايح
(*unmarried*)	*ªaezib* (m)/*mish metgawiza* (f)	عازب / مش متجوزه
sink	*Howd* (m)	حوض
sir	*sayed* (m)	سيد
sister	*okht* (f)	أخت
sister-in-law: my sister-in-law	*nisebti* (f)	نسيبتى
sit (down): he/she sits	*yo'ªod* (m)/*to'ªod* (f)	يقعد / تقعد
sitting (down)	*'aªid* (m)/*'aªda* (f)	قاعد / قاعده
site (*tourist*)	*maªalim* (pl)	معالم
size	*ma'aaes* (m)	مقاس
skate: he/she skates	*yitzaHlaq* (m)/ *titzaHlaq* (f)	يتزحلق / تتزحلق
skates (*roller*)	*ªagal tazaHloq* (pl)	عجل تزحلق
skating	*tazaHloq* (m)	تزحلق
skimmed milk	*laban* (m) *makshooT*	لبن مقشوط
skin	*geld* (m)	جلد
skirt	*gonella* (f)	جونله
sky	*sama* (f)	سماء
sleep: he/she sleeps	*yinaem* (m)/*tinaem* (f)	ينام / تنام
sleeper/sleeping-car	*ªarabayit* (f) *inowm*	عربية النوم

sleeping bag	*sleebing bag* (f)	بسليبينج باج
sleeve	*kom* (m)	كم
slice	*kharTa* (f)	خرطه
sliced	*makhrooT* (m)/	مخروط / مخروطه
	makhrooTa (f)	
slide (*film*)	*slaiyd* (m)	سلايد
slim	*rofaiya^a* (m)/	رفيع / رفيعه
	rofaiya^a a (f)	
slip (*petticoat*)	*'ameeS* (m) *Hareemi*	قميص حريمى
slippery	*mezaHla'* (m)/	مزحلق / مزحلقه
	mezaHla'a (f)	
slow	*baTee'* (m)/	بطئى / بطيئه
	baTee'a (f)	
slowly	*biboT'*	ببطئ
small	*Soghayar* (m)/	صغير / صغيره
	Soghayara (f)	
smell	*reeHa* (f)	ريحه
smell: it smells of . . .	*reeHit . . .*	ريحة . . .
smile	*ibtisaema* (f)	إبتسامه
smile: he/she smiles	*yebtesim* (m)/	يبتسم / تبتسم
	tebtesim (f)	
smoke	*dokhaen* (m)	دخان
smoke: he/she	*yedakhan* (m)/	يدخن / تدخن
smokes	*tedakhan* (f)	
smoked	*midakhan* (m)/	مدخن / مدخنه
	midakhana (f)	
smooth	*na^aim* (m)/*na^ama* (f)	ناعم / ناعمه
sneeze: he/she	*ye^aTas* (m)/*te^aTas* (f)	يعطس / تعطس
sneezes		
snorkelling	*ghaTs* (m)	غطس
snow	*talg* (m)	ثلج
so (*thus*)	*keda*	كده
(*therefore*)	*wi ^aashan keda*	و علشان كده
soap	*Saboon* (m)	صابون
sober	*razeen* (m)/	رزين / رزينه
	razeena (f)	
socialism	*ishtirakaya* (f)	اشتراكيه

socialist	*ishtiraki* (m)/ *ishtirakaya* (f)	اشتراكى/ اشتراكيه
social worker	*mowazaf* (m)/ *mowazafa* (f) *she'oon igtima^aiya*	موظف/ موظفه شؤون اجتماعيه
sociology	*^ailm* (m) *igtimae^a*	علم اجتماع
socket	*bareeza* (f)	بريزه
socks	*shorabaat* (pl)	شرابات
soda (water)	*(maiyit) Sowda* (f)	(مياه) صودا
soft	*na^aim* (m)/*na^ama* (f)	ناعم/ ناعمه
soft drink	*mashroob* (m) *khafeef*	مشروب خفيف
soldier	*^aaskari* (m)	عسكرى
solicitor	*moHaemi* (m)/ *moHamaya* (f)	محامى/ محاميه
solid	*Salb* (m)/*Salba* (f)	صلب/ صلبه
some	*showaya*	شويه
somehow	*biTaree'a aw biokhra*	بطريقه او بأخرى
someone	*shakhSin mae*	شخص ما
something	*shay'*	شئى
sometimes	*sa^aaet*	ساعات
somewhere	*fi makaenin mae*	فى مكان ما
son	*ibn* (m)	إبن
song	*oghnaya* (f)	أغنيه
son-in-law	*gowz* (m) *binti*	جوز بنتى
soon	*qareeban*	قريبا
as soon as possible	*fowran*	فوراً
sore	*moltahib* (m)/ *moltahiba* (f)	ملتهب/ ملتهبه
sorry: I'm sorry	*aesif* (m)/*asfa* (f)	أسف/ أسفه
(regret)	*nadmaen* (m)/ *nadmaena* (f)	ندمان/ ندمانه
sort	*now^a* (m)	نوع
sound	*Sowt* (m)	صوت
soup	*shorba* (f)	شوربه
sour	*HaemiD* (m)/ *Haemda* (f)	حامض/ حامضه
south	*ganoob* (m)	جنوب

souvenir	*tizkar* (m)	تزكار
space	*faraagh* (m)	فراغ
(*universe*)	*faDaa'* (m)	فضاء
spade	*garoof* (m)	جاروف
spanner	*moftaeH* (m) *Sawameel*	مفتاح صواميل
spare	*iDaafi* (m)/ *iDafaya* (f)	إضافي/ إضافية
spare time	*waqt* (m) *iDaafi*	وقت إضافي
spare tyre	*kawetch* (m) *istibn*	كاوتش استبن
sparkling (*wine, water*)	*fawaar* (m)/ *fawaara* (f)	فوار/ فواره
speak: he/she speaks	*yetkalim* (m)/ *tetkalim* (f)	يتكلم/ تتكلم
special	*khaaS* (m)/ *khaaSa* (f)	خاص/ خاصه
special offer	*ªarD* (m) *khaaS*	عرض خاض
specialist	*motakhaSiS* (m)/ *motakhaSiSa* (f)	متخصص/ متخصصه
speciality	*takhaSoS* (m)	تخصص
spectacles	*naDara* (f)	نظاره
speed	*sorªa* (f)	سرعه
speed limit	*Hodood* (pl) *isorªa*	حدود السرعه
spend: he/she spends		
(*money*)	*yeSrif* (m)/*teSrif* (f)	يصرف/ تصرف
(*time*)	*ye'aDi* (m)/ *te'aDi* (f)	يقضى/ تقضى
Sphinx	*abool howl* (m)	ابوالهول
spices	*ªoToor* (pl)	عطور
spicy	*miªaTar* (m)/ *miªaTarra* (f)	معطر/ معطره
spinach	*sabaenikh* (pl)	سباتح
spirits (*drinks*)	*mashroobaet rawHaya* (pl)	مشروبات روحيه
splinter	*shaZya* (f)	شاظيه
spoil: he/she spoils	*yetlif* (m)/*tetlif* (f)	يلف/ تلف
sponge (*bath*)	*safinga* (f)	سفنجه
spoon	*maªla'a* (f)	معلقه

sport	riyaaDa (f)	رياضه
spot	bo'a (f)	بقعه
(place)	makaen (m)	مكان
sprained	malwi (m)/malwaya (f)	ملوى/ملويه
spray	rash (m)	رش
spring (season)	rabeea (m)	ربيع
square (in town)	midaen (m)	ميدان
(shape)	morabaa (m)	مربع
stadium	istaed (m)	استاد
stain	bo'a (f)	بقعه
stainless steel	solb (m) naqi	صلب نقى
stairs	sellim (m)	سلم
stalls (theatre)	daraga 'oola	درجه أولى
stamp (postage)	Taabia (m)/ Tawaabia (pl)	طابع/طوايع
stand (stadium)	minaSa (f)	منصه
stand (up): he/she stands	wae'if (m)/wa'fa (f)	واقف/واقفه
stapler	dabaesa (f)	دباسه
star (in sky; film)	negm (m)/negma (f)	نجم/نجمه
start	bidaya (f)	بدايه
start: he/she starts	yebda' (m)/tebda' (f)	يبدأ/تبدأ
starter (food)	faetiH (m) ishahaya	فاتح الشهيه
state	Haela (f)	حاله
station	maHaTa (f)	محطه
station master	naZir (m) il maHaTa	ناظر المحطه
stationer's	maktaba (f)	مكتبه
statue	timsael (m)	تمثال
stay: he/she stays	yestana (m)/testana (f)	يستنى/تستنى
(in a hotel)	yeskon (m)/teskon (f)	يسكن/تسكن
steak	boftayk (m)	بوفتيك
steal: he/she steals	yesra' (m)/tesra' (f)	يسرق/تسرق
steam	bokhaar (m)	بخار
steamer	baekhira (f)	باخره
steel	Solb (m)	صلب
steep	monHadir (m)/ monHadira (f)	منحدر/منحدره
step	sellema (f)	سلمه

step-brother	*'akh* (m) *mish she'ee'ee*	أخ مش شقيقى
step-children (*husband's children*)	*^aayael* (pl) *gowz*	عيال جوز
(*wife's children*)	*^aayael* (pl) *miraat*	عيال مرات
step-daughter (*husband's child*)	*bint* (f) *gowz*	بنت جوز
(*wife's child*)	*bint* (f) *miraat*	بنت ميرات
step-father	*zowg il 'om* (m)	زوج الأم
step-mother	*zowgit il 'ab* (f)	زوجةالأب
step-sister	*okht* (f) *mish she'e'ti*	أخت مش شقيقى
step-son (*husband's child*)	*ibn* (m) *gowz*	ابن جوز
(*wife's child*)	*ibn* (m) *miraat*	ابن مرات
stereo	*steryo* (m)	ستريو
sterling: pound sterling	*isterleenee* (m)	إسترلينى
steward (*air*)	*moDeef* (m)	مضيف
stewardess (*air*)	*moDeefa* (f)	مضيفه
stick	*laz'* (m)	لازق
sticking plaster	*blaster* (m)	بلاستر
sticky	*milaza'* (m & f)	ملزق
sticky tape	*lazae'* (m)	لزاق
stiff	*gaemid* (m)/*gamda* (f)	جامد/ جامده
still	*saekin* (m)/*sakna* (f)	ساكن/ ساكنه
(*non-fizzy*)	*^aada*	عاده
sting	*las^aa* (f)	لسعه
sting: it stings	*lasa^a* (m)/*lasa^ait* (f)	لسع/ لسعت
stock exchange	*borSa* (f)	بـرصه
stockings	*shorab* (m) *Hareemee*	شراب حريمى
stolen	*masroo'* (m)/ *masroo'a* (f)	مسروق/ مسروفه
stomach	*me^ada* (f)	معده
stomach-ache	*waga^a* (m) *fil me^ada*	وجع فى المعده
stone	*Tooba* (f)	طوبه
stop (*bus etc.*)	*maHaTa* (f)	محطه

stop: he/she stops	*wa'af* (m)/*wa'afit* (f)	وقف/وقفت
stop!	*qof*	قف!
stopcock	*maHbas* (m)	محبس
storey	*dowr* (m)	دور
story	*Hikaya* (f)	حكايه
stove	*forn* (m)	فرن
straight	*mostaqeem* (m)/	مستقيم/مستقيمه
	mostaqeema (f)	
straight on	*ªala Tool*	على طول
strange, stranger	*ghareeb* (m)/	غريب/غريبه
	ghareeba (f)	
strap	*Tow'* (m)	طوق
straw (*drinking*)	*shalimo* (f)	شاليمو
strawberries	*firawla* (pl)	فراوله
stream	*gadwal* (m)	جدول
street	*shaeriª* (m)	شارع
street light	*noor* (m) *ishaeriª*	نورالشارع
stretcher	*na'aela* (f)	نقاله
strike	*iDrab* (m)	إضراب
string	*khayT* (m)	خيط
stripe	*shereeT* (m)	شريط
striped	*mi'alim* (m)/	مقلم/مقلمه
	mi'alima (f)	
strong	*qawee* (m)/	قوى/قويه
	qawaya (f)	
stuck	*malzoo'* (m)/	ملزوق/ملزوقه
	malzoo'a (f)	
student	*Taalib* (m)/	طالب/طالبه
	Taaliba (f)	
studio (*radio/TV*)	*stodyo* (m)	ستوديو
study: he/she studies	*yedris* (m)/*tedris* (f)	يدرس/تدرس
stupid	*ªabeeT* (m)/	عبيط/عبيطه
	ªabeeTa (f)	
style	*isloob* (m)	إسلوب
subtitled	*motargam* (m)	مترجم
suburb	*DaHaya* (f)	ضاحيه
succeed: he/she succeeds	*yengaH* (m)/ *tengaH* (f)	ينجح/تنجح

success	*nagaeH* (m)	نجاح
suddenly	*fag'a*	فجأة
sugar	*sokkar* (m)	سكر
suit	*badla* (f)	بدله
suitable	*monaesib* (m)/ *monasba* (f)	مناسب/ مناسبه
suitcase	*shanTa* (f)	شنطه
summer	*Sayf* (m)	صيف
sun	*shams* (f)	شمس
sunburn	*Darba* (f) *shamsaya*	ضربه شمسيه
sunglasses	*naDara* (f) *shamsaya*	نظاره شمسيه
sunny	*shamsi* (m)	شمسى
sunshade	*shamsaya* (f)	شمسيه
sunstroke	*Darbit* (f) *shams*	ضربة شمس
suntan oil	*zayt* (m) *ilismirar*	زيت الأسمرار
supermarket	*soobar markit* (m)	سوبر ماركت
supper	*ªasha* (m)	عشاء
supplement	*ogra* (f) *iDafaya*	أجرة إضافيه
suppose: I suppose so	*ªala ma aªtaqid*	على ما اعتقد
suppository	*liboos* (m)	ليوس
sure	*akeed*	اكيد
surface	*SaT-H* (m)	سطح
surname	*ism* (m) *il ªela*	اسم العائله
surprise	*mofag'a* (f)	مفاجأه
surprised	*indahash* (m)/ *indahashit* (f)	اندهش/ اندهشت
surrounded by	*moHaaT bi*	محاط ب
sweat: he/she sweats	*yeªra'* (m)/*teªra'* (f)	يعرق/ تعرق
sweater	*bolowvar* (m)	بلوڤر
sweatshirt	*fanela* (f)	فانله
sweep: he/she sweeps	*yeknos* (m)/*teknos* (f)	يكنس/ تكنس
sweet	*Helw* (m)/*Helwa* (f)	حلو/ حلوه
sweetener	*miHali* (m)	محلي
sweets	*Halawayaet* (pl)	حلويات
swelling	*waram* (m)	ورم
swim: he/she swims	*yeªoom* (m)/ *teªoom* (f)	يعوم/ تعوم

swimming	*ᵃowm* (m)	عوم
swimming pool	*Hammaem SibaHa* (m)	حمام سباحه
swimming trunks	*mayo* (m)	مايوه
swimsuit	*mayo* (m)	مايوه
switch	*moftaeH* (m)	مفتاح
switch off: he/she switches off	*yeTfi* (m)/*teTfi* (f)	يطفى/ تطفى
switched off	*maTfi* (m)/ *maTfaya* (f)	مطفى/ مطفيه
switch on: he/she switches on	*yewalaᵃ* (m)/ *tiwalaᵃ* (f)	يولع/ تولع
switched on	*mowalaᵃ* (m)/ *mowalaᵃa* (f)	مولع/ مولعه
swollen	*waerim* (m)/*warma* (f)	وارم/ وارمه
symptoms	*aᵃraad* (pl)	أعراض
synagogue	*maᵃbad* (m) *yahoodi*	معبد يهودى
synthetic	*morakab* (m & f)	مركب
system	*gihaez* (m)	جهاز

T

table	*tarabayza* (f)	ترابيزه
tablet	*Habaya* (f)	حبايه
table tennis	*bing bong* (m)	بنج بونج
tailor	*tarzi* (m)	ترزى
take: he/she takes		
(*bus etc.*)	*yerkab* (m)/*terkab* (f)	يركب/ تركب
(*carry*)	*yaekhod* (m)/ *taekhod* (f)	يأخذ/ تأخذ
(*exam, test*)	*yemteHin* (m)/ *temteHin* (f)	يمتحن/ تمتحن
(*photo*)	*yeSawar* (m)/ *tiSawar* (f)	يصور/ تصور
it takes an hour	*yestaghraq saᵃa*	يستغرق ساعه
taken (*seat*)	*maHgooz* (m)/ *maHgooza* (f)	محجوز/ محجوزه

English	Transliteration	Arabic
take off: he/she takes off (clothes)	ye'la^a (m)/te'la^a (f)	يقلع / تقلع
it is taking off (plane)	iqlaa^a	إقلاع
talcum powder	bodrit (f) talg	بودرة تلج
talk: he/she talks	yetkalim (m)/ tetkalim (f)	يتكلم / تتكلم
tall	Taweel (m)/Taweela (f)	طويل / طويله
tame	aleef (m)/aleefa (f)	اليف / اليفه
tampon	tambon Tibbi (m)	تمبون طبى
tap	Hanafaya (f)	حنفيه
tape (adhesive)	shereeT laza' (m)	شريط لزاق
(cassette)	shereeT tasgeel (m)	شريط تسجيل
tape measure	il metr (m)	المتر
tape recorder	gihaez tasgeel (m)	جهاز تسجيل
taste	Ta^{a}m (m)	طعم
taste: it tastes good	Ta^{a}mo (m) Helw/ Ta^{a}maha (f) Helw	طعمه حلو / طعمها حلو
tax	Dareeba (f)/ Dara^{a}yib (pl)	ضريبه / ضرائب
taxi	taksi (m)	تاكسى
taxi rank	maw'af (m) taksi	موقف تاكسى
tea	shay (m)	شاى
teach: he/she teaches	yeddaris (m)/ teddaris (f)	يدرس / تدرس
teacher	moddarris (m)/ moddarissa (f)	مدرس / مدرسه
team	faree' (m)	فريق
teapot	baraad (m)	براد
tear: he/she tears	ye'aTa^a (m)/te'aTa^a (f)	يقطع / تقطع
teaspoon	ma^{a}la'it (f) shay	معلقة شاى
teat (for baby's bottle)	bazaeza (f)	بزازه
tea-towel	fooTa (f)	فوطه
technical	fanni (m)/fannaya (f)	فنى / فنيه
technology	teknolojya (f)	تكنولوجيه
teenager	morahiq (m)/ morahiqa (f)	مراهق / مراهقه

English	Transliteration	Arabic
telegram	teleghraaf (m)	تلغراف
telephone: he/she telephones	yoTlob (m)/ toTlob (f)	يطلب / تطلب
telephone	tilifown (m)	تليفون
telephone box	koshk (m) tilifown	كوشك تليفون
telephone card	kart (m) tilifown	كارت تليفون
telephone directory	daleel (m) tilifownaet	دليل تليفونات
television	televisyown (m)	تلفزيون
telex	teleks (m)	تلكس
tell: he/she tells	ye'ool (m)/te'ool (f)	يقول / تقول
temperature	daragit il Harara (f)	درجة الحراره
he/she has a temperature	ªando (m)/ ªandaha (f) Harara	عنده / عندها حراره
temple	maªbad (m)	معبد
temporary	mo'aqat (m & f)	مؤقت
tender (meat)	Tari (m)/Taraya (f)	طرى / طريه
tennis	tenis	تنس
tennis ball	korit (f) tenis	كرة تنس
tennis court	malªab (m) tenis	ملعب تنس
tennis shoes	gazmit (f) tenis	جزمة تنس
tent	khayma (f)	خيمه
tent peg	watad (m) il khayma	وتد الخيمه
tent pole	ªamood (m) il khayma	عمود الخيمه
terminal (airport)	maHaTa (f)	محطه
terminus	maw'af (m)	موقف
terrace	tiraas (m)	تراس
terrible	raheeb (m)/raheeba (f)	رهيب / رهيبه
terrorist	fidae'ee (m)/ fida'aya (f)	فدائى / فدائيه
thank you (very much)	shokran (gazeelan)	شكراً (جزيلاً)
that (one)	da	ده
the	il	ال
theatre	masraH (m)	مسرح
their (see Basic grammar, p. 158)		
them (see Basic grammar, p. 158)		
(direct obj)	homma	هم
(indirect obj)	lohom	لهم

285

then	*baᵃdayn*	بعدين
there	*hinaek*	هناك
there is/are	*fi*	فى
therefore	*ᵃashan keda*	علشان كده
thermometer	*termometr* (m)	ترمومتر
these	*dowl*	دول
they	*homma*	هما
thick	*sameek* (m)/ *sameeka* (f)	سميك / سميكه
thief	*Harami* (m)/ *Haramaya* (f)	حرامى / حراميه
thin	*rofaiyaᵃ* (m)/ *rofaiyaᵃa* (f)	رفيع / رفيعه
thing	*shay'* (m)	شئ
think: he/she thinks	*yefakar* (m)/*tifakar* (f)	يفكر / تفكر
(believe)	*yaᵃtaqid* (m)/ *taᵃtaqid* (f)	يعتقد / تعتقد
I don't think so	*maᵃtaqidsh*	مأعتقدش
third	*taelit*	ثالث
thirsty: I'm thirsty	*ᵃaTshaen* (m)/ *ᵃaTshaana* (f)	عطشان / عطشانه
this	*da* (m)/*di* (f)	ده / دى
those	*dowl*	دول
thread	*khayT* (m)	خيط
throat	*zowr* (m)	زور
throat lozenges/ pastilles	*basteel* (pl) *lil zowr*	باستيل للزور
through	*khilael*	خلال
throw: he/she throws	*yermi* (m)/*termi* (f)	يرمى / ترمى
throw away: he/she throws away	*yeDaiyaᵃ* (m)/ *teDaiyaᵃ* (f)	يضيع / تضيع
thumb	*ibhaem* (m)	إبهام
thunder	*raᵃd* (m)	رعد
ticket	*tazkara* (f)/ *tazakir* (pl)	تزكره / تزاكر
ticket office	*shibaek* (m) *il Hagz*	شباك الحجز
tide	*il mad wil gazr* (m)	المدوالجزر

tidy	*monaZam* (m)/ *monaZama* (f)	منظم / منظمه
tie	*karafaTa* (f)	كرافته
tie: he/she ties	*yorboT* (m)/ *torboT* (f)	يربط / تربط
tight	*daya'* (m)/*daya'a* (f)	ديق / ديقه
tights	*shoraab* (m) *Hareemee*	شراب حريمى
till (*until*)	*lighayit*	لغاية
time (*once, twice etc.*)	*marra* (f)	مره
time (*see p. 172*)	*zaman* (m)	زمان
timetable	*gadwal* (m)	جدول
tin	*ᵃelba* (f) *SafeeH*	علبه صفيح
tin foil	*wara'* (m) *alamonyom*	ورق الومونيوم
tinned	*maHfooZ* (m)/ *maHfooZa* (f)	محفوظ / محفوظه
tin opener	*fataeHa* (f)	فتاحه
tip (*in restaurant etc.*)	*ba'sheesh* (m)	بقشيش
tired	*taᵃbaen* (m)/ *taᵃbaena* (f)	تعبان / تعبانه

tissues	*wara' naᵃim* (pl)	ورق ناعم
to	*ila*	إلى
toast	*towst* (m)	توست
tobacco	*Tonbaq* (m)	طنباق
tobacconist's	*bitaᵃ isagayir* (m)	بتاع السجاير
today	*inaharda* (f)	النهارده
together	*sawa*	سواء
toiletries	*adawaet izzeena* (pl)	أدوات الزينه
toilet(s)	*towalit* (m)	تواليت
toilet paper	*wara' towalit* (pl)	ورق تواليت
toilet water	*maiyit towalit* (f)	ماية تواليت
toll	*Dareebit moroor* (f)	ضريبة مرور
tomato	*TamaTim* (m)	طماطم
tomb	*ma'bara* (f)	مقبره
tomorrow	*bokra* (m)	بكره
tongue	*lisaen* (m)	لسان
tonic water	*maiyit tonik* (f)	مياه تونيك
tonight	*ilayla* (f)	الليله

too	*kamaen*	كمان
tool	*adae* (f)	اداه
tooth	*sinna* (f)	سنه
toothache	*waga* (m) *sinaen*	وجع سنان
toothbrush	*forshit* (f) *sinaen*	فرشة سنان
toothpaste	*ma*ᵃ*goon* (m) *sinaen*	معجون سنان
top (*summit*)	*qemma* (f)	قمه
on top of	*fow' il qemma*	فوق القمه
torch	*baTarayyit* (f) *noor*	بطارية نور
torn	*ma'Too*ᵃ (m)/	مقطوع/ مقطوعه
	*ma'Too*ᵃ*a* (f)	
total	*magmoo*ᵃ (m)	مجموع
touch: he/she touches	*yelmis* (m)/*telmis* (f)	يلمس/ تلمس
tough (*meat*)	*qasi* (m)/*qasya* (f)	قاسى/ قاسيه
tour	*gawla* (f)	جوله
tour: he/she tours	*yelif* (m)/*telif* (f)	يلف/ تلف
tourism	*siyaHa* (f)	سياحه
tourist	*sayiH* (m)/*sayHa* (f)	سايح/ سايحه
tourist office	*maktaeb* (m) *siyaHa*	مكتب سياحه
tow: he/she tows	*yegor* (m)/*tegor* (f)	يجر/ تجر
towards	*fitigae*	فى الاتجاه
towel	*fooTa* (f)	فوطه
tower	*borg* (m)	برج
town	*madeena* (f)	مدينه
town centre	*wesT il balaed* (f)	وسط البلد
town hall	*il baladaya* (f)	البلديه
tow rope	*Habl gar* (m)	حبل جر
toy	*le*ᵃ*ba* (f)	لعبه
track (*path*)	*Taree'* (m)	طريق
(*rail*)	*sekka* (f) *Hadeed*	سكه حديد
tracksuit	*traksoot* (m)	تراك سوت
trade union	*itiHaed* ᵃ*omael* (m)	اتحاد عمال
traditional	*taqleedi* (m)/	تقليدى/ تقليديه
	taqleedaya (f)	
traffic	*moroor* (m)	مرور
traffic jam	*takados* (m) *il moroor*	تكدس المرور

English	Transliteration	Arabic
traffic lights	isharaat (pl) il moroor	اشارات المرور
trailer	maqtoora (f)	مقطوره
train	'atr (m)	قطار
by train	bil 'atr	بالقطار
training shoes (trainers)	gazma kawetch	جزمة كاوتش
tram	tromaiy (f)	ترام
tranquilliser	mohadi' (m)	مهدئ
translate: he/she translates	yetargim (m)/ tetargim (f)	يترجم/ تترجم
translation	targamma (f)	ترجمه
travel	saffar (m)	سفر
travel: he/she travels	yisaefir (m)/ tisaefir (f)	يسافر/ تسافر
travel agency	wikaelit saffar (f)	وكالة سفر
travellers' cheques	shikaet siyaHaya (pl)	شيكات سياحيه
travel sickness	dowar (m) saffar	دوارسفر
tray	Sanaya (f)	صينيه
treatment	ⁱilaeg (m)	علاج
tree	shaggara (f)	شجره
trip	reHla (f)	رحله
trousers	bantalown (m)	بنطلون
trout	samak il aTrooT (m)	سمك الأطروت
truck	looree (m)	لوري
true	saHeeH (m)/ saHeeHa (f)	صحيح/ صحيحه
that's true	saH	صح
try (attempt): he/she tries	yeHawil (m)/ tiHawil (f)	يحاول/ تحاول
try on: he/she tries on	ye'ees (m)/te'ees (f)	يقيس/ تقيس
T-shirt	tishert (m)	تشيرت
tube (underground)	anbooba (f) metro il anfa' (m)	انبوبه مترو الانفاق
tuna	toona (f)	تونه
tunnel	nafa' (m)	نفق
turn: he/she turns	yeHawid (m)/ teHawid (f)	يحود/ تحود

turn off: he/she turns off (*light*)	*yeTfi* (m)/*teTfi* (f)	يطفئى / تطفئى
twice	*maritayn*	مرتين
twin beds	*sereerayn* (pl)	سريرين
twins	*taw'am* (pl)	توأم
twisted	*mabroom* (m)/ *mabrooma* (f)	مبروم / مبرومه
type (*sort*)	*now*[a] (m)	نوع
type: he/she types	*yeTba*[a] (m)/ *teTba*[a] (f)	يطبع / تطبع
typewriter	*'aela katba* (f)	أله كاتبه
typical	*namoozagi* (m)/ *namoozagaya* (f)	نموزجى / نموزجيه

U

ugly	*qabeeH* (m)/ *qabeeHa* (f)	قبيح / قبيحه
ulcer	*qorHa* (f)	قرحه
umbrella	*shamsaya* (f)	شمسيه
uncle	*ankil*	انكل
uncomfortable	*mish moreeH* (m)/ *mish moreeHa* (f)	مش مريح / مش مريحه
underground (*tube*)	*metro il anfa'* (m)	مترو الأنفاق
under(neath)	*taHt*	تحت
underpants	*libaes* (m)	لباس
underpass	*mamar* (m)	ممر
understand: he/she understands	*faehim* (m)/*fahma* (f)	فاهم / فاهمه
I don't understand	*mish faehim* (m)/ *mish fahma* (f)	مش فاهم / مش فاهمه
understood	*mafhoom* (m)/ *mafhooma* (f)	مفهوم / مفهومه
underwater	*taHt il maiya* (f)	تحت المياه
underwear	*malaebis dakhilaya* (pl)	ملابس داخليه
undress: he/she undresses	*ye'la*[a] (m)/*te'la*[a] (f)	يقلع / تقلع

unemployed	*ªaaTil* (m)/*ªaaTla* (f)	عاطل/عاطله
unfortunately	*lil 'asaf*	للأسف
unhappy	*zaªlaen* (m)/*zaªlaena* (f)	زعلان/زعلانه
uniform	*yooniform* (m)	يونيفورم
university	*gamªa* (f)	جامعه
unleaded petrol	*banzeen* (m) *min ghayr roSaaS*	بنزين من غير رصاص
unless	*ila iza*	إلا إذا
unpleasant	*ghayr mostaHab*	غير مستحب
unscrew: he/she unscrews	*yeftaH* (m)/*teftaH* (f)	يفتح/تفتح
until	*Hatta*	حتى
unusual	*mish ªadi* (m)/ *mish ªadaya* (f)	مش عادى/مش عاديه
unwell	*moreeD* (m)/ *moreeDa* (f)	مريض/مريضه
up	*fow'*	فوق
upper	*aªla* (m & f)	أعلى
upstairs	*fow'*	فوق
urgent	*mistaªgil* (m)/ *mistaªgila* (f)	مستجل/مستعجله
urine	*bowl* (m)	بول
us	*iHna*	إحنا
use	*istiªmael*	استعمال
use: he/she uses	*yistaªmil* (m)/ *tistaªmil* (f)	يستعمل/تستعمل
useful	*mofeed* (m)/ *mofeeda* (f)	مفيد/مفيده
useless	*mish mofeed* (m)/ *mish mofeeda* (f)	مش مفيد/مش مفيده
usually	*ªadatan*	عادة

V

vacant	*faaDi* (m)/*faDya* (f)	فاضى/فاضيه
vacuum cleaner	*hoover* (m)	هوفر

English	Transliteration	Arabic
vacuum flask	*tormos* (m)	ترمس
valid	*saaliH* (m)/*salHa* (f)	صالح/ صالحه
valley	*waedi* (m)	وادى
valuable	*qayim* (m)/ *qayima* (f)	قيم/ قيمه
valuables	*ashya' qayima* (pl)	أشياء قيمه
van	*ªarabaya* (f) *na'l*	عربة نقل
vase	*vaasa* (f)	فازة
veal	*bitello* (f)	بتللو
vegetables	*khoDar* (pl)	خضار
vegetarian	*nabaeti* (m)/ *nabaetaya* (f)	نباتى/ نباتيه
vehicle	*ªarabaya* (f)	عربيه
vermouth	*vermoot* (m)	ثرموت
very	*'awi*	قوى
vest	*fanella* (f)	فانله
vet	*biTari* (m)/ *biTaraya* (f)	بيطري/ بطريه
via	*ªan Taree'*	عن طريق
video cassette	*shereeT vidyo kassett* (m)	شريط فيديو كاسيت
video recorder	*tasgeel* (m) *vidyo*	تسجيل فيديو
view	*manZar* (m)	منظر
villa	*villa* (f)	فيلا
village	*qarya* (f)	قريه
vinegar	*khal* (m)	خل
vineyard	*mazaeriª koroom* (pl)	مزارع كروم
virgin	*ªazra'* (f)	عزراء
Virgin Mary	*maryam il ªazra'*	مريم العزراء
visa	*visa* (f)	ثيزا
visit	*ziyaara* (f)	زياره
visit: he/she visits	*yezoor* (m)/*tezoor* (f)	يزور/ تزور
visitor	*Dayf* (m)/*Dayfa* (f)	ضيف/ ضيفه
vitamin	*vitameen* (m)	ثيتامين
vodka	*vodka* (m)	ثودكا
voice	*Sowt* (m)	صوت
volleyball	*volleebowl* (f)	قولى بول

voltage	*volt* (m) *il kahraba*	فولت الكهرباء
vote: he/she votes	*yintaekhib* (m)/	ينتخب/ تنتخب
	tintaekhib (f)	

W

wage	*ogra* (f)	أجره
waist	*wesT* (m)	وسط
waistcoat	*Sidayri* (m)	صديرى
wait (for): he/she waits	*yestana* (m)/*testana* (f)	يستنى/ تستنى
waiter	*garsown* (m)	جرسون
waitress	*garsowna* (f)	جرسونه
waiting room	*Hogrit* (f) *ilintizaar*	حجرةالأنتظار
Wales	*waylz* (f)	وايلز
walk: he/she walks	*yemshi* (m)/*temshi* (f)	يمشى/ تمشى
he/she goes for a walk	*yetmasha* (m)/ *tetmasha* (f)	يتمشى/ تتمشى
walking stick	*ªaSaiya* (f)	عصاه
wall	*HayTa* (f)	حائط
wallet	*maHfaza* (f)	محفظه
walnut	*ªayn* (f) *gamal*	عين جمل
want: I want, would like	*ªayiz* (m)/*ªayza* (f)	عايز/ عايزه
war	*Harb* (f)	حرب
First/Second World War	*il Harb* (f) *il ªalamaya il 'oola/tanya*	الحرب العالمه الأولى/ الثانيه
Six Day War	*Harb yonyo*	حرب يونيو
warm	*daefi* (m)/*daefya* (f)	دافئى/ دافئه
wash: he/she washes	*yeghsil* (m)/*teghsil* (f)	يغسل/ تغسل
he washes up	*yeghsil il mawaªeen*	يغسل المواعين
washable	*qabil* (m)/*qabila* (f) *lil ghaseel*	قابل/ للغسيل
wash-basin	*HowD* (m)	حوض
washing	*ghaseel* (m)	غسيل
washing machine	*ghassaela* (f)	غساله
washing powder	*Saboon* (m) *ghaseel*	صابون غسيل

293

washing-up liquid	*Saboon* (m) *mawa^aeen*	صابون مواعين
wasp	*Daboor* (m)	ضبور
wastepaper basket	*sabat* (m) *zibaela*	سبت زباله
watch	*sa^aa* (f)	ساعه
watch: he/she watches	*yetfarag* (m)/ *titfarag* (f)	يتفرج / تتفرج
watchstrap	*ostayk* (m)	أستيك
water	*maiya* (f)	مياه
mineral water	*maiya ma^adanaya*	مياه معدنيه
distilled water	*maiya m'aTara*	مياه مقطره
water heater	*sakhaen* (m)	سخان
watermelon	*baTeekha* (f)	بطيخه
waterfall	*shallael* (m)	شلال
waterproof	*watarproof* (m & f)	ووتر بروف
water-skiing	*watarskee* (m)	تزحلق مائى
wave *(sea)*	*mowga* (f)	موجه
wave: he/she waves	*yeshaewir* (m)/ *teshaewir* (f)	يشاور / تشاور
wax	*sham^a* (m)	شمع
way *(manner)*	*Taree'a* (f)	طريقه
(route)	*Taree'* (m)	طريق
this way, that way *(direction)*	*il Taree' da*	الطريق ده
way in	*dekhool* (m)	دخول
way out	*khoroog* (m)	خروج
we	*iHna*	إحنا
weather	*gaw* (m)	جو
weather forecast	*inashra* (f) *il gawaya*	النشره الجويه
wedding	*zifaef* (m)	زفاف
week	*izboo^a* (m)	اسبوع
weekend	*weekend* (m)	ويك اند
weekly	*izboo^aee* (m)/ *izboo^aaya* (f)	اسبوعى / اسبوعيه
weigh: he/she weighs	*yewzin* (m)/*tewzin* (f)	يوزن / توزن
weight	*wazn* (m)	وزن
well	*kwayyis* (m)/ *kwayissa* (f)	كويس / كويسه
as well	*kamaen*	كمان

well done (steak)	**maZbooT**	مظبوط
(congratulations)	**mabrook**	مبروك
Welsh	**min waylz**	من وايلز
west	**gharb** (m)	غرب
western	**gharbee** (m)/	غربى/ غربيه
	gharbaya (f)	
wet	**mablool** (m)/	مبلول/ مبلوله
	mabloola (f)	
wetsuit	**badlit** (f) **ghaTs**	بدلة غطس
what (is)?	**ay**	ايه؟
wheel	**ᵃagala** (f)	عجله
wheelchair	**korsi** (m) **lil**	كرسى للمقعدين
	moqᵃadeen	
when?	**imta**	متى؟
where (is/are)?	**fayn**	فين؟
which?	**ay**	أى؟
while	**baynama**	بينما
whisky	**wiski** (m)	ويسكى
whisky and soda	**wiski bil sowda**	ويسكى بالصودا
white	**abyaD** (m)/**bayDa** (f)	أبيض/ بيضه
(with milk)	**bilaban**	باللبن
white coffee	**'ahwa bilaban**	قهوه باللبن
who?	**meen**	من؟
who is it?	**meen howa** (m)/	من هو؟/
	meen haya (f)	من هى؟
whole	**kaemil** (m)/**kamla** (f)	كامل/ كامله
why?	**lay**	ليه؟
why not?	**lay la'**	ليه لا؟
wide	**waeseᵃ** (m)/**wasᵃa** (f)	واسع/ واسعه
widow	**armala** (f)	أرمله
widower	**armal** (m)	أرمل
wife	**zowga** (f)	زوجه
my wife	**miraati** (f)	مراتى
wild	**motawuHish** (m)/	متوحش/ متوحشه
	motawaHisha (f)	

win: he/she wins	*yeksaeb* (m)/ *teksaeb* (f)	يكسب/ تكسب
who won?	*meen kesib*	مين كسب؟
wind	*reeH* (m)	ريح
windmill	*TaHoonit* (f) *hawa*	طاحونة هواء
window	*shibaek* (m)	شباك
(*shop*)	*vatreena* (f)	فترينه
windsurfing	*TazaHloq* (m) *shira*ⁱ	تزحلق شراعى
windy: it's windy	*hawa* (m) *gaemid*	هواء جامد
wine	*nebeet* (m)	نبيت
wine merchant	*baya*ᵃ (m) *nebeet*	بياع نبيت
wing	*ginaH* (m)	جناح
winter	*isheta* (m)	شتاء
with	*ma*ᵃ*a*	مع
without	*min ghayr*	من غير
woman	*sit* (f)	ست
wonderful	*hayil* (m)/*hayla* (f)	هائل/ هائله
wood	*khashab* (m)	خشب
(*forest*)	*ghaeba* (f)	غابه
wool	*Soof* (m)	صوف
word	*kilma* (f)	كلمه
work	*shoghl* (m)	شغل
(*job*)	*shoghlaena* (f)	شغلانه
(*task*)	*ma'mooraya* (f)	مأموريه
work: he/she/it works	*yishtaghal* (m)/ *tishtaghal* (f)	يشتغل/ تشتغل
world (*n*)	*idonya* (f)	الدنيا
(*adj*)	ᵃ*alami* (m)/ ᵃ*alamaya* (f)	عالمى/ عالميه
worried	*'al'aen* (m)/ *'al'aena* (f)	قلقان/ قلقانه
worse	*awHash*	أوحش
worth: it's worth . . .	*'eemto* (m)/ *'eemet-ha* (f) . . .	قيمته/ قيمتها . . .
it's not worth it	*mayestahilsh* (m)/ *matistahilsh* (f)	مايستهلش/ ماتستهلش

wound (*hurt*)	*garH* (m)	جرح
wrap (up): he/she wraps	*yelef* (m)/*telef* (f)	يلف/ تلف
write: he/she writes	*yektib* (m)/*tektib* (f)	يكتب/ تكتب
writer	*kaetib* (m)/*katba* (f)	كاتب/ كاتبه
writing paper	*wara' kitaeba* (m)	ورق كتابه
wrong (*incorrect*)	*ghalaT* (m & f)	غلط

X

| X-ray | *ishae^aa* (f) | إشاعه |

Y

yacht	*yakht* (m)	يخت
yawn: he/she yawns	*yetaewib* (m)/ *tetaewib* (f)	يتشائب/ تتشائب
year	*sana* (f)/*sineen* (pl)	سنه/ سنين
leap year	*sana kabeesa* (f)	سنه كبيسه
yellow	*aSfar* (m)/*Safra* (f)	أسفر/ سفره
yes	*aywa*	أيوه
yesterday	*imbariH* (m)	إمبارح
yet	*Hata il'aen*	حتى الآن
yoghurt	*zabaedi* (m)	زبادى
you (*see* Basic grammar, *p. 158*)	*inta* (m)/*inti* (f)	أنتَ/ أنتِ
young	*soghayar* (m)/ *soghayara* (f)	صغير/ صغيره
your(s) (*see* Basic grammar, *p. 158*)		
youth	*shabaeb* (pl)	شباب
youth hostel	*bayt* (m) *ishabaeb*	بيت الشباب

Z

zebra crossing	*aoboor* (m) *ilmoshaeh*	عبور المشاه
zip	*sosta* (f)	سوسته
zoo	*Hadeeqit il Haiyawaenaet* (f)	حديقة الحيوانات
zoology	*ailm il Haiyawaen* (m)	علم الحيوان

NOTES

EMERGENCIES

(*see also* Problems and complaints, *page 151*)

You may want to say

Phoning the emergency services

The police, please
il bolees min faDlak/faDlik

The fire brigade
il maTafi

An ambulance
il is^aaef

There's been a robbery
HaSal Ser'a

There's been an accident
HaSal Hadsa

There's a fire
fi Haree'a

I've been attacked/mugged
Had i^atada ^aalaya

I've been raped
Had ightaSabni

There's someone ill
fi waHid ^aayaen (m)/
fi waHda ^aayaena (f)

There's someone injured
fi waHid itgaraH (m)/
fi waHda itgaraHit (f)

It's my husband
gowzi

It's my wife
miraati

It's my son
ibni

It's my daughter
binti

It's my friend
SaHbi (m)/*SaHbiti* (f)

Please come immediately
ta^aaloo fowran

The address is . . .
il ^aenwaen . . .

My name is . . .
ismi . . .

ALL-PURPOSE PHRASES

Hello
ahlan wa sahlan

Goodbye
ma ªassalaema

Good morning
SabaH il kheer

Good evening
misa' il kheer

Good night
tisbaH ªala kheer (to m)/
  tisbaHi ªala kheer (to f)

Yes
aywa

No
la'a

Please
min faDlak (to m)/
  min faDlik (to f)

Thank you (very much)
shokran (gazeelan)

Don't mention it
il ªafw

I don't understand
mish faehim (m)/*fahma* (f)

I speak very little Arabic
batkalim ªarabi baseeT

I don't know
mish ªarif (m)/*ªarfa* (f)

Pardon?
la mo'akhza

Would you repeat that,
  please?
kamaen marra min faDlak/
  faDlik

More slowly
bishwaysh

Again, please
taeni min faDlak/faDlik

Can you show me in the
  book?
momkin tiwareenee fil
  kitaeb

Can you write it down
  (here)?
momkim tiktibha (hena)

Do you speak English?
inta bititkalim ingleezi (to
inti bititkalimi ingleezi (to

My telephone number is . . .
nemreti . . .

Where is the police station?
fayn maHatit ibolees

Where is the hospital?
fayn imostashfa

At the police station/hospital

Is there anybody here who
  speaks English?
fi Had hena biyetkalim
  ingleezi

I want to speak to a woman
ªayza akalim waHda sit

May I speak to the British
  Embassy?
momkin akalim isifara
  ilingleezaya

I want a lawyer
ªayiz/ªayza moHaemi

You may hear

fi ay
What is the matter?

HaSal ay
What has happened?

ismak wi ªenwaenak/
  ismik wi ªenwaenik
Your name and your address

Hanib ªat ªarabayit bolees
We will send a police car

Hanib ªat ªarabayit maTafi
We will send the fire brigade

Hab ªat ªarabayit is ªaef
I am sending an ambulance

The police

ismak/ismik ay
What is your name?

ªenwaenak/ªenwaenik ay
What is your address?

HaSal ay
What happened?

HaSal fayn
Where did it happen?

momkin towSif li . . .
Can you describe . . .?

ta ͨala/ta ͨali ma ͨana li ism ibolees
Come with us to the police station

inta ma'booD ͨalayk/inti ma'booD ͨalayki
You're under arrest

The doctor

(*see* Health, *page 140*)

biyewga ͨ fayn
Where does it hurt?

ba ͨalak/ba ͨalik 'ad ay keda
How long have you been like this?

ba'alo 'ad ay keda
How long has he been like this?

ba'alha 'ad ay keda
How long has she been like this?

laezim tiroH imostashfa
You will have to go to hospital

Emergency shouts

Help (me)!
ilHa'ooni

Police!
bolees

Stop!
qof

Stop thief!
imsik Harami

Fire!
Haree'a

Look out!
khod baelak (to m)/
khodi baelik (to f)

Danger! Gas!
khaTar gaez

Get out of the way!
ifsaH iseka (to m)/
ifsaHi iseka (to f)

Call the police
oTlob/oTlobi ibolees

Call the fire brigade
oTlob/oTlobi imaTafi

Call an ambulance
oTlob/oTlobi il is ͨaef

Call a doctor
oTlob/oTlobi doktowr

Get help quickly
oTlob/oTlobi mosa ͨda bisor ͨa

It's an emergency
Halit Tawari'